MULTINATIONAL ENTERPRISES – FINANCIAL AND MONETARY ASPECTS

Société Universitaire Européenne de Recherches
Financières (SUERF)

MULTINATIONAL ENTERPRISES- FINANCIAL AND MONETARY ASPECTS

edited by

J. S. G. Wilson   and   C. F. Scheffer

with contributions from

Lord O'Brien   W. A. P. Manser
G. Y. Bertin   John Mellors
F. H. Brittenden   Sylvain Plasschaert
John H. Dunning   Sidney E. Rolfe
Jack Hendley   Sieghardt Rometsch
J. Koning   Edward Thielemans
A. J. W. S. Leonard   Patrice de Vallée
Nils Lundgren   Donald W. Vollmer

1974
A. W. SIJTHOFF — LEIDEN

ISBN 90 286 0124 4

Library of Congress Catalog Card Number: 74-77133

Printed in the Netherlands.

PREFACE

One of the main purposes of the Société Universitaire Européenne de Recherches Financières, which was established in 1964, has been to organise from time to time Colloquia on subjects of general interest to our members; this we would describe as 'research in action'. The present volume makes available the papers presented to the Colloquium held at the University of Nottingham in England in April 1973. In addition to the papers presented to the several Commissions, we have included the Opening Address given by the then Governor of the Bank of England (The Rt. Hon. Lord O'Brien of Lothbury, GBE, PC) and the General Report presented by the Rapporteur-General (Professor S.E. Rolfe of the Massachusetts Institute of Technology). Also, since it was stimulated by our discussions in Nottingham, we have reprinted as an Appendix John Mellors' article on "Multinational Corporations and Capital Market Integration", originally published in *The Bankers' Magazine*. We take this opportunity of recording our thanks both to the author and the Editor of *The Bankers' Magazine* for their kind permission to do so.

SUERF already has a widely ranging membership consisting—on the corporate side—of the leading banks and similar institutions in Western Europe, in addition to which it is supported financially by the central banks in those countries. Several non-financial multinational enterprises have also joined the ranks of SUERF. On the personal side, membership is comprised mainly of academics interested in monetary economics and institutions or of economists employed in financial institutions and related activities. In this way, SUERF assists in building bridges between the world of practical finance and the more cloistered pursuits of the study of financial institutions and policies in our Universities. In part, this is the function of the Colloquia, but in addition from time to time research papers contributed by members of SUERF are circulated, as well as information relating to research within its general field and currently being undertaken in the Universities of Western Europe.

Finally, SUERF aims to sponsor and encourage original research—within the limits of the resources available—and the publication of the results. Through this present volume—and the earlier volume on *The Future of the International Monetary System* (which reported the proceedings at our first Colloquium at Guldenberg in April 1969)—we hope to reach an even wider audience and to inform the world about the nature of SUERF activities.

In connection with the preparation of this volume, we would wish to express our appreciation to the Executive Secretary of SUERF, Miss M.C. Hinkenkemper, and to Miss Linda Bolton and Miss Annelies Vugs for all their help in the preparation of the text for the printers and for assistance with the reading of the proofs.

J. S. G. Wilson   *C. F. Scheffer*
University of Hull   Katholieke Hogeschool, Tilburg
England   The Netherlands

TABLE OF CONTENTS

VIII

ABOUT THE EDITORS AND THE AUTHORS

J.S.G. Wilson (editor) is Professor of Economics & Commerce, University of Hull and President of the Société Universitaire Européenne de Recherches Financières (SUERF).

C.F. Scheffer (editor) is Professor of Business Finance, University of Tilburg and Secretary-General of the Société Universitaire Européenne de Recherches Financières (SUERF).

The Rt. Hon. *Lord O'Brien* of Lothbury, G.B.E., P.C., at the time he opened the Colloquium was Governor of the Bank of England.

G.Y. Bertin is Professor and Maître de Recherches at the Centre National de la Recherche Scientifique, Rennes.

F.H. Brittenden is Head, Treasurers General, Shell International Petroleum Company Limited, London.

John H. Dunning is Professor of Economics, University of Reading.

Jack Hendley is Joint General Manager, Midland Bank Limited, London.

J. Koning was at the time of the Colloquium Director, Philips Finance Company, Eindhoven.

A.J.W.S. Leonard is Group Treasurer and Director, Shell International Petroleum Company Limited, London.

Nils Lundgren is Research Associate, Institute for International Economic Studies, Stockholm.

W.A.P. Manser is Economic Adviser, Baring Brothers & Company Limited, London.

X

John Mellors was at the time of the Colloquium Lecturer, University of Reading.

Sylvain Plasschaert is Professor at the Universities of Antwerp and Louvain.

Sidney E. Rolfe is Professor at the Center for International Studies, Massachusetts Institute of Technology, Massachusetts, U.S.A.

Sieghardt Rometsch is Vice-President and Assistant General Manager, The Chase Manhattan Bank N.A., Frankfurt am Main.

Edward Thielemans is Director, Kredietbank NV, Brussels.

Patrice de Vallée was at the time of the Colloquium a Management Consultant in Paris.

Donald W. Vollmer was at the time of the Colloquium Vice-President, Multinational Division, Bank of America, London.

Part I

General Introduction

Chapter I

MULTINATIONAL ENTERPRISES *

by the Rt. Hon. *Lord O'Brien* of Lothbury, G.B.E., P.C.

Introduction

The fourth in this valuable series of SUERF international conferences is a particularly significant one for us, being the first one to take place in the United Kingdom and the first one to take place under a United Kingdom chairman. So it gave me especial pleasure when your President invited me to give the opening address. Professor Stuart Wilson is an old friend of ours in the Bank of England, and I am happy to be here to support him in this very worthwhile venture.

The Bank of England has always been in sympathy with the objectives of SUERF and have supported your society from the outset, indirectly and through the membership of a number of our senior executives. We feel that conferences such as this, which bring together representatives of the academic world and those involved in the day-to-day operational and decision-making aspects of the topics discussed, are particularly valuable. The development of a continuing dialogue of this kind can only be of mutual benefit and lead to greater insight into the problems and their implications on the part of all involved. I am glad to say that it is something to which we in the Bank of England have given particular attention in recent years.

The conference which opens today deals with a topic which is peculiarly appropriate for such a meeting of minds. Multinational enterprises have been the subject of a great deal of comment in recent years but much of this has been vitiated by the adoption of partisan viewpoints or hampered by incomplete data. This is particularly true of the financial aspects of the operations of such companies. The attention which this conference is to focus on these aspects is valuable in itself, and also of particular interest to central bankers. While we are naturally interested in the overall rôle of multinational

---

* *Text of an address given by the Governor of the Bank of England at the Colloquium, organised by the Société Universitaire Européenne de Recherches Financières, at the University of Nottingham on 11th April 1973.*

3

enterprises in our national economies, their influences on financial flows and markets are the aspects with which we are most intimately concerned.

However, multinational enterprises do not generally form an identifiable statistical category—they certainly do not in the United Kingdom—and all of us concerned with their operations find it difficult from time to time either to substantiate or to controvert some of the rather sweeping claims and allegations made about their operations. For this reason, therefore, I welcome the addition to informed and impartial analysis which I am sure will come out of this conference. I am confident it is going to produce worthwhile results and I am only sorry that other pressing commitments make it impossible for me to participate in the remainder of your deliberations.

Why the growing interest?

The co-ordination of operations on an international scale, under a centralised ownership and management, is no new thing. We in the United Kingdom have experience of this field reaching back to the Hudson's Bay Company, the East India Company, and other chartered companies of the 17th and 18th centuries. In more modern times, banks, shipping lines, and latterly oil companies have been for generations a familiar element in the international business scene. Only the last, perhaps, can be deemed to fall within the narrower definition of multinational enterprises underlying the current debate—which I take to be operations embracing manufacture or extractive industry in a number of different countries. Why, then, the growing interest and concern which has been evinced about the operations of these enterprises in recent years? How do companies of this kind, and the environments in which they operate, differ from, say, before the Second World War?

I would single out four factors which together come close to making the difference one of kind rather than degree and go some way to explain the attention which these companies are currently receiving.

First and foremost, of course, is the element of sheer size. This is the product of rapid growth combined with mergers and a high rate of investment overseas. The output of multinational companies is currently expanding at around 10 per cent. per annum—twice as fast as world G.N.P. and if anything faster than the growth of world trade. This explains why multinational companies are steadily growing more powerful relative to the smaller economies, and accounts for the frequently-heard forecast that in a decade or two world business will be dominated by perhaps as few as 300 companies. This is a situation which needs to be taken seriously by all national authorities, and particularly by the smaller economies. Few such territories are unaffected. In recent years multinationals concerned with extractive industries have broadened their operations to take in new territories where their particular com-

4

modity has been discovered. At the same time, rising standards of education and productivity have widened the range of countries in which manufacturing corporations are able to set up centres of production.

Second has been the long campaign to liberalise capital movements during the post-war period. A key objective in the field of international finance, until quite recently, has been the dismantling of wartime and pre-war controls which interfered with the freedom of movement and choice in both current and capital transactions. The success of this policy, pursued steadily through the '50s and '60s, facilitated an unprecedented growth of world trade with concomitant benefits to developed and developing countries alike. In recent years, de-stabilising capital flows have from time to time necessitated the reintroduction of controls, normally temporary, in some countries. But it is still broadly true that the move towards greater capital freedom has been a major change in the international financial environment, and one without which the multinational corporations would not have been able to build up their present sophistication in international money management.

Third, the expansion of international business has been accompanied by the development of world-wide banking networks, on a more sophisticated level than hitherto, to ensure that financial services are available to meet the needs of the biggest international companies. Similarly, the growth of the Eurocurrency markets has provided a new range of facilities for mobilising short or long-term funds, or investing them, in a form consistent with the international outlook of the multinational companies, and largely free of national restrictions. These facilities, allied to vastly improved communications networks and the development of electronic data processing, have put at the disposal of the sophisticated company treasurer new and more efficient machinery for cash transmission and the deployment of liquid assets.

Fourth, there is nowadays a growing sensitivity in most countries to social and political issues generated by the activities of multinational enterprises. This can be seen in the vigorous representations made from time to time by groups interested in environmental and ecological questions, and in the reaction of national and international trade unions to questions of labour relations and employment policy. The communist-inspired World Federation of Trade Unions is holding this week in Santiago a conference to examine ways of undermining the multinational enterprises. The International Confederation of Free Trade Unions, to which our own Trades Union Congress is affiliated, has declined to take part, but that can be attributed more to the sponsorship of the Santiago conference than to any lack of sensitivity to the underlying issues. In some countries, governments have intervened to limit the degree of foreign control of key sectors of industry or otherwise to preserve the national interest. This problem is potentially more embarrassing in the smaller territories, where it is sometimes seen as having neo-colonial overtones. Strictly speaking, the problem arises as a result of private foreign direct investment rather than

5

from the activities of multinational companies as such; the two issues tend to become confused because of the predominance of such companies in investment in sensitive areas.

These and other factors have led many people to question whether the interests of multinational enterprises do not diverge from those of host governments, and—more importantly—whether their power is such as to represent a significant reduction in the sovereignty of the host government in the situation where such divergence occurs. Before I go on to examine and comment on some of the specific areas of concern where this divergence of interest may emerge in the financial field, I would like to make two points that arise out of the general considerations I have just outlined.

In the first place, "bigness" is part of a modern trend towards bigger units and greater interdependence; this is evident in both the political and economic fields. This trend is a fact of life which is not going to be reversed—though it may well slow down. It behoves us therefore to attempt squarely to evaluate the benefits and disadvantages of such expansion, to see how the benefits can be maximised and the disadvantages controlled and reduced to a minimum. In the context of multinational enterprises, such evaluation includes political, economic, social and ecological elements; and trade unionists, consumers and others have a contribution to make as well as economists and public servants.

The second general point to which I would draw your attention is the fact that the biggest companies have a reputation and a "good name" which they need to maintain. They cannot afford to engage in confrontations with government or become involved in lengthy wrangles with government departments to the detriment of their good name as responsible organisations. Nor indeed can they flout public opinion indefinitely with impunity. This is not to say of course that saintliness will characterise their every action. It does mean, however, that they will usually be at least as scrupulous as their domestic counterparts, if not more so, in keeping their operations within the law and the bounds of defensible commercial practice.

Areas of concern

I turn now to the examination of some specifically financial aspects of the operation of multinational enterprises which have given rise to criticism and comment. Many will no doubt be dealt with elsewhere in more detail as the conference proceeds. My purpose now is mainly to open up these areas for discussion, and in so doing to comment on some of the misconceptions which I find on occasion confuse the debate.

Some of these areas I must admit are not a central banker's immediate concern (except indirectly as far as they affect the balance of payments). For that reason, I will refrain from substantive comment. But I feel that at least a passing reference is called for to three topics. The first is the question of marketing arrangements, under which access to particular export markets is sometimes reserved to particular members of a multinational group, thus depriving an individual subsidiary of possible exports—to the detriment of its host country's balance of payments performance. The second is the general question of capital investment policy; whether by switching productive capacity internationally, the giant multinationals can wield undue influence through their ability to slow down or speed up investment. Both these are primarily the concern of the Department of Trade and Industry, but they raise interesting questions of the interaction of legitimate commercial judgment and the natural concern of governments for the national interest.

A third topic of this kind is the multinational groups' practice of allegedly maximising profits in lower tax areas, at the expense of profits in higher tax areas. This can be done by the adjustment of prices between members of the same group, assuming that the pattern of intra-group trade (in both goods and services) lends itself to such a practice. In some cases, however, we know that multinational groups prefer to fix prices to a large extent on an arm's-length basis, i.e. as if between unconnected buyers and sellers. In the United Kingdom, supervision of these matters is primarily the concern of other regulatory bodies than the Bank. I therefore confine myself to commenting that they illustrate again how a principle generally accepted in domestic matters—that "no-one is obliged to so arrange his affairs as to allow the Revenue to insert the largest possible shovel into his store",—can give rise to contention when applied at the global level.

I turn now to matters of a more directly central banking interest.

I should like to start by taking up the question of the much-publicised ability of multinational groups to shift their liquid assets around in times of exchange crisis in such a way as to protect their interests—and in the process to accentuate the pressure on exchange markets. The recent dollar crises have led to renewed comment on the rôle of multinational enterprises in these recurring surges of short-term capital. A study just published by the United States Tariff Commission puts a figure of $268 billion on the liquid assets (at the end of 1971) of bodies participating in the international money markets, of which some 70 per cent. were held by United States multinational corporations and banks. No doubt today's figures would be considerably higher. Of course not all these funds are freely available for transfer—the assets of one body may be the liabilities of another; and working capital has to be retained or made good from somewhere. But $268 billion was more than twice as large as total world reserves at that time ($122 billion) and the sudden redeployment of even 1 per cent. of this total would be sufficient to cause a noticeable disturbance in the exchange markets.

The exact rôle of multinational corporations in the sterling crisis of June

1972 and the more recent international crises of February/March 1973 has still to be evaluated. However, there is no doubt that transfers of liquid balances by multinational companies did account for an important part of the transfers which eventually led to the floating of the pound, the devaluation of the dollar, the floating of the yen, and the situation of widespread floating in which we now find ourselves. Perhaps the fact that a devaluation of the dollar against all currencies appeared imminent, and most of the biggest multinationals are United States controlled, had something to do with the size of these flows during the recent crises.

It would be wrong to assume that the international cash management policies of all multinational corporations are dominated by the search for short-term gain through currency speculation. But in situations of exchange market uncertainty, where the options appear to be all one way, normal prudence would suggest defensive policies designed to protect assets against loss. These considerations apply not to multinational corporations alone but to all companies whose trading is not wholly domestic. What distinguishes the multinational companies is their greater opportunity to switch funds from one currency to another and perhaps the greater sophistication they are able to employ in doing so.

The same features of greater opportunity and sophistication also characterise the ability of multinational companies to make use of another technique for shifting the currency composition of assets and liabilities—the practice of "leading and lagging". Payments or receipts for international transactions may be hurried forward or delayed in the hopes of profiting, or avoiding a loss, from a change in exchange rates. If there is substantial international trading within the group, a multinational company will have more opportunity to engage in leading and lagging than will purely national concerns dealing with foreign trading partners at arm's length.

A third way in which, it is sometimes suggested, multinational groups may adapt their practices in response to exchange market developments is in their policy over profit remittances. For example, they may hasten to declare and remit abnormally large dividends from subsidiaries in countries threatened with devaluation. Whatever may be the practice of individual companies, this suggestion is not in fact borne out by aggregated statistics, as analysed in Professor Lee Remmers' useful work *"The Strategy of Multinational Enterprise"*,[1] or by a more recent study by Mr Manser of Baring's *"The Financial Role of Multinational Enterprises"*.[2] In any case—as far as the United Kingdom is concerned—remittance is only allowed subject to certain limitations

1. Michael Z. Brooke and H. Lee Remmers, *The Strategy of Multinational Enterprise: Organisation and Finance*, Longman, 1970.

2. W. A. P. Manser, *The Financial Role of Multinational Enterprises*, Cassell/Associated Business Programmes Ltd., 1973

and after proper provision for tax has been made.

There has been a tendency to point the finger at multinational companies because they have the most obvious scope for redeployment of liquid assets and the organisation of "leads and lags". One of the questions which this Colloquium might consider is whether the difference between multinational and domestic companies in those respects is fundamental, or simply one of degree. It would certainly be unwise for the United Kingdom authorities to ignore the extent to which purely domestic companies can seek the protection of those devices. In any event the problem of short-term international capital flows seems to me to raise wider questions still. They reflect a failure in international adjustment which has reached a point where the business and financial communities are no longer confident that they can afford to deny themselves the protection against loss that is available—and act accordingly. Whatever we may seek to do by direct action to moderate such flows, we should not ignore the imperative need to tackle problems of international maladjustment at the root, through timely corrective policies domestically and, where necessary, externally.

There are many interesting questions about direct action to control capital flows that could be studied. Some are philosophical, what we ought to be trying to do. How far does the national interest diverge from that of the individual company or group? How should the balance in official policy be struck, between controlling capital flows and responding to them with adjustments in other instruments of policy? But matters of principle cannot be the only guide: the practical issues are likely to be dominant. We in the United Kingdom have long had certain types of control over capital movements, while leaving many transactions relatively free. This has not prevented very large short-term capital flows. And the same applies to the experience of most other countries. Some types of external transaction are impossible to control closely without a degree of supervision that is almost unacceptable. This suggests that controls are probably not a complete answer to the problem of mobile capital flows. Nevertheless, it can be argued that a degree of control is of some assistance. The world is still groping its way towards a solution of this difficult problem. I shall therefore pass these questions to you without further comment on my part.

I turn now to a more domestic topic—the interaction of credit control and monetary policy with the operations of multinational enterprises.

As I have said before, companies of this kind are not normally treated as a specific category in United Kingdom statistics or policy decisions; in the eyes of the Exchange Control, for example, companies are either resident, resident but non-resident-controlled, or non-resident. There are some limitations—not onerous—on borrowing in the United Kingdom by the middle group. In general, however, multinational companies have never been discriminated against in United Kingdom credit control policy and administration; except for some

Exchange Control purposes, they are treated "on all fours" with other British companies.

Have they—that is to say the subsidiaries in the United Kingdom of foreign multinational parent companies—succeeded however in evading the impact of restrictive policies in the past?

Various studies have demonstrated that such subsidiaries, once they are established on a firm footing, rely mainly on internally-generated cash flow and local borrowing sources, such as the banks, for the bulk of their finance; capital from elsewhere in the group is conventionally the smallest element. It will be appreciated that cash flow and local borrowing are sources of funds which are usually available to all companies equally. On the other hand, access to funds from elsewhere in the group when local borrowing becomes more difficult or expensive can put a multinational affiliate in an advantageous position.

As regards bank finance, I have no reason to believe that multinational subsidiaries have been treated in a discriminatory way at times of credit stringency. However, the standing and "name" of the group as a whole, and the explicit or implicit guarantee of the parent company, might be said to give them a slight advantage, as compared with a domestic company of similar, size and function.

Against this must be set the fact that it is difficult for such firms to raise long-term capital by public issue in the United Kingdom—as it is, for various reasons, in most domestic capital markets. On the other hand, access to the Eurobond market has been increasingly in recent years a useful source of funds for international (including United Kingdom-based) groups; despite the growing number of borrowers taking advantage of this market not many purely national firms are big enough.

For some years now such groups have been taking a substantial proportion of Eurobond issues (nearly 40 per cent., for example, over the period 1964-68). These are largish sums, but still fairly modest in comparison with the total domestic credit made available in, say, North America plus the United Kingdom and Western Europe.

To sum up therefore it may be argued that multinational subsidiaries have a slight edge over similar domestic companies at times when credit is being rationed. But I have no reason to think that such companies' borrowing has operated to the detriment of United Kingdom monetary policy or credit control in the past (which when exercised selectively was after all usually aimed at consumption and speculation rather than industrial activity generally).

My remarks up to this point have focussed—as indeed this conference as a whole is to do—on what are after all rather limited areas of a multinational group's overall activity. One should always remember that they are in business to mine or process or manufacture something and then to sell it. They expand their operations to improve their production and marketing capacity, not to take advantage of some (perhaps short-lived) variation in tax rates or exchange arrangements. For the most part, the complexities of life which confront the multinational companies as a result of financial variations between the countries in which they operate are accepted much more as a necessary evil than as providing scope for bigger and better manipulations. No one criticises a national group of companies, which operate purely in one country, if they so arrange matters between the members of the group as to maximise profits or protect themselves against currency losses. Such self-protection is equally natural to a group that operates across frontiers. Trouble comes when such actions are seen to be at variance with national objectives; and it is then that difficult questions arise for policy.

Concluding remarks

The debate on whether the operations of multinational enterprises confer a net benefit overall takes a different form in relation to host countries on the one hand, and to home-based countries on the other. It is a debate that will no doubt continue for a very long time without reaching a definite conclusion. We in the United Kingdom have had long experience of both rôles. Our general view is that on both counts companies of this kind tend to be sufficiently above average in their technological know-how and managerial drive to generate economic advantages for both home and host country. Professor Dunning's recent study for The Economist Advisory Group, for example, showed that between 1957 and 1970 affiliates of United States companies accounted for one third of the increase in United Kingdom exports. Their net contribution to the United Kingdom balance of payments, on both current and capital accounts, was of the order of £600—700 million in 1970. However, there are other matters which need to be weighed in the balance; some of them we have already considered and some lie outside the terms of reference of this conference. The commercial interests of a multinational enterprise may not coincide with the national interest of a country where it operates; and further work remains to be done on how best such conflicts of interest can be reconciled, so as to preserve national objectives without necessarily killing the goose that lays the golden eggs.

I doubt myself whether international controls or legislation provide the answer, although there may be a case for a freer interchange of information between fiscal authorities and other supervising agencies in different countries. After all, subsidiaries of foreign parent companies have to comply with domestic government policy and legislation just as domestic companies do. They are therefore subject to the same curbs in fields such as company legislation, monopoly and merger policy, exchange control, and general employment and investment policy.

11

The enlargement of the European Community will lead over time to a measure of harmonisation in these important fields, and (more importantly) in fiscal and monetary matters also. As this development takes place, the difficulties which at present face multinational companies operating under a variety of systems will diminish with a consequent gain in efficiency—and a reduction in the temptation to take advantage of such variations. There are already signs that United Kingdom industry is increasingly eager to expand its international operations through mergers across European frontiers. In the banking field, we expect to see more cross-frontier mergers in Europe to provide better and more co-ordinated facilities in step with developing industrial and commercial needs. For our part, we announced in November that a more liberal régime would apply, from the date of our joining the Community, to mergers and participations involving the "marriage" of European banks with British banks (including merchant and overseas banks). At the same time, the "open door policy" in relation to the establishment in London of branches and subsidiaries of reputable non-E.E.C. banks will be maintained.

The improvements in the international monetary system which are now being vigorously pursued have among their objectives the improvement of the adjustment process and the minimising of de-stabilising capital flows. The Committee of Twenty Deputies have now set up a special study group to concentrate on the latter aspect of the problem. The events of recent months have lent extra urgency to this debate, and among the techniques being closely examined are the various possibilities in the field of capital controls. In this context the rôle of multinational corporations will be closely scrutinised.

Now I would like to raise our sights somewhat beyond our present difficulties, to a time when reform of the international monetary system is a reality. When the objective of finding a proper balance between stability and flexibility of adjustment is attained, the incentive, and the need, for multinational companies to engage in the operations that have been criticised in recent years may be significantly reduced. This will enable them to concentrate more exclusively on their real business, of contributing to higher standards of living not only in the host countries but also, through increases in world trade, in the developing countries. This in turn should lead to an improvement in the quality of life for all the peoples of the world.

Chapter II

THE MULTINATIONAL ENTERPRISE

oy *Edward Thielemans*

The phenomenon of the internationalisation and integration of economic life constitutes along with the advance of technology, a basic datum of our age, constantly spurring on the research workers, businessmen and political leaders to revise their opinions and to give a new direction to their policy.

Economic thinking, and especially economico-political thinking, however to a large extent continues to be determined by national considerations. Expressions such as national economy, national product and national income, balance of payments and foreign trade are among the principal operational notions which condition economic policy and which serve to give an understanding of economic reality. Is not the enterprise regarded by many, in the first place, as a component of the national economy? And in cases where the company extends its field of activity beyond the borders of the national economies, it may be wondered whether the macro-interests of the national economy and the micro-interests of the company coincide in all respects.

Prior to World War II, there was much discussion about the controversial question of free trade or protectionism. Although the official attitude since then has been in favour of the freedom of international trade, this problem is not yet solved, despite all the progress made in this direction. The politically organised community still has the last word and in certain circumstances puts its own interests (real or imaginary) before those of others.

This explains why protectionism is still in existence and even on the ascendant, and also why the governmental attempts to achieve economic and political integration are often held in check for quite some time, and in any case progress too slowly, in the opinion of those who think that unification and the formation of larger aggregates are in line with historical development.

It appears, however, that by the direct action of enterprises, the situation is now undergoing thorough changes.

The centre of gravity of the internationalisation and integration of business activity and national economies is shifting from trade to the production factors themselves. International movements of goods seem to be eclipsed by international production, while foreign trade seems to be lagging behind and even to be replaced by direct investments abroad. The total value of the international production of companies with foreign operations is said already to exceed by far the exports of goods from the principal countries and, above all, it is said to be increasing much more rapidly. The internationalisation of the production structures would thus already be far advanced.

This internationalisation is the work of companies which deem their own national economy and national political community to be inadequate to enable them to develop all their possibilities, to quench their thirst for expansion or even to safeguard their long-term viability. They select a wider, international field of action. They give themselves an international structure and thus embark on a development which may be of very great importance both for themselves and for the economic and political communities.

They have already been given a variety of names: international company, anational, plurinational, multinational, transnational, supranational company, and even worldwide or planetary company. What lies behind this multiplicity of labels? And what do these forms of companies represent for the communities in which they operate?

Definition

The multinational enterprises are in correlation with two basic trends in the modern economy: the tendency towards enlargement of scale and the tendency towards internationalisation and integration.

The *enlargement of scale* relates to the big enterprise resulting from international growth and different forms of concentration. They provide the advantage which must make it possible to produce more cheaply, to pay higher wages, to make bigger profits, to effect larger investments, to penetrate more deeply into new technical fields, to manufacture new products and constantly to conquer new markets.

Internationalisation and integration make radical changes to the image and life of economies and countries, bring them together into larger units, perhaps even into a world economy and, in the distant future, a political world system.

Both trends come together in the multinational enterprise, which derives its growth and development from the limitations of the national market and endeavours to acquire the advantages of the large enterprise at a transnational or even world level by the internationalisation of its market and corporate structure. At the level of the enterprises, the process of breaking out of the national framework occurs in different stages.

A first step will be to find outlets abroad by exporting, while the company's production and organisation remain purely national. By selling in foreign countries as well, the company widens its market, acquires the possibility of coping with fluctuations in demand and ensures a greater continuity and more ample growth opportunities. The subsequent stages may be: the set-

14

ting-up of a trading system abroad (representatives, exclusive agency agreements, sales bureaux and distribution network of its own), cooperation with or participation in foreign companies, setting up production units in foreign countries (e.g. by assembly lines or production under licence and finally the gradual development of a whole network and system for industrial and commercial activities in different countries with the corresponding organisation and control structures which may show a great diversity.

The multinational enterprise is in fact situated in the last stage of this break-through process, whereby the enterprise gives up the national structure, in its many aspects, for an international structure with a view to approaching the different markets in the most rational and efficient way, economically speaking.

The different phases of multinationalisation or internationalisation may, but need not necessarily be consecutive. They may indeed overlap each other as well. This overlapping occurs mainly in the last stages and it is there that a wide diversity may be encountered. Indeed, a company may be multi- or international as regards its affiliates, but national as regards management, ownership or organisation structures, and it should also be pointed out that many intermediate nuances are possible.

Thus, Professor Richard Robinson, of Harvard, makes a distinction between the international, the multinational, the transnational and the supranational enterprise:[1]

— *the international enterprise:*
one in which all operations with foreign countries are centralised in a separate department and which is prepared to apply every possible type of strategy to penetrate foreign markets, even going so far as direct investment.

— *the multinational enterprise:*
one in which operations with foreign countries—as regards both structure and policy—are on the same footing as domestic operations, and the management is prepared to use the available resources for the company's purposes, without thereby paying attention to national borders. Ownership and central management are in the hands of persons from the country of origin of the multinational company; its decisions are therefore nationally inspired.

— *transnational enterprise:*
a multinational enterprise which is managed and owned by persons of different nationalities. The decisions are thus no longer guided by national considerations.

— *supranational enterprise:*
a transnational enterprise without legal nationality: it may be registered only with an international institution set up by virtue of an international conven-

1. Richard D. Robinson, *International Business Policy*, New York 1964 and *International Management*, 1967.

tion, which supervises the enterprise and levies taxes on it.

In the same field and taking as a point of departure the psychological attitude of the management, Professor Perlmutter distinguishes three types of international enterprises:[2]

In the *ethnocentric* international enterprise, based on the country of origin, the affiliates are strictly subordinated to the parent company. The central management imposes its views on the local companies, either because it is rather distrustful in its attitude towards the countries where it operates, or because it deems that it has the best organisation and decision-making formulae and that it can apply the same methods and techniques with just as much success in foreign countries as in its own country. The managerial posts are entrusted to persons of the same nationality or culture as those of the parent enterprise.

In the *polycentric* international enterprise, oriented towards the country where the branch is located, the local situations are regarded as a kind of individuality. The enterprise aims to adapt itself to the pluralistic world and to identify itself to a certain extent with the national interests of the respective countries. The key positions are held by persons of the country in which the establishment is situated. The solution of the problem is left to the initiative of the local managers.

Lastly, the *geocentric* international enterprise has a world orientation. The top posts in the parent company are entrusted to a cosmopolitan elite of managerial staff, recruited in the different branches. In this way, the decisions are less linked to the limitations resulting from the national surroundings of head office and branches. The geocentric enterprise is based not only on a greater confidence in the personnel of the affiliates, but also on a more intense exchange of persons and information in both directions between the affiliates and the parent company. The cosmopolitan elite of managerial staff ensure coordination, thus making it possible to disengage the local companies from their corresponding surroundings.

The transnational enterprise of Robinson and the geocentric type of Perlmutter are obviously closely related, and may in many respects be regarded as a model, but in fact are met with only rarely. It is sometimes said that only the International Red Cross fulfils the criteria laid down in this respect. Nestlé, Royal Dutch-Shell, Unilever and Agfa-Gevaert perhaps come closest to this definition, although the last three have rather the character of "binational" enterprises.

The majority of internationally operating enterprises may be regarded, at the very most, as multinational enterprises, according to the Robinson crite-

2. H. V. Perlmutter, "L'Entreprise Internationale: trois conceptions", *Revue Economique et Sociale* 1965, May, University of Lausanne, pp. 151-165.

ria, and are rather of the ethnocentric than of the geocentric type. S. Rose[3] came to the conclusion that in the 150 United States companies examined, only 1.6 per cent. of the top managerial staff were not of American nationality, while this percentage was 20.7 per cent. for the personnel as a whole.

It may be said that the majority of the internationally operating companies still have a genuine nationality: they are American, British, German, French, Dutch, Japanese, Swiss, Belgian, etc. enterprises, which also produce abroad. This does not prevent these enterprises from being considered as multinational companies. The terms "multinational" and "international" are moreover frequently used to designate one and the same fact, i.e., enterprises having or controlling production units in different countries the activities of which units they coordinate.[4]

Relative importance

In order to measure the degree of "multinationalisation" of an enterprise, the basis generally taken is the ratio between its assets abroad and its total corporate assets, or the same ratio as regards turnover, profits and employment. The statistical material in this field is far from complete. Nevertheless, it appears from the available data that production abroad, in the case of many large enterprises, has already come to occupy a large place.

The best statistical material relates to the United States enterprises with interests abroad. According to a survey made by N. Bruck and F. Lees[5] for the 500 largest United States Corporations (*Fortune* list), it appears that in 1964 the sales, profits, assets, production or employment abroad, in the case of 77 of them, already represented 25 per cent. or more of the aggregate of the enterprise, and that in the case of 199, i.e., 40 per cent., this proportion amounted to 10 per cent. and over.

S. Rolfe, in his basic report on international companies prepared for the Congress of the International Chamber of Commerce in 1969,[6] by a study of

3. Sanford Rose, "Rewarding strategies of multinationalism", *Fortune*, September 1968, pp. 100-105 and 180-182.

4. The recent report of the Tariff Commission *Implications of multinational firms for world trade and investment and for U.S. trade and labor*, report to the Committee on Finance of the United States Senate and to its sub-committee on International Trade, February 1973, concludes, after a survey of the terminology and its historical evolution: "Hence to reduce the definitional problem to manageable proportions, the study will focus on all U.S. firms engaging in foreign direct investment in production facilities" (p. 83).

5. Nicholas K. Bruck and Frances A. Lees, "Foreign Content of U.S. Corporate Activities", *Financial Analysts Journal*, September-October 1966, pp. 127-132.

6. Sidney E. Rolfe, *Les sociétés internationales*, basic report for the XXIInd Congress of the International Chamber of Commerce, Istanbul, May-June 1969, p. 15 and pp. 180-183.

the balance sheets and other data, has endeavoured to ascertain for which of the 200 largest non-American corporations of the *Fortune* list the assets, turnover, profits, employment, etc. abroad represent 25 per cent. and over of the aggregate of the enterprise.

This would be the case for some fifty of them, but taking account of other indications such as the number of production plants abroad in order to offset the lack of data, Rolfe thinks that the number must be almost the same as that of the United States corporations, i.e. 77 of the 500 largest.

The lists established by *Fortune* relate only to the largest enterprises, but apart from these there are many others which have set up branches in foreign countries.

Thus, S. Rolfe points out that, in a list of foreign companies having interests in the United States drawn up by the Department of Commerce, twenty pages out of thirty-one are devoted to enterprises not appearing on the *Fortune* list and not yet included in one or another easily available publication. Furthermore, the study by the Tariff Commission on multinational companies reveals that, according to the Bureau of Economic Analysis of the Department of Commerce, there were in 1966 a total of 3,400 American firms having a network of 23,000 affiliates abroad. (The latter figure may be compared to the figure of 8,000 affiliates of major American enterprises quoted by Professor Vernon for 1970 (against 2,300 in 1950), in his work *The multinational spread of U.S. enterprises: Sovereignty at Bay.*)

It is a wellknown fact that the statistical material from American sources on direct investments is the best in this field. According to the Department of Commerce, American direct investments abroad rose from $12 billion in 1950 to $32 billion in 1960 and $78 billion in 1970 ($86 billion in 1971). As for direct foreign investments in the United States, the respective figures are $3.4 billion for 1950, $6.9 billion for 1960 and $13.2 billion for 1970.

This relates only to direct American investments abroad and direct foreign investments in the United States; in other words, direct non-American investments outside the United States are not included in these figures.

The OECD has made a more global study relating to direct foreign investments made by enterprises of the eleven countries which are members of the Development Assistance Committee, i.e. Belgium, Canada, the Federal Republic of Germany, France, Italy, Japan, the Netherlands, United Kingdom, United States, Sweden and Switzerland. In this study, the book value of the direct foreign investments by the countries which are members of the Development Assistance Committee was estimated at $90 billion at the end of 1966, of which $55 billion for the United States and $35 billion for the other countries. Although this figure is substantial, it is nonetheless an underestimate, falling far short of the actual amount. In the first place, it relates solely to investments which have been made through the intermediary of the exchange institutes which means, for example, that the investments financed by loans abroad have not been taken into consideration. It is probably more important to know that the real value of these investments quite widely exceeds the value at which they were entered in the accounts at the time of the actual investment.

According to the Reddaway report,[7] the difference for the direct foreign investments of Great Britain would have reached an average of 36 per cent. at the end of 1964. If, following the example of S. Rolfe, this appreciation ratio is applied to the other non-American investments, the amount mentioned above would need to be increased from $35 to $47 billion. The direct United States investments have developed mainly in the course of the past fifteen years; it is therefore thought likely that the difference between their real value and the value at which they were entered in the accounts is not so great.

In any case, it appears from these figures that the internationalisation of the production structures, which is one of the chief characteristics of the multinational company in the widest sense, has already assumed quite substantial proportions. This becomes still more evident if the international production—i.e., the production effected in foreign branches—is compared with international trade.

J. Polk[8] has calculated that the value of the production of the affiliates of United States companies abroad amounts to double the book value of the United States direct investments, i.e., respectively $120 billion and $60 billion for 1967. This production value considerably exceeds the value of United States goods exports, which amounted to $32 billion in 1967. It also exceeds the gross national product of all other countries, apart from the United States and the Soviet Union.

S. Rolfe has applied the 2:1 ratio put forward by J. Polk to the OECD estimates concerning the foreign investments of the industrial countries.[9] Taking account of the value of the production of foreign enterprises shares of which are held in portfolio by other companies, he arrives at a rough estimate of $240 billion for the total value of the international production. This is almost double the amount of the exports of goods ($130 billion) by the leading industrial countries in 1967.

These figures have shown an appreciable increase since then, but it is the fact that international production is perhaps twice as great as international trade that deserves special emphasis.

7. W. B. Reddaway, in collaboration with S. J. Potter and C. T. Taylor, *Effects of U.S. Direct Investment Overseas, Final Report*, Cambridge University Press, 1968.

8. J. Polk, "The New World Economy", *Columbia Journal of World Business*, January 1968, p. 8.

9. Sidney E. Rolfe, "The International Corporation in Perspective", in *The Multinational Corporation in the World Economy*, edited by S. E. Rolfe and W. Damm, 1970, p. 9.

On the basis of the more complete data, covering a period of many years, on American investments abroad, it may be said that the direct investments occur to an ever-increasing extent outside the basic commodity industries and the developing countries; indeed, the investments in manufacturing industries and the tertiary sector in the industrial countries have developed most rapidly in the past ten years, which clearly points to an incipient interconnection of the production apparatus and a spreading of the corporate structure throughout the world.

The very rapid and considerable increase in American direct investments over the past twenty years meant that attention has been concentrated rather one-sidedly in this direction and made the existence of an international network of United States enterprises look like an "American challenge".

In fact, however, it is a question of the emergence of a new international economic structure, in which the international or multinational enterprises are proceeding to take their place, under pressure from economic and not from political motives.

This place will definitely not be of modest dimensions, but is by no means certain whether it will develop to such an extent as some people would be inclined to forecast. It is sometimes asserted that within a few years three quarters of the world production facilities will be in the hands of between 300 and 400 big multinational enterprises. This figure is based on an extrapolation of the existing growth paces of of planned rates of growth of these enterprises by comparison with the average growth rates of the national economies. One thus comes to the conclusion that within multinational companies an ever greater concentration of production and production factors will take place. After all, this view corresponds with what was previously said, and what is still sometimes said, about concentration within the national economy. The actual development has so far contradicted this forecast, because new enterprises are constantly coming into being in new sectors of activity and because existing enterprises acquire new growth opportunities thanks to innovations which they themselves carry out or which are passed on to them by others.

The big enterprise has not become entirely preponderant in the framework of the national economy, but it has indeed contributed to the fact that the local markets have to a large extent intermingled, and that integrated national markets have thus come about. It is an undoubted fact that this process has been able to go ahead on a wider basis and more speedily than would have been possible in a structure of very numerous small local enterprises. The big company indeed regards the whole national market as its field of operation, both for the sale of its products and for the attraction of production factors and the location of its branches.

A similar contribution may be expected from the multinational enterprises at the international and the world level. Regarded from a purely economic point of view, the expansion over the frontiers in no way differs from domestic expansion. It is the same motives which intervene in both cases: the need for sales outlets and expansion, the various advantages resulting from enlargement of scale, the big firm's need for independence vis-à-vis the uncertainties of the market, and the subjection of the enterprise to a long-term development plan.

In this sense, it is certainly correct to regard the multinational companies ¡as the prolongation of the big firm, or rather as the form in which the latter emerges, which is made possible and necessary by developments outside the enterprise (technical progress, e.g., in respect of communication facilities and transport) and within the enterprise e.g., the growth of the firm.

It is a fact that the multinational company has to develop its activities in a much less homogeneous milieu because, by the fact of going beyond the national borders, it is confronted with other political communities, each having its own legislation and regulations and in most cases showing a wide diversity as regards culture, language, psychology, etc. Naturally, the multinational enterprise will, in many respects, be less familiar with the milieu than its local competitors, and this is undoubtedly a handicap for it. However, the fact that it prefers to canvass foreign markets by the decentralisation of production rather than a further increase in exports indicates that there are advantages in so doing.

Specific advantages

The big multinational enterprise enjoys in the first place the advantages of scale for research and development in respect of production technique and marketing. In this connection, it is interesting to point out that the multinational enterprises which, as regards production establishments, are most internationally spread, are to be found rather in the consumer goods sector than in the investment goods sector.

Among the investment goods, the differences in scale indeed make themselves felt mainly at the production level and the scope of the production unit itself is thus of essential importance. The producers of investment goods therefore often stick to a few production centres whence exports are made to the different countries. These enterprises can increase the number of their branches only according as the sales possibilities expand. Certain producers with very large sales figures have already developed a whole system of subcontracting and assembly within their enterprises. The components are produced in various optimum production units located in different countries, and are assembled into the finished product in another unit. Examples of this are found, *inter alia*, in the computer industry and the motor industry. The formation of common markets and free trade areas has naturally encouraged this tendency towards product specialisation in the framework of geographically dispersed enterprises. The old theory of comparative costs, according to which trade between two countries develops on the basis of the relative cost advantages, thus finds a modern illustration in the framework of the multinational enterprise.

In the case of consumer goods, the advantages of scale are located rather in the commercial field, *i.e.* at the level of marketing and more particularly of market testing in respect of its receptivity to the product, in its various aspects and qualities, and to the planned advertising. The launching of mass-produced goods calls for enormous marketing costs which in most cases can only be borne by large enterprises. The advantage of the big multinational company in this field seems to lie mainly in the fact that the tests performed on a given market yield experiences that can be useful to a certain extent on other markets, which means that considerable savings in cost are possible, as well as valuable time-saving, factors which may be at least as important on competing markets.

By reason of its spreading over different countries and markets, the multinational company also enjoys the advantage of being able, up to a certain point, to escape from the uncertainties of the market. Impelled by the necessity for planning, it endeavours, like all big enterprises, to eliminate uncertainty and dependence as much as possible. Its international spread decreases its dependence in respect of price fluctuations, uncertainties and difficulties in raw materials supply, marketing of its products, transport, etc. On-the-spot production makes it less sensitive to the difficulties which often face exporters. The multinational enterprise thus acquires a life of its own, and a certain independence vis-à-vis its surroundings.

Another important advantage of the multinational company is the ample experience which it may have at its disposal by reason of the fact that it has to deal with so many different situations. It can apply this experience in new markets, countries and fields of activity.

Furthermore, it can draw on a much greater reserve of available production factors than the national enterprise or it can make better use of the various possibilities that are offered in different countries and markets.

In some cases, it is precisely the wish to have available certain production factors that are relatively scarce and expensive in the firm's own country, that spurs on a company to become established abroad. The idea of a larger reserve is also valid as regards financial activity. By its presence in different countries, the multinational enterprise has access to the various money and capital markets. This means that, in certain circumstances, it can borrow where the conditions are most attractive at the time and can place available liquid resources on the markets which offer the highest interest rates.

It is obvious that the multinational enterprise is thus better placed than anyone else, thanks to a centralised financial management, to make good use of the differences in time and space occurring between the financial markets, both as regards availability and as regards cost of financing resources. Thus, the multinational companies have played a prominent role in the development of the Eurobond and Eurocurrency Markets.

Furthermore, by manipulating the reciprocal supplies of goods, pricefixing and terms of payment among the different branches, the multinational company may occupy an advantageous position in certain circumstances as regards exchange risks and taxation burden. Its international character also enables the multinational enterprise to make maximum use of the financial, fiscal and other advantages which countries often offer to promote investments on their own territory.

The multinational company as a source of autonomy

This brief survey of the main advantages of the multinational company brings out the fact that it is actually active in three dimensions. First of all, the national dimension of the parent company, whence it extends its activities over the world and which takes decisions on the strategically important points and determines the arrangement of the whole. In the second place, the dimension of foreign countries, which is fragmented by political, economic and sociological boundaries, and which is occupied by the multinational enterprise via its local establishments. And lastly, the multinational company's own specific dimension, created by itself via its internal organisation and structure.

This threefold dimension gives the multinational enterprise a greater degree of independence vis-à-vis its environment and thence offers its possibilities which are not available, or at least are available to a lesser extent, to the national enterprise.

On the other hand, it is a fact that each of these three dimensions has its own characteristics which must be brought into line with each other. The possibilities of tensions and even conflicts are great. The multinational company must limit these tensions to the fullest possible extent and make the influence of the enterprise's own dimension on the two other dimensions as great as possible; in other words, it must try to avoid the disequilibria, distortions and checks which hinder the optimum utilisation of the available resources.

It is thus obvious that it is confronted with two types of problems: on the one hand, those which are peculiar to the enterprise itself and which are connected with the organisation and exercise of authority and on the other, those which stem from the fact that the multinational company breaks out of the limits of national states and economies.

Internal problems

The multinational enterprise exercises its activities against a geographically extensive background, which moreover shows a great diversity. First of all, it has to overcome the distance factor. This applies as well—although to a lesser degree—to any national enterprise from a large country, even if this enterprise does not develop beyond the frontiers. It is therefore not surprising that the multinational companies attach great importance to good communications facilities when choosing the places of their branches.

The widespread establishments must be brought together and kept together in a whole which operates well at the level of planning, decision-making, operations and control. Numerous organisational set-ups are applied and are in full course of development.[10] It is possible to distinguish two major types of organisational patterns.

In the first type, the responsibility for the allocation and management of the resources at international level rests with a separate international department in the parent company or possibly even with a company specially incorporated for this purpose. This international department has wide powers in the framework of the general objectives of the parent company. Its members form a sort of pool of managers who, coming both from the parent company and from the branches, are prepared and competent to occupy responsible positions at any point whatever in the entire group.

A second type, which may be regarded as more developed from certain points of view, has a more integrated character. In it, the structural distinction between domestic and foreign operations is abandoned in favour of an organisational pattern in which the central management outlines the policy for the whole group in a truly international perspective, and coordinates and supervises the execution of this policy.

The actual structure of the international department in the first type and of the central management in the second type may be functional, geographical or product-based.

The different models may also be combined. In practice, the organisation models seem to present a very great variety by reason of the fact that each enterprise adjusts its organisation to its own needs and objectives.[11]

10. P. De Bruyne, *Entreprises et marchés d'outre-mer*, Louvain 1966, pp. 336-355 and L. Vansina, *De Internationalisatie van de onderneming, Ondernemingspolitiek en Economische Integratie*, Negende Vlaams Wetenschappelijk Economisch Congres, 1969, pp. 319-321 with detailed bibliography. See also Business International Corporation, *Organizing the worldwide corporation*, January 1970.

11. See E. de Martino and Bruce E. Searle, "Operating on a Global Basis, Today and Tomorrow" in *Columbia Journal of World Business*, September-October 1972, pp. 51-61. This article is based on a survey of two hundred American and European multinational enterprises.

24

The complexity and geographical spreading of the multinational company obviously endanger the speed and efficiency of decision-making, execution and supervision, as well as the exercise of authority and responsibility. In so far as it is lacking in aggression and efficiency in these fields, it runs the risk of being outstripped by national enterprises in certain circumstances. This would then form one of the possible limitations for the expansion of big multinational companies. In this connection, we may refer to the role which the computer may play in order to maintain an overall view of the organisational structure of these big dispersed enterprises and to render their supervision efficient.

Another difficulty for the multinational company lies in the diversity of the milieu in which it is bound to exercise its activity. It is not an easy matter to become aware of this diversity and to take account of it. This depends not only on the international qualities of the managers, but also on the way in which the headquarters of the company put into effect the highly important coordination and control of the whole set-up.

Indeed, the activities of the different branches must be integrated into a single whole, if the multinational enterprise wants to acquire its own dimension. It is here that the problems of the relationship between the multinational enterprises and the national economies arise.

External problems

The problems resulting from the emergence of multinational or foreign companies in national economies are very complex. They also differ from one country to another and even in a single country, they differ in time or according to the countries from which the enterprises originate.

A great many of these problems are situated at the level of the so-called national independence, and more especially economic independence. In this connection, stress is laid on the danger that vital decisions may be taken by enterprises which are outside the national community and which do not come under the national regulations, for example, decisions concerning the continued existence of the local branch, its expansion, activity, employment, orientation, exports, etc. It is feared that, in the framework of a multinational company, national interests in the economic and social field could be subordinated to the interests of the enterprise itself or of the country of origin. In particular, American affiliates are often the subject of criticism or suspicious doubt, which is mainly ascribable to the large scope of the United States enterprises by comparison with others and to the very marked increase in their direct foreign investments in the past twenty years.

In fact, only a few examples of such subordination are known; nevertheless, it cannot be denied that there is always a latent possibility to its occurring. As a consequence of what was stated above about the multinational enterprise's own dimension, it was even obvious that, according as the different local branches are integrated into the overall strategy of the international enterprise which becomes genuinely multinational or transnational, they gradually lose their local or national character. Whether this will harm the national economy or not is quite another question.

But in any case, more sensitivity will be shown towards the decisions of affiliates of foreign enterprises concerning activity, employment, supply of products, *etc.*, than towards the decisions of national enterprises. In many countries, we have witnessed recently labour and trade union campaigns against multinational companies which had decided to proceed to certain reorganisations of the group that were likely to have repercussions on employment in specific affiliates or regions. It also seems that it is above all the presence and global strategy of the multinational companies that give an incentive to the formation of trade union groups at the international level.

The structure of the corporate management and of the ownership of capital is closely connected with the national or foreign character of the enterprise. Ethnocentric managements (to use Perlmutter's term), whereby the leading posts are occupied solely by foreigners, often come in for criticism. In this connection, the term "neo-colonialism" is even sometimes used. However exaggerated this may be, it nevertheless points to the existence of certain tensions and sensitivities which the multinational enterprises have to take into account.

Similar problems arise with regard to the ownership of capital. In most cases, the multinational companies—and especially those of American origin—prefer to hold the entire share capital of their foreign establishments or controlled firms, and this again raises questions, in the countries concerned, about the possibilities of participation in ownership, management and distribution of profits.

Recently, it is mainly problems connected with the balance of payments and the autonomy of the national interest and credit policy that have come to the fore. It is not so much a matter of the problems which may arise from a more or less centrally decided partition of the markets or from the fixing of prices for reciprocal supplies among the different branches of the multinational company, but rather of the repercussions which the foreign exchange, credit and investment operations of the big multinational enterprises may have on the national balance of payments, gold and exchange reserves, the position of the currency, the volume of liquid assets and the interest rate and credit policy.

Obviously, the leads and lags and the purchases and sales of foreign exchange in connection with expected devaluation and revaluation are not confined to the multinational companies; they may also originate from national enterprises wishing to protect themselves against variations in exchange rates or to profit therefrom. But owing to the international background against which they operate, by their spread over various countries and monetary zones, as well as by the scope of their commercial operations and of the resources they manage, the multinational enterprises are extremely well placed for this purpose. The same must be said of the borrowing and investment operations beyond the frontiers, for reasons of interest rate conditions and the availability of credit on the different markets. Both factors may be considerable obstacles to the balance of payments policy, as well as the credit policy, the level of interest rates, the availability of liquid assets and the contra-cyclical interest, liquidities and cyclical policy of the national governments. The foreign operations of multinational companies may thus give rise to numerous problems for the national economies, and the above considerations leave out of account the problems connected with competition for existing national enterprises and with labour relations.

Despite this, the authorities and public opinion in the industrial countries, where the penetration of the multinational enterprise is now most pronounced, are in general positively disposed. Indeed, there is an awareness of the close link between the freedom of movement of goods and economic integration, on the one hand, and the internationalisation or multinationalisation of production and corporate structures, on the other.

The principal measures to slow down the tendency of enterprises to spread over different countries are moreover found in the United States and the United Kingdom, where the government is trying to check direct investments abroad owing to the repercussions of the capital outflows on the balance of payments. In the United States, the multinational companies have become the target of harsh criticism on the part of the labour unions, which accuse them of depriving American workers of jobs by moving their production to lower-wage countries (job drain) and by re-exporting to the United States products manufactured abroad. [12]

These accusations led to the submission of the famous Hartke-Burke Bill, providing for steps to be taken against the multinationals in the following fields: taxation, capital operations with foreign countries, customs duties and the control of these enterprises.

12. It should be noted that these assertions do not seem to be borne out by the facts. The survey made by Professor Stobaugh of Harvard with a representative sample of American multinational companies in the manufacturing industry sector seems to show that direct investments abroad have created, in the aggregate, more jobs than they caused to be lost and that if these investments had not taken place, the employment losses would have been substantial, for the simple reason that it would have been impossible to maintain the position on the foreign markets by exports from the United States. (See David W. Ewing, "Multinational companies on trial", *Harvard Business Review*, May-June 1972, pp. 131-132). The report of the Tariff Commission concludes, after a detailed analysis, that the activity of the American multinational companies has had a positive influence on employment in the United States (pp. 645-672).

As regards the "host countries", on the other hand, it remains correct to say that in general, the majority of them are making efforts rather to attract foreign investments with a view to certain national objectives of a social and economic nature which are at present well served by the activity of the foreign branches. It is indeed fully realised what a great significance foreign direct investments can have for the solutions to regional development and reconversion problems. It is also realised that they may have favourable effects on employment, renewal and diversification of the industrial structures, reinforcement of the export position, contribution and dissemination of technology and management, increase of the rate of growth of production and income-formation, etc. This does not alter the fact that, even apart from Canada and Australia, the authorities are beginning to show concern about the foreign presence in their economies, either because it is sometimes deemed to be excessive or because it affects so-called vital sectors.

Future and policy

It would be useless to try to weigh up the advantages and drawbacks of the multinational companies under various aspects. The multinational enterprise exists—in any case, if there is a genuine wish to agree on the meaning of the term—and it is probable that an ever growing number of enterprises will acquire the same character.

Among the numerous factors which encourage its creation and expansion, it is particularly important for the future to stress the scope of the efforts made in the field of research and development.

Technological progress and the pressure of competition will constantly give rise to increasing budgets for research and development, which will need to be spread over larger total turnovers. These turnovers presuppose vast markets, the penetration of which can be achieved to an ever decreasing extent by exports alone. The spreading of production units throughout the world, which has considerably gained in intensity in the past twenty years, especially as regards United States companies should therefore proceed further. It may be expected that the European and Japanese companies will be very active in this field in the coming years.

The direct investments of European and Japanese enterprises have already greatly increased in recent years. (14 per cent. per annum against 10 per cent. for American direct investments). We are still far from a European and Japanese invasion of the Unites States, to which some observers are already starting to refer, but it must probably be expected that investments and acquisitions of control by European and Japanese firms in the United States will be stimulated by successive devaluations and revaluations and by the effect of certain currency floats which have profoundly changed the parity ratios and the relative cost of these operations. Furthermore, the same reasoning leads to the conclusion that American direct investments could show a certain slowdown. At the same time, the European and Japanese enterprises will most probably increase their activities outside their countries of origin.

In any case, it may be stated as a tendency that the world economy—or considerable portions thereof—is moving towards a more corporate-minded structure. If this tendency persists, international economic relations will gradually be based to a lesser extent on national economies which exchange goods, services and capital among themselves and will come to depend increasingly on multinational enterprises which will organise the international division of labour and specialisation, as well as the flows of goods, services and capital in their own midst. Their direct action on the application and remuneration of usable production factors and the opening-up of markets and opportunities would thus become a more and more important factor for integration and for the dissemination and increase of prosperity. This leads certain observers to consider the multinational companies as the beginning of a new worldwide politico-economic system.

However, it cannot be forecast to what extent such an evolution will in fact be implemented. The development towards a free circulation of goods and capital has already been interrupted on several occasions, but each time fortunately has got under way again. It is therefore perfectly possible that the multinational companies will in future encounter obstacles that offer such resistance that they will have to learn to live with them and seek other means of ensuring their expansion or viability. Indeed, it may very well be imagined that according as their relative importance increases they will arrive at economic and political limits and that political power will be the winner in case of conflict. In addition, the beneficial contribution by the multinational companies to the economies in which they have become installed could precisely render the authorities of these countries less dependent on them and thus increase the degree of freedom of action for these authorities in respect of them.

Multinational enterprises extend beyond the frontiers and beyond the national economies and, with a view to maintaining their position and their growth, they have to develop a strategy of their own and to acquire a certain independence. This entails risks of tensions between them and the political communities which have their own objectives, conceptions, legislation and requirements.

Both will have to learn to make allowances for each other, so that conflicts and upsets can be limited as much as possible, in the interest of the development of the multinational enterprises themselves as well as of the economic growth and development of prosperity in the countries and regions.

The multinational companies will thus have to realise that, despite their possible technological advance and great economic significance, they cannot occupy a preponderant position in the economy of a country or in really vital sectors without this leading to a reaction sooner or later. In their corporate strategy and policy, they cannot remain insensitive to the objectives of the economic and social policy and the laws and customs of the countries concerned. To the greatest possible extent, they should allow the communities in which they are established to participate in ownership and management. In fact, the majority of the plurinational enterprises are still very nationally-slanted in these two respects. But their genuine multinationalisation cannot be otherwise than to their advantage. They will be able to draw managerial talent and capital form a world reserve and to adapt themselves more adequately to the great diversity of all the regions of the world in which they operate, and will be better equipped to discover and develop their potentialities. This should enable them to integrate themselves better and more easily in the environment and the respective communities, which in the final analysis is one of the foremost social tasks for every enterprise, without which it can hardly perform its economic role successfully.

As regards the national governments, it may be expected that they will not make a point of reducing the mulitnational companies to an aggregate of national enterprises in which the specific factors of planning, decision making and operation on a global scale would be lacking. They cannot force these enterprises to operate in their countries; they can only keep them out by imposing on them either prohibitions of obligations which would run counter to their fundamental interests. Then, however, the national economy does not benefit from the favourable effects of the activity of the multinational enterprise and abandons these advantages to other economies. This is at present the case for numerous countries which are competing for foreign investments.

In the presence of international enterprises, the national authorities will have to learn to practise an international policy as well, at least in fields of capital importance for the multinational company such as anti-trust legislation, taxation, company law and legislation on concentration, patent law, interest and credit policy. There is a great deal to be done here with respect to harmonisation and unification, which shows that the multinational company is a factor of integration.

The problem arises in an especially acute way in Europe, and more particularly within the European Economic Community. The E.E.C. Commission has put forward some valuable orientations in a Memorandum on the industrial policy of the Community, the objective being to promote the creation of transnational European enterprises, meaning by this term enterprises which not only operate in various European countries and outside them as well, but whose capital and management are also in European hands and whose decision centre is located in Europe. It should be noted that, in the opinion of the Commission, the formation of transnational enterprises and the possible support measures in this respect should not remain limited to the large enterprises, but would also need to extend to the medium-sized firms which often show more dynamism and greater capacity for adjustment and are quicker to seize new opportunities offered by market developments and innovations.

By way of conclusion to these comments on the multinational company, attention should be drawn to certain recent developments concerning the penetration and activities of large multinational enterprises in the Eastern countries. This penetration occurs essentially by means of contractual arrangements relating to production and co-production, management, performance of all kinds of services, etc. The host countries are owners of the enterprises, the presence of the foreign enterprise is limited in time and the contracts can be renegotiated after a certain period. In fact, it amounts to replacing ownership relations by contractual relations, with the remuneration of the multinational company taking the form of a fee instead of dividends and accumulation of assets.

Similar formulae probably lend themselves to applications in other countries. Obviously, they mean a profound change of approach by comparison with the "classic" direct investment. In the opinion of certain observers, [13] they will gradually replace the present forms of expansion of the multinational companies, starting with the developing countries. This would mean that the heyday of the multinational firm which we are now witnessing is almost over. The future will show whether this is so.

13. Peter G. Gabriel, "Adaptation: the names of the MNC's game", *Columbia Journal of World Business*, Nov.-Dec. 1972, pp. 7-14.

Chapter III

THE GROWTH OF MULTINATIONAL ENTERPRISES—A LOOK INTO PAST AND FUTURE

by *G. Y. Bertin*

It is a commonplace to note that the experience over the past fifteen years has established the power of what are usually—and perhaps wrongly—named multinational enterprises.[1] The following current data will suffice to identify the multinational phenomenon: an overall turnover of $600 billion a year;[2] over 80,000 subsidiaries all over the world;[3] an average growth rate of 10 per cent. per annum, i.e., nearly twice as much as the average rate of growth, and some $130 billion of "free" capital reserves.[4]

Neither the difficulties known in the past few years, nor the monetary crisis of 1970-73, nor the last slump in the United States of America (1970) have slowed down the rise of multinationalization. Whereas the rates of expansion were slowing down on domestic markets, the rate of growth in foreign markets has remained comparable to that of preceding years.

It would appear, however, from various symptoms that the most active phase of multinationalization is probably over and that we have now perhaps stepped into a different era.

The present moment is a good time to take stock—all the more so since we may now look back over the past fifteen years and better appreciate the main trends of this complex phenomenon. In this context, there is much useful information to be found in the official reports of experts' conferences and meetings of specialists.[5]

1. We do not wish here to enter into terminological arguments about what multinational, international, or transnational firms respectively represent. (Refer here to Y. Aharoni, "On the Definition of a Multinational Corporation", *Quarterly Review of Economics and Business*, Vol. II, 1971). By multinational firm is therefore meant a company, an important part of whose business (20 per cent.) is carried on abroad and which owns a more or less widespread network of production subsidiaries.

2. 1973 estimation after J. Polk (see R. Vernon, "Multinational Enterprise and National Security", *Adelphi Papers*, 1971).

3. Amongst which, in 1970, 39,633 were American. Source: *Reporting Data on Foreign Corporations*, U.S. Treasury Department International Service, 1973.

4. Declaration by U.S. Senator Church in Commission (February 1973) (figures revalued).

5. Ref.: Rennes Symposium on "The Growth of the Large Multinational Firm" (September 1972) and Brissago Symposium.

Initially, we will study the general trend of the process. Three fundamental questions deserve some attention:

The first concerns the prospects of multinationalization: will the movement keep on at the same speed, or is it likely in the near future to alter its course or its nature, thus leading back to a phase such as we have known in the past, when international relations assumed a contracted form?

Secondly, it is unquestionable that multinationalization is no longer in 1973 what it used to be only ten years ago. The course it has followed has greatly modified the pattern of relations and the structure of trade thus influencing future growth. It is therefore essential to describe how it operates.

Finally, and this has been repeatedly confirmed by recent events—the relations between large worldwide firms and national states have deeply disrupted the international economie game. Is it now possible to identify their lines of action and reaction and also the division of responsibilities and the consequences that may follow?

Before tackling each of these different points, one should recall a few of the important features without which the definition of multinational growth might be misinterpreted.

Two of these remarks relate to the transformation of the general context; the third concerns the recent evolution of large companies.

Internationalization, or even multinationalization, has become a current element in growth. Foreign growth does not merely concern a few hundred firms, but indeed several thousand. This extension has two aspects: on the one hand, firms whose growth had hitherto been purely on a domestic level have "discovered" foreign countries; on the other, numerous so-called "average-sized" firms have in their turn become multinational. Statistics are very revealing on this particular point. In 1960, less than 2,000 American firms invested abroad; over 8,000 do so now.[6] In 1965, there were 200 Japanese firms; in 1972, over 1,400.[7]

What started as a somewhat limited ans secondary development has turned into a massive process. Obviously, neither its mechanism, nor its specific characteristics, nor the result can any longer be the same .

The second remark is that the world in which the multinational firms have evolved has also changed. Shrunken by technical progress, it has become both more open and more conscious of the potential impact of the phenomenon. It wants to take advantage of "free trade" for itself, in the name of the liberal ideal to which all the main countries officially subscribe; and at the same time, it wishes to limit the destructive or the excessive sharpness of its effects, thus adopting a Neo-Keynesian, if not a mercantilist, attitude.

The rules of the game and the way it operates confirm that the predomi-

6. U.S. Treasury Department and *U.S. Survey of Current Business*.
7. M.I.T.I.: "Les investissements japonais à l'étranger", 1972, French edition.

nant economy is still all powerful. The situation also highlights the limits and the uncertainties of the international game and the heavy costs that will have to be borne by all sides. Along with the evolution in the general background, we find an evolution in the objectives and behaviour of multinational groups. The size of the average group and its international spread have both considerably increased. Nowadays, the large multinational firm comprises 50 to 200 "foreign" subsidiaries, making 30 per cent. to 90 per cent. of its sales and manufacturing 20 per cent. to 75 per cent. of its output outside its country of origin. It controls international assets three or four times greater than twelve years ago;[8] the "small" multinational firm owns only from two to ten or so subsidiaries and its foreign assets rarely exceed $50 million but it has become multinational within a shorter space of time and its progress has been more rapid.[9]

The multinational enterprise operates in a competitive atmosphere where above all it is most important not to be left behind by a competitor, i.e., to maintain or attain the minimum size. It also wants to maintain a growth rate which enables it to hold the same relative position—or even to improve upon it. Expansion in the world's regional markets provides a line of growth. It is the only factor that allows the firm both to strengthen it position and to draw the most profit from economies of scale in the production field as well as in some aspects of management.

But the one-dimension linear growth is no longer sufficient. The larger groups already know its limitations. The direct pressure of competition, along with the market's opportunities, and the indirect pressure of imitation and technological innovations create a certain amount of risk; beyond a certain point, the relevant risks reach an exceedingly high level, thus reducing the prospects of long-term growth. The large firm can no longer be just multinational. It must also be multi-dimensional, not only because this makes possible profits from external effects and integration, but also because in doing so the large firm proportionally reduces the risks linked to the growth of the original sector and to its own growth.

Beyond a certain phase in its development, the large modern company is therefore doomed to an "all-round strategy"—which is the only one that can guarantee a stable enough growth rate and an acceptable level of risk.

Both the facts outlined and the attitudes of the main protagonists seem to converge towards two essential points: the unavoidable character of this expansion and the equally absolute necessity to counter its consequences or at least to reduce its uncertainties. Seen in this light, the problem of the growth

8. In 12 years (1959-1971) the consolidated figure for world turnover has on average been multiplied by 3; the foreign turnover by 4–G.R.E.F.I., "La croissance des SMN, note sur les tendances 1969-1971" (1972 roneotyped).

9. G. Y. Bertin, "L'expansion internationale des grandes entreprises", *La documentation française, travaux et recherche*, no. 25, 1972, 124 pp.

of the multinational enterprise is merely a reflection of the tensions that derive from it.

Basically, multinational growth is far from reaching an end and its evolution can be expected to keep on at a sustained pace.

The various general indications available on the evolution of the firms' foreign assets confirm the stability of their growth rate around the average figure over the past 12 years, i.e., approximately 10 per cent. per annum.[10] The slight drop from 10.5 per cent. per annum (1950-1960) to 9.4 per cent. (1960-1970) is scarcely significant.[11] Specific data on the selected multinational firms confirm this tendency: this shows that progress has kept up a steady rate of 60 per cent. per period of 4 years since 1959.[12] Expected short-term or medium-term growth does not show further slackening.[13]

Although such plans have a mere indicative value in the present state of things, a great number of arguments strongly support the thesis of steady growth.

Large multinational firms have not yet reached the limits of their international expansion. Only a few important firms, even in the United States, henceforth plan to concentrate their expansion only on their domestic markets; at the same time only a few of these have yet reached a high degree of internationalization. With regard to market orientated firms, the ideal limits theoretically consist in distributing the world sales in proportion to the size of respective markets. Within these limits, many American multinational firms want to keep on increasing the foreign element in their overall activities. In order to do so, a steadier growth and a better distribution of assets are just as important as preoccupation with profit or with one's competitive position.

Under these conditions, the expected 40 to 45 per cent. of consolidated turnover figure quoted in the reports of numerous firms does not seem unreasonable and might be attained during the current decade.

As for European multinational enterprises, they are—with a few exceptions—even further from attaining such a distribution, if European investment is considered as purely domestic. In the case of Japanese firms, the process of multinationalization is only just beginning and the prospects of growth are very bright.[14] The "catching up" process of non-American multinational firms can thus provide a large potential for further multinationalization in the future.

10. Refer here to: *U.S. Survey of Current Business*, November-December 1972, chronical J. Freidlin and A. Kupo.

11. 93rd Congress, Committee on Finance, U.S. Senate: "Implications of Multinational Firms for World Trade and Investment and for U.S. Trade and Labor", February 1973, 930 p.

12. G.R.E.F.I., *op. cit.*, p. 5.

13. *Survey of Current Business, op. cit.*

14. M.I.T.I., *op. cit.*: $10 billion in 1975-26 in 1980.

Secondly, over the past few years, the internationalization process has been widely extended to medium-sized firms. This should continue. But these firms still represent a small (about 20 per cent.), though growing, proportion of world business, especially in Europe.

Even though newcomers may be of a different nature or behave quite differently from traditional multinational firms, their mere existence backs up the existing trend by amplifying it and strengthening its foundations.

This mechanistic view of multinational growth actually coincides with the investors' deepest motivations. Further investigation shows that, for the most part, the urge to expand abroad remains extremely strong.

We are now more aware of the factors that play a part in determining direct investment, even though it is still difficult to disclose their respective influences. Among the determinants studied by J. H. Dunning, [15] some are less important than is usually thought. Apart from some areas, the attraction of a low wage level, [16] often counteracted by low productivity, has played only a seemingly minor part in past expansions.

On the other hand, factors like tariff or structural barriers, market size, the wish to be nearer the consumer, or close to the supplier maintain their full strength.

In reality, most studies consider profit as most important as a criterion for good investment, whether it is anticipated or regarded "ex post".

Now, prospective profits drawn from foreign operations, though not as bright as they formerly were, remain greater than on many home markets—provided that these operations have the advantage of a monopolistic position in the field of technology, commerce, or management.

With regard to American direct manufacturing activity, the profit rate calculated on the base of adjusted earnings, varies over time between 11.5 per cent. and 12 per cent. in underdeveloped countries and 11 per cent. and 12 per cent. in developed countries; [17] it means that its level is 2 to 4 points higher than that attainable in the United States. Similarly, despite a serious drop over these past years, due to political and technical reasons, primary producers (e.g. mining and oil industries) still retain adequate profitability. Furthermore, we are merely quoting average figures: margins on new "monopolized" products often being greater. This persisting difference provides the best guarantee of multinational expansion in so far as the parent company derives from it a substantial and stable proportion (up to two-thirds) of consolidated profits.

15. J. H. Dunning, "The Determinants of International Production" in C.N.R.S. (G. Y. Bertin, ed.) *The Growth of the Large Multinational Corporation* (Rennes Symposium) forthcoming edition.

16. This is not G. Adam's opinion: "New Trends in International Business: World-wide—Sourcing and Dedomiciling", *Nota Economica*, 1971.

17. *Survey of Current Business, op. cit.*

It is nevertheless true that, for a large group, the expanding and deepening of foreign markets is a very good way of reducing the risk of a capital loss. This risk may also be reduced in part by the expansion of multinational firms into new areas (e.g. the developing interests of American multinationals in the countries of the Far East and South-East Asia).

A final positive argument stems from the race to capture natural resources, since they tend to become scarce either through exhaustion or national take-over.

Although multinational growth prospects remain wide open, there is no proof that the stimulus will remain as strong as it was in the past and that the existing trend will not level off somewhat. But conditions will change anyway.

A degree of saturation and even disinvestment may take place in the most intensively penetrated markets (e.g. in Europe).

Moreover, the growth process is more than ever linked to general economic and political conditions. The pace of United States new investment will possibly slow down at a time when European (mostly German) and Japanese investment can be expected to increase in line with their respective positions in their balances of payments.

Finally, it is not likely to remain identical to what it used to be.

The possibility cannot be excluded that its main axes may shift, albeit slightly: to start with, there has been a relative shift of foreign investment from the oil industry to manufacturing industries in spite of the new discoveries in the North Sea and possibly in South-East Asia.

Next a geographical shift; the more developed countries, especially Europe, have hitherto been the preferred grounds for expansion. Doubtless, they will remain so under the present conditions of risk and profit. But new markets (Brazil, Australia, South-East Asia, Africa, etc.), which often progress twice as quickly, will gradually become more attractive for the average multinational firm.

The impact of axial shift is considerable: even if the changeover is only noticeable over a decade, several billion dollars "set free" on the market may be redirected towards new areas. Indeed, past experience, and preferential capital movements [18] within one large sector—e.g. that of energy—or between markets providing a similar potential demand, seem to point to possible areas for future international investment; yet, to some extent, they leave this growth a degree of freedom.

Multinational growth and direct investment by one country (or one area) in another should not be considered as a single phenomenon. New investment tends to be financed by contributions from outside. But growth can, up to a point, feed itself from local sources. In reality, the experience of American

18. Cf. the concept of close-circuit financing (M. Byé).

firms proves that the financial market structures and the wish of parent firms to keep control of foreign operations have hitherto helped to maintain the external share in financing subsidiary growth at a steady level (40 per cent.).[19] But these again are average global figures and the reality may turn out differently with a change in the respective positions of United States and European financial resources.

Finally, classical direct investment may not be the only long-lasting formula.[20] Although it is hardly likely that many large firms will follow Kaiser's example, some American multinational enterprises may be tempted to do so under indirect pressure of trade unions and government and by fear of rising cost of investment and wages in Europe. It is also possible to see a certain amount of international investment take the shape of technical and commercial assistance backed by investment of public funds. American negotiations with the USSR, China or other socialist countries will hold surprising outcomes in store. . .

In these ways, the terms and conditions of multinational growth are going through important changes, the origin of which can be traced briefly to the main concern of multinational firms: preserving in the best possible way their potential for future growth and looking for the cheapest ways of entering new markets.

A few years ago, the possession by a firm of any monopolistic advantage was in itself enough to guarantee a sustained international growth, as long as the firm also had the real or potential means to support it. Such advantages still exist—as many cases ranging from IBM to Michelin will prove. Yet, the shortening of the time within which it is successfully possible to imitate technology, and the fact that multinational enterprises are being faced by an increasing number of competitors on a local or world scale, will restrict future prospects and weaken expansion based on a single line of production. Those multinational enterprises operating branches promising future expansion and a high level of profit, with difficult entry conditions, can maintain a steady "linear" growth without fearing that their overall performance will fall below that of their main competitors.

On the other hand, the success of purely conglomerate multinational growth is without doubt not as clear as some would often like to emphasise. Real conglomerates, whose activities have only one common objective—that of making money—are in the main American, and multinational growth applies only to a restricted part of their activity. Other firms, incorrectly called conglomerates, exploit technical or commercial complementarities within one

19. *Survey of Current Business, op. cit.*
20. This results from the growing demand for international investment in socialist countries.

large industrial sector. Only a few very large multinational enterprises (e.g. ITT) have an international conglomerate strategy.

However, a definite tendency towards conglomerate growth is undeniable and it will almost certainly be even more so in the future. The main influences whose effects are both noticeable and long-lasting can be easily listed:

The wish to save money through vertical integration leads multinational enterprises to open up, down-stream from the production line, new markets from which new diversification appears possible.

The fact has become clear that economies of scale are more considerable and more directly applicable in financial or organization matters than in the technical field—especially in the management of a largely international group.

Some evolution has taken place in the concept of the market. It no longer revolves around a product or a range of products but centres on a combination of complementary yet technically separate needs such as the big industrial building, energy, or the general foodstuffs market, etc. The strategy of large firms then encourages them to control both the *confluent markets* (i.e., the final product markets) and the *affluent markets.*

The long-term risks increase for the non-diversified firm, due to techniques and branches becoming more rapidly obsolete, the smaller number of new growth opportunities that may be met, and above all to apprehension regarding the outcome of an efficient international anti-trust policy.

These elements combine so as to induce the main industrial groups to diversify their activity around their main line of expansion. Numerous recent examples confirm this tendency, which is becoming a rule among some branches (e.g. mechanical industries, food industries, etc.). [21] Moreover, the diversification process of the main branch or within that main branch is greatly increasing (from 12 per cent. to 16 per cent. between 1963 and 1971 in a selection of nearly 230 multinational firms), [22] confirming this evolution.

Now this coincides with the wish to penetrate new markets in the cheapest possible way in order to alter at the same time the aspects of multinational growth.

Strategy creating new production units takes fullest advantage of competition between states in order to lessen setting-up costs. In the same way, a buying-up strategy lessens penetration costs, and above all shortens the time the firm will take to become operative on the market. This external growth represents around 80 per cent. of the growth of the large firms, and over 50 per cent. in Europe. [23] Should the "opportunities" for such an investment

21. G. Y. Bertin "Multinational Growth, Oligopoly and Competition", C.N.R.S., *op. cit.*

22. G.R.E.F.I. "Sociétés multinationales et diversification", March 1973, and a forthcoming study (Bus. Int., Geneva).

23. See Scherer, *Industrial Economics* and articles by A. P. Weber on concentration.

decrease in the long-run, once restructuring of the more open sectors is well on the way, they can and should be compensated by an increasing transfer of assets or "industrial divisions" from one group to another. In this way, both considerations of short-term profit and the need to provide against increased industrial risks, combine to push multinational firms towards greater flexibility.

Yet this process hardly takes place except in the more advanced countries. Reducing penetration cost or risks in more exposed areas—i.e., developing countries and, in particular, in countries with a socialist economy—implies the effective use of new nostrums restricting the stakes of the multinational groups while preserving their essential interests or their profits. Trying to obtain contracts for technical and financial aid without a contribution of capital, etc. is the logical way out. The firm raises the value of such factors that it and international markets are possibly most short of: [24] technique and management, i.e. qualified personnel. Thus its very substance, its capital, is immobilised and subjected to hazard.

It now clearly appears that the reaction of multinational enterprises against uncertainty and potential risks is to diversify their strategy to the greatest extent possible. Yet, owing to this fact, the changeover to greater diversification and flexibility has considerable *consequences for the internal structures* of multinational firms as well as for *the structures of the economies* within which they operate.

The multinational firm is trapped by the necessity: (1) to guarantee sufficient freedom of management to a body that is tending to increase both in size and in complexity and (2) to ensure both an efficient and well-coordinated management. It is difficult to reconcile both objectives and this results in a large variety of formulas being selected—ranging from complete centralization to complete decentralization. However, an increasing number of multinational enterprises are opting for a "grid" type structure founded both on the recognition of the product division and the existence of regional headquarters. This confirms that operational flexibility tends to be the prevailing tendency.[25] Yet one may wonder whether what is gained in flexibility will not be paid for in terms of a certain clash of interest between general management (especially the financial management), on the one hand, and technical and commercial management at the local level, on the other, though it may be driven to it one day by the very size of the group and by a complex of isolationist circumstances.

During the past decade, owing to multinationalization, the most tightly

24. E. T. Penrose, "The Growth of International Corporations and Their Changing Role in Under Developed Countries", C.N.R.S.

25. L. Franko, "Organizational Structure and Allocative Efficiency in European M.N.C.", C.N.R.S.

closed national structures have completely disintegrated. Can we say therefore that this leads to greater competition? This is by no means certain. "Frozen" national oligopolies have been replaced by one international oligopoly, which is often extremely lively when markets are either opening up or coming together. This kind of activity is very far from subsiding and the entry of new competitors is likely to keep it going. Yet at the regional level–e.g. in Europe, Latin America, etc.–the movement tends to crystallize slowly and everything points to an accentuation of this process.

The penetration of outside multinational firms, especially American ones, has been followed by a two-fold concentration movement. [26] The first centred around the newcomers; the second around threatened local firms. A temporarily increasing number of competitors on a national market reinforces in fact the relative positions of the leading firms. This clearly appears to be the case in comparative studies on the structure of countries or of large regions, or if one investigates world classifications consolidated by type like those published by *Fortune*. A large number of top multinational firms have their positions both reinforced and expanded. [27]

Several objections may be made at this point: reinforcement of multinational firms may stimulate oligopolistic concentration. Indeed, the world concentration level seems, in some branches, to be receding, and oligopolistic conflict has been resumed, due to the growth of Japanese or European firms. [28] Groups' subsidiaries often have divergent if not conflicting interests and politics. Finally, the structural pattern goes unchanged in so far as multinational firms depend upon a widespread network of subcontractors and complementary industries. Yet, despite the fact that technical concentration should not be confused with financial concentration, structures are tightening up: this leads to group alliances, partial or temporary consolidations, official or secret agreements, if competition looks too intensive or too expensive. This logically derives from a certain stabilization of markets.

Finally, limitations on the development of an excessive concentration of multinational enterprises are of two kinds:
(1) management efficiency which may lead to the profitable giving up of activities that have become marginal owing to new geographical or sectoral orientations being taken by the groups; and
(2) those which are more pressing and more uncertain, viz., legislative restrictions imposed by national states in the name of their own interests, or under this pretence.

26. A. Bienaymé, "Grande entreprise nord-américaine et concurrence", C.N.R.S.
27. A. Jacquemin et M. Cardon, "Les plus grandes entreprises de la C.E.E. et la Grande-Bretagne–structures, performances et politiques de concurrence", C.N.R.S.
28. J. H. Dunning, *op. cit.* p. 32.

It is an understatement to say that relations between multinational firms and national states have become a major preoccupation. The limitations of their respective powers are widely discussed each time international economic difficulties arise, and multinational enterprises are often accused of being the catalysts if not the cause of the trouble. The last monetary crisis (1973) provides us with a very good example, as do local conflicts like the "Roche case".

Yet, on reviewing the past decade, one may be impressed, as was Raymond Bertrand,[29] by the small number of open conflicts resulting from the emergence of the multinational phenomenon. Only the developing countries (e.g. Chile and the oil producing countries) have known serious conflicts, while, if one excepts conflicts arising from international monetary instability, more advanced countries were mostly spared—although they suffered a certain amount of tension (e.g. in Canada).

The advantages enjoyed by multinational enterprises may play a part in this situation. In a world where scarce factors such as capital, technique, and organization are in great demand and where their supply is limited—partly for artificial reasons—the supplier holds a strong position. It is all the more so, since he is the only one to offer a "block of productive combinations" through direct investment. Moreover, the multinational enterprises enjoy a threefold advantage: (1) their financial and technical dimension; this warrants access on preferential terms to the available resources and a good bargaining position; (2) most essential, the ability to shift rare factors; and (3) last but not least, the ability to make the first move in the strategic game, i.e., being able to choose the most favourable terms for their expansion from the range offered by the bidding countries and the firm's country of origin.

In this context—some foresee the come-back of a new wild capitalism—states are forced to retreat and the world's economic space tends to be organized along the main lines chosen by multinational enterprises.

In reality, most conflicts occur in two areas, both highly sensitive for firms and/or states.

The first cause of difficulties and the most direct one is linked with what, generally speaking, may be called "mobility": i.e., essentially mobility of capital, resources, and financial supplies, mobility of technical processes and even of production units. For example, in the financial field, any remaining hindrance is paid for not only in terms of an increase in risk but also in addition as an extra cost of transfer or "supplementary opportunity". We know the importance that multinational enterprises grant to freedom of action in what is regarded by them as essential, i.e., free use or transfer of

29. Raymond Bertrand, "Société multinationales et investissements directs dans leurs rapports avec les états", O.C.D.E. Document, 15 March, 1972.

42

profits and freedom in making the main decisions regarding current management, since their own performance depends upon them. On the other side, national states willingly admit that they should guarantee a certain amount of mobility. Except in underdeveloped countries, no serious difficulty has ever arisen as far as transfer of current profits is concerned. Yet they do not accept such mobility as would lead them to grant to multinational enterprises preferential terms and eventually to compromise general policy objectives. However, this mobility is an inherent part of the working of a multinational enterprise and its effects are occasionally amplified because of their own considerable weight. Movements of funds or financial manoeuvres often amounting to hundreds of millions of dollars are thus directly involved. Consequently, it is the concept of mobility itself which is involved—should one accept complete mobility and allow economies of scale full play, which would encourage a better distribution of factors? Or is it, on the other hand, advisable to control mobility in the name of a limited local optimum whose only merit would be to prevent the sudden appearance of disequilibrium? With inevitably restricted scope for intervention, states are strongly tempted to reinforce existing regulations. They do not realize that its real efficiency is not due to its force but rather to the extent of the area within which it is applied and which is limited to their national boundaries.

Yet, rather than mobility, the real point of controversy remains the delimination of the multinational enterprises' powers. This preoccupation manifests itself in direct investment regulations and in the development of anti-trust legislation.

The problem does not arise today under the same conditions as existed even a mere ten years ago. Since states recognize the almost exclusive advantages deriving from multinational firms and the multinational process, they are no longer systematically hostile to their presence. Yet the sharing of profits from direct investment sometimes appears to them to be unrealiable, unequal and unevenly spaced in time. This is why primary production countries strongly express the wish to "retrieve" ("*récupérer*") their own national resources; this is also why they wish to secure a minimum profit in advance, or at least to reduce "the trade-off" ("*le coût de contrepartie*") by asking for guarantees as soon as the investor steps in. Canadian legislative proposals follow this line of action; other Western countries (such as Mexico and Australia) may resort to it again.

However, in spite of some move towards a renewal of nationalism, the latter measures have only a restricted effect in an open economic world; although they impede outside contributions, they never successfully check the expansion of multinational enterprises on a local scale.

Ex-post interventions would bring entirely different forces to bear upon the expansion of multinational firms. In fact, it is the only kind that could slow down secondary expansion, but in so doing it would be necessary to transgress the officially inviolable (though often challenged) principle of equal rights between nationals and non-residents.

In practice, the "Continental Can" case has been typical. The decisions made reveal the limitations on state action: practical limitations, inasmuch as these can prevent the state from taking advantage of economies of scale and restrict the power of its own multinational firms in relation to other countries; there are also political limitations.

Owing to the spreading of the multinational phenomenon, the conflict between multinational enterprises and national states is shifting to the level of international relations. Neither spasmodic intervention nor specific action against multinational firms will suffice, considering that, in the United States, for instance, over half of the trade in goods and four-fifths of the capital movements are directly linked with the operations of multinational firms. [30] Discussing their terms of expansion ought to be part of an inclusive negotiation taking into account every aspect involved: trade, employment, monetary balance, etc. Yet finding the equation for the problem is not easy: national states wish to retain the benefits of multinationalization, but they are not necessarily prepared to bear its costs. The advantage drawn by the United States from "business surplus" (*l'excédent commercial et financier*) due to operations of multinational firms is one thing. The disequilibrium in employment which results is another; [31] states live off multinational firms, but they are also paralysed by them. So, they must take up their options . . . or . . . give up and let the system work.

In reality, the reason for this complex problem is that the ideal solution ought to be both satisfactory for individual states and compatible with easy trade between countries.

It is easy to believe that the answer lies in the hands of liberalism, even if unavoidable mistakes have to be compensated for here and there—by investment codes or "rules of good conduct". But then one forgets that the game of liberalism is not a "pure" game, and is therefore imperfect inasmuch as states exist and do not intend to commit suicide. One may also rely upon the strength of "compensating powers". Multinational or transnational unions (*organisations syndicales*) show the way by submitting precise and united programmes. [32] The setting up of co-ordinated worldwide banking networks could be another kind of "compensating power". This will probably not be sufficient. One may think, as many do, [33] that production and trade organization may in the near future require the setting up of a neutral and unchallen-

30. Implications on multinational firms . . . *op. cit.*
31. *Ibid.*
32. "Les sociétés multinationales", C.S.I. Report, Brussels.
33. See in particular: J. H. Behrman, "Industrial Development Through the Multinational Enterprise"; H. Arndt, "International Corporation and Economic Power" in C.N.R.S.

44

ged authority, i.e., a Council or Settlement Court that could at least offer suggestions and resolve minor conflicts.

In conclusion, finding a formula bypasses the question of multinational firms. This seems to be dissociated from a complete remodelling of the international monetary and banking institutions. [34] It is also true that the problem is political and despite the progress of non-American firms, it concerns above all the relations between the United States and Europe. Finally, the relative positions of multinational firms and states have still to be established. We may think (see C. P. Kindleberger [35]) that the world to come will be made up of specialized areas placed side by side—e.g. distribution, culture, or production; each under a separate management organisation (multinational corporation, national state, etc.). We may also judge (see S. H. Hymer [36]) that one particular structure is more stable than another and that perhaps multinational firms are already past their "prime". Whichever opinion one may choose. there is no doubt that solutions, not just palliatives, will have to be found and put into effect without any further delay.

34. It is worth noting that there is a certain amount of similarity between the situation existing at the end of the 20th Century and that experienced by industrial countries in the early 19th Century, when central banks were first established.

35. C. P. Kindleberger, "Size of Firms and Size of Nations" (Rennes Symposium).

36. S. Hymer, "The Internationalization of Capital" in C.N.R.S.

Part II

*Financial management of
multinational corporations*

Chapter IV

FINANCIAL ASPECTS OF A MULTINATIONAL COMPANY

by *J. Koning*

> When I was a boy
> World was simpler spot:
> What was so was so, what was not was not
> Now I am a man
> World have changed a lot
> Some things are nearly so, some things are nearly not

From: *"The King and I"*

Introduction

In this paper it is presumed that the reader is familiar with the fundamental problems and theories of financial management, hence no detailed definitions and explications will be given of commonly known terms as assets (capital goods), shares, bonds, financial structure and so on.

As the external and macro-economic financial aspects of a large multinational enterprise are dealt with in a very clear and extensive way in the co-paper of Mr. A. J. W. S. Leonard, this paper will pay more attention to the internal, micro-economic aspects, namely the specific difficulties arising in a multinational enterprise in arriving at optimal financial decisions.

To understand the behaviour of a multinational enterprise it is necessary to distinguish between a multinational and an international company. Whereas a domestic enterprise does business within the national borders only, an international company is a domestic enterprise that also does business over the national frontiers, in the form of exporting and importing, granting of technical and other assistance to non-nationals, lending and/or borrowing abroad and so on. It may even have affiliates or subsidiaries abroad, but all this does not make it automatically a multinational. As a matter of fact most multinationals consist of a Central Holding Company, in a certain mother-country, and a number of subsidiaries abroad, looking just like many internationals. The main characteristic of a multinational enterprise however is that its subsidiaries abroad (hereafter referred to as "national organizations")

49

want to integrate themselves as deeply as possible in the national economies of the countries where they are situated. They do not only try to make use as much as possible of local labor, local suppliers, local capital markets and so on, but they even want to behave in the same way and assume the same responsibilities as every other local national company doing business abroad. It may be clear without saying so that this multinational philosophy may and often will give rise to a conflict of interests between a national organization and the Central Holding Company as well as between a national organization and other national organizations, which situation in principle, does not exist in a pure international enterprise and, if it arises, will certainly be dealt with otherwise.

Consequently a multinational enterprise is always, by definition, an international enterprise, but not every international is a multinational.

In this paper, a multinational enterprise is defined as a group of manufacturing and selling companies, dealing in many articles or article-groups (product divisions), situated in a number of countries, with a Central Holding Company and/or a Central Management Company, making use as much as possible of the international division of labor and specialisation of production (specialized supply centers) and desiring to integrate as much as possible into the national economies of the countries concerned. Further, it is assumed that the product divisions have a central management which has world-wide responsibility for production and selling of the articles concerned and that the National Organizations have a local management, responsible for the groups' performance in their country. Product division-management as well as national organization-management report directly to Central Management.

The basic financial aspects of an enterprise are well known, they are: a) the estimation of and decision on the future capital needs for research, development, manufacturing and selling; b) the continuous research of and contacts with the capital markets about the sources, quantities, prices and so on of the capital available for this enterprise; and c) the elaboration of the desired long-term financial structure. Once these three points have been decided upon, financial management turns into financial engineering, in fact the obtaining from the sources mentioned in b) at the lowest possible costs of the capital needed for a) in the right form, the right amounts, at the right moment, for the right period at the right place, bearing in mind the desired financial structures.

The above-mentioned financial aspects of an enterprise have other characteristics than their purely financial one. There is the problem of responsibility for instance. The assessment of future capital requirements—(a)—is a joint-responsibility of technical/commercial managers and the financial manager together. The acquisition of capital—(b + c)—is the exclusive responsibility of the financial manager. Another point is the future decision-period. Long-term financial policy is mainly concerned with the desired financial structure.

Short-term financial policy boils down to the actual cash in hand, which is no longer a management-problem. In between the financial manager tries to earn his daily bread.

From the foregoing it may be clear that solving the financial problems of a domestic enterprise is not an easy task. Internationality and multinationality give it additional dimensions. Some of them will be discussed below.

Assessment of future capital requirements

Generally speaking the estimation of future capital requirement is done via a) precalculated balance sheets or b) a consistent system of budgeting or c) by a combination of a) and b). Strong preference has to be given to method c).

The isolated precalculation of balance-sheets (via ratios) gives insufficient information. Balance sheets are snapshots of a situation at a certain moment, no information is obtained of what happens between balance sheet dates. Moreover, the extrapolation of ratios is a dangerous way of prophesying. A consistent system of budgeting (method b) gives information on the operational development to be expected and enables the financier to establish a budget of the future incoming and outgoing flows of money, which is the basis for his financial management. However, no information is obtained via this method about the development of the structure of the enterprise, which the financial manager has to know to be able to decide upon his long-term management, i.e., the decision about the future financial structure.

Hence method c) is to be preferred. Starting with the balance sheet at the beginning of the planning period, linking the budgets to it and thus ending up with the precalculated balance sheet at the end of the planning period, gives the maximum possible information.

As a matter of fact, this planning has to be done for a period sufficiently long (3-6 years) to enable financial management to feed back financial constraints to the plans, if the planned development of activities (sales, production, investments and so on) results in such an additional capital requirement that providing for it is either not possible or would result in a too expensive financial structure, given the expected overall return on capital invested.

The larger the enterprise and/or the more it is spread geographically, the more delegation of responsibility and even of initiative has to be granted and the more complicated the above described procedure becomes. In a large international/multinational enterprise it may be so long before all plans of product divisions and national organizations are consistent with each other, and even after such consistency has been achieved, the information and reaction on deviations from the plans may take so long to be communicated, that sometimes the whole machinery threatens to come to a grinding halt. Such a situation has to be avoided at any price, because it brings the financial manager into an impossible situation. In such a case, he is not only left completely in the dark as far as additional (positive or negative) capital requirements are concerned, but he also cannot form an opinion about the question of what financial safety margins are necessary.

Simultaneous use of operational research, linear programming, ratio-network models, etc. can be very helpful, but they give mainly enterprise-wide, consolidated information and in an international/multinational enterprise the financial manager has to know also "where and when". Moreover, apart from the fact that such a financial solution is extremely expensive, no amount of liquid resources (traditionally the first line of financial resistance) can be considered large enough to resist all the attacks a large enterprise can open on itself.

The best solution for a large international enterprise is to establish, in addition to a considerable amount of centrally managed cash resources, an international system of non-used credit-lines, from local banks as well as from international banks. As prevention is always better than cure, every large international ought to drive relentlessly towards the introduction of an—yet still not available—enterprise-wide integrated system of electronic data processing to shorten information and decision time-lags.

In this paragraph, which is concerned with the forecasting of future capital requirements special attention has to be paid to the so-called fixed assets. Whereas amounts invested in raw materials and semi-manufactured items normally bear a close relationship to production, and investments in finished articles and accounts receivable follow the volume and value of sales, there is in principle, with regard to these balance sheet items—apart from currency aspects, which will be treated later on—no difference between a domestic enterprise and an international/multinational one. However, with regard to investments in fixed assets, in other words the creation of productive capacity, international and multinational companies have, contrary to domestic enterprises, to decide upon the country of settlement. On the one hand, they will aim at the creation of large, specialised supply centers; on the other hand, it will probably be impossible for them to establish all their productive capacity in one country. But, where an international enterprise could aim at a limited number of geographical spread supply centers, for a multinational company this would go against even its basic philosophy.

The ideal situation for a multinational enterprise would be such a geographically balanced spreading out of its productive capacities that in every country where it is active the money value of production plus profit thereon would equal the money value of local sales. In the case of specialized production, a lot of articles to be sold in a certain country would then still have to be imported, but as a consequence a corresponding part of the local production would then have to be exported, which would neutralize the balance of

52

payments impacts. From a financial point of view, this would in many respects facilitate the solution of many problems set out in the paper of Mr. Leonard. However, for many reasons, varying from country to country and from article group to article group, even in very large multinational enterprises such a situation cannot be reached. Except perhaps for a very few of the bigger countries, there will for a long time to come remain importing and exporting countries, but a multinational enterprise must constantly be aware of this and try to distribute its expansion investment as evenly as possible. The financial manager has to conform to this philosophy as much as possible, and accept the consequential financial complications thereof.

Financial structure

The enterprises' ultimate aim being continuity, (including growth) one of the basic objectives of financial management in general is to maintain a good reputation on the capital markets. A deterioration of this acceptability decreases the available financial alternatives and probably increases the cost of capital.[1]

The financial image of an enterprise and consequently its entrée on the financial markets, is determined by many factors. The most important, besides the size of the enterprise, are the financial past performance, profitability, growth-expectations, cash-flow considerations and the financial information.[2]

Although financial management cannot completely determine all factors governing the financial image,—capital suppliers do have their own opinions— one of the best means to create and to maintain a sound financial position is to formulate against the background of its overriding goals a long-term financial structure for the enterprise concerned, to make this conception well known, internally as well as externally, to explain clearly and in good time the deviations that occur and the changes that may become necessary in the future. In this way, everybody concerned (internally and externally) can analyse and evaluate his position and draw the necessary conclusions. -

Such a long-term financial structure comprises not only, on the one hand, the desirable interrelations between assets as shown in the balance sheet and, on the other hand, the composition of the liabilities and of the net worth, but also the criss-cross relationships, and the links between balance sheet, profit and loss account and cash flow.

1. In this respect one must not forget that on many financial markets the price to be paid is partly a result of negotiation between the suppliers of capital and the enterprise.
2. The better information a capital-supplier receives about the actual situation and about the expected future developments of the enterprise, the more he will be prepared to make his resources available at a reasonable price.

Formulating the long-term financial structure to be aimed at is not an easy decision, as such a framework has to be a synthesis (or a compromise) between often conflicting purposes, such as considerations about:

a. ownership rights, to maintain operational lines of command;

b. elasticity, to be able to provide for unexpected increases in the capital requirements or to dispose of unexpected surpluses;

c. financial power of resistance (solvency), to ensure the financiability of the enterprise in case of temporarily occurring unfavourable developments of sales and/or profitability;

d. profitability, in fact trading on the equity, to minimise the costs of capital and to offset the disadvantage of inflation.

Improving the elasticity of the financial structure by taking in more short-term credits may decrease the desired ratio between equity and liabilities. Improving the financial solvency increases the cost of financing and diminishes the flexibility and decreases the insulation against inflation.

In the case of international and multinational enterprises, when considering the above-described complicated problem of deciding on the long-term optimal financial structure, the financial manager has to deal with the consolidated overall picture of the enterprise, and also simultaneously with the financial framework of the national organizations, which complicates the situation still more. As a matter of fact, there exists a two-way interdependent relationship between the consolidated structure and the financing of the national organizations. On the one side, the consolidated figures are the sum total of the financial structures of the national organizations, on the other side, one has, within the framework of the total structure, a certain liberty with regard to the financial structure of an individual national organization. In both international and multinational enterprises the consolidated picture will be the predominant aspect but in a multinational enterprise much more consideration has to be given to the national organizations financial structure than in an international one. An international company will first design the consolidated picture and adapt the financial structures of its national organizations accordingly. A multinational enterprise will first design the nationally seen optimal financial structure of its national organizations, and only then impose deviations if the resulting consolidated status is thought to be, or likely to become, unacceptable in the eyes of the worldwide financial opinion.

As a possible consequence of the foregoing, an international company will not easily accept third-party local shareholding in its national organizations, whereas a multinational enterprise, although for many reasons normally not inviting such third-party participations, will hesitatingly tend to accept them if they fit into the philosophy and the "normal" circumstances of the countries concerned.

These local third-party participations restrict organisational, operational and financial freedom and increase considerably the problems of attribution and allocation of profits and of dividend policy, for the enterprise as a whole and for the national organizations concerned. It is for this reason amongst others, that multinational enterprises will try to have their holding company shares quoted on as broad a geographical scale as possible. Doing this, they open for inhabitants of as many countries as possible, the opportunity of taking an interest in that multinational enterprise as a whole, which is more preferable for them than to have an interest only in the national organization working in their country.

Another aspect of this subject is that in many countries regulations are in force which limit the possibilities of obtaining short- and/or long-term credits. Sometimes such regulations apply for all enterprises situated in a country, sometimes they only apply for "foreign" enterprises. In both cases the national organization of an international/multinational company may (indirectly) be forced to accept local participations to obtain the status of a "national" company or it has to be financed by equity capital to a larger extent than objectively deemed desirable. The first alternative has already been hinted at above. The second alternative may oblige the financial manager of the central company either to accept an unwanted impact on the consolidated financial structure or to force other national organizations to finance themselves with more short/long-term loaned capital than is objectively deemed desirable in those countries. In the last mentioned situation, local capital suppliers may feel the financial structure of those other national organizations has become too weak and they will consequently ask for additional guarantees from the Groups' Central Holding Company.

In countries with persistent inflation, be it creeping or running, special attention has to be paid to the financial structure of the national organizations concerned.

In such countries, one of the best solutions to aim at is a financial structure whereby nominal assets (accounts receivable, liquid assets) are kept as small as possible and are financed with at least an equal amount of local credits. This may not always be possible because of existing, anti-inflationary creditregulations and, in any case, it is an expensive solution. If this financial policy is not possible, or is too expensive, it is still better to bring in loans from abroad than to finance nominal assets with equity capital. Inflationary countries may have to devalue their currency from time to time and a tax-credit can be obtained for the loss on funds loaned from abroad, which is normally not the case for equity capital. The way the adaptations of the financial structures of national organizations in inflationary countries will affect the consolidated position cannot be stated in advance, but at the same time it is clear that this aspect must always be borne in mind.

One of the most important questions accompanying the design of an optimal long-term financial structure is how fast the enterprise can grow from a financial point of view. This problem has quantitative as well as qualitative and geographical aspects.

It goes without saying that, once for the enterprise as a whole the desired ratio between equity capital and liabilities is arrived at, the expansion of sales will require a proportional increase in equity capital (provided the turnover-speed of capital employed cannot be improved) either by the issue of new shares or via retained profits.

In the context of this paper, it will be assumed that for many reasons large international enterprises cannot regularly carry through adequate issues of new shares, so the required additional equity capital has in fact to come from retained profits. By means of computerized simulation models it is not very difficult to establish the interrelationship between various probable growth patterns and the allied profitability expectations which have to be compared with the profitability required to stay within the framework of the chosen overall financial structure.

In a dynamic international/multinational organization a continuous flow of propositions for future developments will emanate both from the product divisions and from the national organizations. To be able to analyse, evaluate, compare, rank and select all those alternatives, the first condition is to introduce a uniform evaluation procedure for the whole organization. This procedure has to be applied by all parts of the enterprise which are authorized to send in plans for the future.

The second condition is that the ranking and selection is decided upon centrally, bearing in mind the strategic objectives and the necessity to equalize marginal profitability and the so-called "cut-off rate" in the form of the firms' cost of capital, which is identical with the above-mentioned long-term profitability requirements; this will be discussed below.

The third condition for a well-balanced expansion program is that as a rule the product division-plans must have priority over the national organization-plans as far as the allocation of production-facilities is concerned, but that the national organizations (which have the marketing responsibility) must have first priority in commercial plans.

In this way, it can happen in an international/multinational organization that for commercial reasons in a certain country it is necessary to create a certain industrial image, to obtain for instance, the indispensable cooperation of the authorities, whereas from a manufacturing point of view the creation of an often only small local production unit is scarcely justified. In an international enterprise, probably the industrial opinion will win, in a multinational enterprise, very often the commercial view must be paramount and the consequent decrease in average profitability be accepted, because the enterprise wants "to be there" or has "to stay there", since withdrawing is even more "expensive". The financial consequence must be that, given the required overall profitability, either in other sectors (commercial or technical), or in other countries, the cut-off rate has to be increased or a certain deterioration of the overall financial structure must be accepted, which is for financial continuity reasons possible for a limited period of time only. Moreover, as set out in Mr. Leonards' paper, it will be clear that the financing of the above type of national organization can cause special problems, at least during the first years of the industrialization process in that country.

If the expansion program of the total enterprise requires anyway an increase of the production potential of a certain product or group of products, the best solution for the situation described is to establish a full-size supply-center for those products in that country, to arrive at the lowest possible production costs, and to export the locally unrequired production surplus to other national organizations. However, it will be clear that in the light of total capacity needed, this procedure cannot be followed in every country and that it would be purely accidental if the export thus generated coincides with the balance of payments equilibrium indicated on pages 52 and 53.

Moreover, in many countries there may not be a sufficient and/or adequate labor supply, or local costs may be too high compared with other countries, so that profitable export of the production surplus may not be feasible. Finally, from a financial point of view it is not always possible to find sufficient local finance for such an industrial operation and capital must be brought in from or via the concern-center.

If all the mentioned negative aspects accumulate, the price to be paid for "being there" becomes rather high from an isolated financial point of view, as such a development would most probably not meet the required minimum profitability and consequently bring pressure to bear upon the financial structure somewhere else in the multinational enterprise.

The foregoing holds especially true for the so called Developing Countries, but even in advanced industrial countries some or all of the above indicated circumstances may present themselves for certain specific products.

In Developing Countries there normally exists a small but growing market for a broad mixture of the final products of an international/multinational enterprise, but "local for local" production is often difficult to realize because in general these countries can offer for the most part an (abundant) supply of unskilled labor only and possess no capital market of any significance.

From an industrial point of view these countries allow for the establishment of a rather simple production activity of an assembling character and a limited range only. In the eyes of the enterprise such countries clearly belong to the group of net-importing countries, but their balance of payments cannot bear a big net import-balance. This situation severely restricts the expansion of the enterprise, unless an ever increasing credit is granted by the Concern Center, which is in most cases physically not possible or very expensive, and not without danger from a currency point of view.

A true multinational enterprise will realize that investing capital in developing countries means working for the future and therefore it must be willing, be it not on an unlimited scale, to invest capital, financed in hard currency, in industrial and commercial activities in those countries of the third world, from which no positive result or only a small one can be expected for a long time to come because of inflation and other reasons. All the above indicated phenomena of balances of payments, local third-party participations, allocation of profits, distribution of dividends, relatively important financing by the Concern Center via equity and/or long and short-term loans, can become actual and have to be solved, not only ad hoc but also on the basis of a long term philosophy and confidence.

Allocation of the cost of capital

This problem has to be approached from the viewpoint of the responsibility of the financial manager, whose task it is inter alia to attract the capital the company needs. The financial manager is operating on markets where scarce capital is being negotiated at a market price. This goes of course for loan capital, but is also valid for equity capital. If the yield on shareholding is continuously below the expectations of the investors, the suppliers of venture capital turn away from the shares of the company concerned.

In order to ensure continuity the financial manager has to see to it that the capital markets remain open to his company. Therefore he is responsible for his company earning the rate of return that suppliers of capital demand and as a consequence the financial manager will have to see to it that market prices of capital (which are based on scarcity) find expression in daily business management. Irrespective of the question whether the price to be paid for equity capital is theoretically also a real cost price component, it is obvious that the operational managers should be charged, or at least confronted with, the costs related to the employment of all kinds of capital.

It seems unnecassary to dwell upon the prices of the borrowed funds, i.e., the interest to be paid, as here more or less objective market prices prevail. As most enterprises also have at their disposal a sizeable amount of non-interest bearing liabilities and provisions, the average interest cost of total liabilities lies below the level of interest paid on interest-bearing funds.

To shareholders, an alternative to investing in risk-bearing equity capital is the granting of risk-avoiding long-term loans and therefore they require on equity capital the same interest as paid for on long-term loans plus a risk-premium.

For decision calculations, this risk premium has to be included in the cost of total capital. In performance reporting (ex post calculations), however—when the risks have already had their impact on the business—the risk premium must be eliminated as an element of the cost of capital. Thus, the financial manager passes on to the operational managers the equity capital at the rate of interest paid for long-term loans. The financial manager cannot speak of profit as long as this interest has not been earned; the profit that results after deduction of the latter amount is directly related to the venture risks taken.

In order to make the compensation to shareholders comparable to that to the suppliers of borrowed funds, two corrections are necessary:

1) Suppose the interest percentage for long term loans is 8 per cent. This represents the nominal compensation of, for instance, 4 per cent. for saving, plus 2.5 per cent. for compensation for inflation, plus 1.5 per cent. for running a certain debtor's risk. If companies do not determine profit on a nominal base, but on the basis of replacement value, the 2.5 per cent. compensation for inflation has to be discarded when calculating the interest part of the price of stockholders' equity. So the 8 per cent. for loans is identical to 5.5 per cent. for equity.

2) The interest percentages mentioned, of 8 for loans and 5.5 for equity are net. Unlike the interest cost for loans, which is tax deductible for the enterprise, the interest on equity is not, so—at a taxation rate on profits of for example 50 per cent.—the said percentage of 5.5 for equity becomes 11 per cent. before taxes.

The average cost of capital can now be computed as follows:

Assuming a debt/equity ratio of 60 : 40, an average taxation on profit of 50 per cent., interest on equity of 5.5 per cent. net, interest on debt of 8 per cent. and an interest bearing/non-interest bearing funds ratio of 5 : 3, the average cost of capital amounts to

$$0.40 \times \frac{5.5 \text{ per cent.}}{1 - 0.50} + 0.60 \times 5/8 \times 8 \text{ per cent.} = \text{approximately } 7.5 \text{ per cent.}$$

The cost of capital of 7.5 per cent. as calculated above has to be applied to all assets at book value to be able to meet the claims of the suppliers of capital.

The above indicated 7.5 per cent. represents the average cost of capital for the enterprise as a whole and has to be considered as the bare, rock bottom minimum that has to be earned on assets (Return on Capital Invested). For budgetting and decision purposes, a higher percentage of return on capital invested is required as a cut-off rate, depending on the desired growth rate and the financial structure to be maintained.

In an international enterprise it is not unlikely that the result indicated above of calculating the cost of capital will be applied uniformly throughout the business, the enterprise being considered as a homogeneous entity. However, in a multinational enterprise it is necessary to differentiate between the average cost of capital in one country and another and probably even between one kind of activity and another, which means differentiation per product division. This implies that instead of applying the enterprise's averages, the cost of capital for a certain national organization has to be based on local rates of interest, local tax rates on profit, and the local financial structure. Moreover, the kinds of activity (for instance manufacturing, selling, sales financing, real estate business) in that particular country have to be taken into account by configurating the normative capital structure of the national organization concerned.

The capital structure of a national organization is not an arbitrary one. It is determined largely by the composition, the liquidity and the marketability of the assets. For the purpose of this analysis it is thus conceivable to develop a more or less refined system of normative ratios between the various kinds of assets and the correponding composition of liabilities and net worth. For example, the item "non-consolidated companies" will have to be financed by equity capital. There must also be a close relationship between stocks and accounts payable (i.e. non-interest bearing funds) and it is an accepted rule that accounts receivable are financed to a much greater extent with borrowed funds than plant and equipment. Further, there is the ratio of current assets to current liabilities and the financial press frequently mentions the norm that equity must equal fixed assets.

To illustrate the above with a simple example showing the consequences for the cost of capital of calculating different local interest rates, different local tax rates and different financial structures, based upon different types of activities, one can assume the existence of a Holding Company with two subsidiaries, A and B, which have different activities and which are located in different countries. Assume further that the enterprise-wide "interest" on equity is 5.5 per cent. net and that the only structural norm applied is that equity capital equals fixed assets.

	Enterprise (consolidated)	Subsidiary "A"	Subsidiary "B"
fixed assets	40	10	30
current assets	60	20	40
stockholders' equity	40	10	30
liabilities	60	20	40
debt/equity ratio	1.5 : 1	2 : 1	1.33 : 1
rate of interest	5 %	6 %	4.5 %
tax rate	50 %	58 %	47 %

Thus the cost of capital comes down to 7.4 per cent. for the Concern as a whole and for the subsidiaries "A" and "B" respectively to 8.4 and 7.0 per cent.

The classic thesis that the determination of the financial structure is beyond the influence of an operational manager and consequently he cannot be held responsible for the ensuing costs of capital, does not hold true. Every operational manager determines by his decisions the extent, the nature and the length of the investments for which he is responsible. For a multinational enterprise, this is a very important conclusion, because it implies that it is necessary to assign to every national organization its own (normative) financial structure on the basis of its activities and the related investments and thus to arrive at a differentiation of the cost of capital.

Flows of funds

To enable financial management to formulate, within the framework of the designed long-term financial structure, a financial plan for the next "period" (e.g. a day, a week, a month, a quarter, a year) and to enable it also to react quickly and adequately to divergences from the plan (which are inherent in all planning), a system must be designed to "translate" the information about future and realized activities (research, development, production, sales, stocks, profitability, etc.) into information about the corresponding flows of funds into, out of, and within the enterprise. The financial manager has to know how the enterprise functions as a money-household and how its flows of funds react on technical, commercial and other decisions, for "what ultimately counts is cash".

The first stage of a financial plan includes the formulation of a provisional overall plan to provide for the capital needed by the enterprise as a whole during the next period. For the later years of a long-term plan, this overall picture is sufficient but for the first year(s) to come one has to go into details to ascertain whether within the total picture any bottlenecks or unwanted surpluses loom up in any country which may threaten the execution of the total plan or may lead to needless expensive constructions. This spliting-up of the provisional overall plan should be done in this way so that—after analysis of the flows of funds resulting from the plan—the optimal constellation of these flows can be determined. To find this optimal constellation, one has to start from the hypothetical situation which would exist if within the enterprise there were only a circulation of goods and services and no internal payments at all, so that financial transactions would occur with third parties only. Then the supply-center countries would show a financial deficit and all other national organizations where sales exceed local out-of-pocket production costs, would show surpluses. If national frontiers did not constitute financial barricades, it would be easy in this hypothetical situation to transfer the surplus funds to the deficit countries and to cover the eventually remaining overall deficit on those markets, and in such ways that, against the background of the desired long-term financial structure, the least expensive form of financing results.

In actual fact this hypothetical solution of the financial problem, which certainly would lead to the lowest overall average cost of capital, is not feasible. In practice, the enterprise is tied by many external restrictions and official regulations which curtail the transfer of funds and/or cause additional costs, depending on the transfer-channels to be used. Ergo it is necessary to devise the "cheapest" combination of transfer-channels—within the framework of the above constraints—to arrive at an equalization of the expected geographical financial surpluses and deficits.

In general, in an international/multinational enterprise the following transfer-channels are available:
1. payments for imported/exported goods and services;
2. payments for technical, commercial, legal and managerial knowhow;
3. transfers of interest and dividends;
4. transfers of loans and repayments thereof;
5. transfers to increase or decrease equity capital of national organizations.

Each of these transfer-channels has its own specific capacity and its specific costs.

The first constraining departure from the above described hypothesis is that the enterprise is not allowed to circulate freely goods and services on an international basis without payments. Customs and fiscal regulations stipulate that exported goods have to be invoiced, as a rule with a certain profit which can be taxed in the exporting country. On the other side, the importing country wants to charge import duties on the same goods and also levies a taxable profit when those goods are sold or re-exported. Without any doubt, a very difficult problem comes up for discussion here. For the enterprise the profit on an international transaction is the difference between the final proceeds of the goods on the market and the sum total of all the costs spent in the preceding stages. Hence the level of internal international invoicing implies a division of the total profit over the countries concerned (which may be many), each demanding a part of it. Moreover, this is not only a question of conflicting interests between the fiscal authorities of the various countries concerned, but also a problem for the Customs and the Inland Revenue in the same country. To stick as close as possible to the above-mentioned hypothesis, the present analysis of the flows of funds has to start with the minimal level of invoicing that customs and fiscal authorities in the countries concerned will accept. Any increase of invoice prices above this level will probably cause additional costs.

The transfer-channel for technical and other assistance provided within the enterprise is also governed by official regulations. In some countries such payments are not transferable at all, sometimes they are not tax-deductible; in other cases, a source-tax is levied on the transfer. It may be clear that any increase of the price of these services charged above the hypothetical zero-level, may bring about additional costs.

The transfer-capacity of the dividend-channel is subject to two constraints. The first is that local authorities protest—and the status of the national organization as a national organization will be injured if an unusually large part of the profit made in that country is distributed. Unless specific (tax-) regulations justify a relatively large distribution of profit, it will not be advisable to distribute more than half of it. In many cases it should be even less. Within the amount left by the above, it is necessary to determine how much dividend can be transferred without causing additional costs as compared with retaining the profit. The system of taxation in the countries concerned has to be taken into account, profit-tax-rates, source taxes, and so on.

A very peculiar situation arises if a national organization for one reason or another has taken in local shareholders, who expect a dividend on their investment, while at the same time the national organization is perhaps not very profitable and/or the transfer of dividends to the parent company is relatively very expensive. Perhaps a multinational enterprise will appreciate this consideration more than an international one.

Mutatis mutandis the foregoing is also valid as far as transfers of interest, loans and equity capital are concerned.

Along the above lines it is possible to establish the absolute minimum of the transfer-costs of every open transfer-channel and its capacity at that level of costs. Any additional transfer will then cause additional costs. If, for example, more is transferred via the import/export channel, additional costs will be incurred in the form of extra import-duties, less export-premium and the like, and plus or minus costs incurred in the form of shifting profit tax from one country to another.

As the foregoing constitutes an optimization problem, it is possible to arrive at a configuration of transfers which minimizes the total costs as a percentage of the total amount transferred. Then the marginal costs of this configuration have to be compared with the opportunity costs, which are the costs of borrowing additional capital by the parts of the enterprise that are in deficit.

The pattern of flows of funds drafted in this way constitutes the last stage of the financial planning. Combined with the above mentioned precalculated balance sheets, a complete picture is obtained of expected future financial events. As a matter of fact it remains necessary to repeat the whole procedure periodically on a revolving basis. Moreover, the realization of the planning must be pursued carefully to detect unexpected deviations quickly so that supplementary measures can be taken in good time.

In a really large international/multinational enterprise, doing business in many countries and making use of many specialised supply centres—at least two or more for every group of technically related products (e.g., one for the Common Market, one for E.F.T.A., one for Latin America)—there exists a very complicated and extensive network of internal exchanges of goods and services, and optimizing the corresponding flows of funds, as described above, is easier said than done.

In order to reduce the complexity of this problem, it is advisable to direct all payments to and from concern-enterprises situated in a certain country via a central clearing house, to compensate as far as possible opposite flows of funds and pay the remaining balances only, and then to introduce an international internal clearing system, comprising as many countries as possible, to aim at the same result internationally.

Even then it remains very difficult to get a good insight, "on line and real time", into the overall international currency position, the latter being of first importance, especially these days. Theoretically, it should be possible to establish an enterprise-wide information system, informing the financial concern center to the minute of all currency positions and of the changes in them, but such a system is hardly operational today. Therefore, apart from the above indicated nominal equilibrium in the financial structures of the national organizations it looks practical to instruct all the national organizations to make out where possible their international invoices in their own national currency. That way the current currency risks are concentrated with the importing enterprises. As creditors have the first initiative and responsibility for the payment—the debtor often having to demand payment and so being in the weaker position—the importing national organizations should automatically try to avoid losses on currency fluctuations and plan their transfers accordingly, in that way reducing the total currency risks for the multinational enterprise, without the necessity for continuous central intervention.

Chapter V

FINANCIAL MANAGEMENT OF A MULTINATIONAL ENTERPRISE

by *A. J. W. S. Leonard and F. H. Brittenden*

You will notice that the title of this paper uses the expression "multinational enterprise" which I think is more appropriate than the description "multinational corporation" which is sometimes used. The latter incorrectly implies the existence of a single company, whereas I shall be concerned with an international group of companies. Even in its preferred form the expression "multinational enterprise" has a variety of meanings in current use and, when loosely applied, has given rise to serious misconceptions, for example that such an enterprise operates outside the control of national jurisdictions, which is the opposite of the truth. I would offer the definition, which fits the circumstances of my own group, of a group of companies which trade in a number of different countries and currencies, financing their operations on a worldwide basis, with a central company fulfilling the role of banker to the group as a whole. Companies of such a group have many financing problems which do not exist for a single national group. These may be summarised as the need to gather resources from the various countries of operation for investment worldwide for the benefit of the group as a whole and one of the main aims of management is to achieve freedom, flexibility and economy in the two-way flow of funds thus generated.

As I have said, the definition suggested is appropriate for the Royal Dutch/Shell Group of Companies but I would emphasise that an important fact about so-called "multinational enterprises" is their diversity, both in the nature of their operations and in their corporate and financial structures. The fact that we, the Royal Dutch/Shell Group of Companies, come to be counted amongst the multinational enterprises has been born of the physical realities of the oil industry. We have had no choice in the matter, and, though current fashion would have it as a recent phenomenon, we have been a multinational enterprise for the last fifty years or so. Certainly outside North America and the Communist Countries oil is found and produced in areas without markets capable of absorbing it and has therefore to be transported in bulk to the refining centres located nearer the final consumer of the resultant oil products.

In this paper, I will firstly give a brief outline of the structure of the Royal

Dutch/Shell Group of Companies and of some of the problems to which this gives rise. The main theme of the paper will, however, be an assessment of the relationship which we expect to obtain in the next few years between the capital needs of the companies of a large international group in the oil industry and the international resources of money which are available to finance them. Lastly, I will explain some of the problems associated with the efficient deployment of funds which become available to us.

Royal Dutch in Holland and Shell Transport in the United Kingdom are the parent companies of the Group, owning 60 per cent. and 40 per cent. respectively of the Group assets and income. They have no trading activities but rely for their income on dividends paid to them by two Holding Companies, Shell Petroleum N.V. in Holland and Shell Petroleum Company Limited in the United Kingdom. The Holding Companies in turn own between them all the shareholdings in Group or associated companies. It is the function of the Holding Companies to receive income in the form of dividends or interest from Group companies worldwide and to make available the finance required by those companies, either as share capital or as loans. Because of our exchange control situation, which I will mention later, it is a matter of indifference, apart from taxation considerations and the need to provide the parent companies' dividends, whether cash flows from operating companies to the United Kingdom or to Holland. This provides a form of financial unity. An important, and indeed unique, role is also played by our Service Companies in London and The Hague. Within this structure, we are a Group of diverse companies, each in its own sphere of activity, and having identifiable nationality and independence of action, albeit influenced by the operations carried out by other companies affiliated to it. The structure of this group has grown out of a recognition of the dangers of becoming martyrs to an ideal of over-centralised and over-rigid management practices in a world where the need for a rapid appreciation of ever changing national political and economic circumstances is paramount. The only practicable method of operation for us is based upon and originates with the separate integrity of each operating company. This has been reinforced by the need to work within the individual legal frameworks in force within national frontiers and to preserve the fiscal integrity of each segment of the business, which requires mind and management to be and be seen to be exercised by and in the companies subject to any particular regime.

For everyday financial control, the group structure requires that accounts be presented in conformity first with national laws and practice and secondly in a format which enables overall consolidation and inter-company comparisons to be made. It also brings into unwelcome prominence the subject of transfer prices, which in the context of a functionally integrated group operating entirely within national confines are of importance only for management accounting; but in their international context they regulate the fiscal

66

base and thereby fall under the scrutiny of the fiscal authorities. Where oil products are actively traded in an open market—such as that in the Gulf of Mexico—few difficulties arise, but prices naturally give rise to more active enquiry where no similar bench mark exists. An accusation which, in this respect, is often levelled against multinational enterprises is that they juggle transfer prices and consequently the distribution of profit to take advantage of low tax areas. But while we see no reason to make high tax payments voluntarily, the scope for measures of this kind is in practice extremely limited. Certainly advantage is taken of those possibilities available to mini-mise the effect of double taxation—mainly opportunities presented in double taxation agreements—and the incentive to do so is high bearing in mind the extremely high rates of tax payable in production areas of the Middle East and elsewhere.

Taxation problems commonly arise where funds flow from the countries of operation where the profits are made to the central holding company from which investment funds are obtained. Payments of dividends, interest and royalties may give rise to withholding taxes in the country of operation and the level of these taxes may vary depending on the existence and scope of double taxation agreements between the country from which they are paid and the home country. In our case, the existence of two Holding Companies based in the United Kingdom and Holland presents a further complication, but also an opportunity to mitigate double taxation, in that tax treaty ar-rangements may differ between the United Kingdom and Holland in relation to any particular third country.

Capital in rapidly rising amounts is needed to provide sufficient capacity to meet growing energy demands. Whatever relative emphasis we give to the future importance of leisure, automation, heavy industry, services, conserva-tion etc., a dominating common element is the need for an abundance of primary energy and, at least for the medium-term future, that means oil and gas.

Allied to higher volumes is the prospect of higher unit capital costs in most phases of the business. The constant renewal of the resource base of the oil industry is driving us from the land deeper and deeper into the sea; wells on land can cost more than £250,000 while, in the inhospitable waters of the North Sea and of the Atlantic waters of Eastern Canada, the figure can exceed £1m. Added to this are the demands made on us to up-grade our products in use and to provide better refinery and distribution hygiene to protect the environment. Further, the gains in productivity to be made by increasing the size of tankers and refinery units are becoming less significant. We are consequently witnessing the reversal of the downward trend in unit costs which in the past has overcome the impact of inflation. The burden of capital expenditures will therefore become relatively heavier in future. It is estimated by the Chase Manhattan Bank that the capital expenditure of the oil industry outside the Communist countries in the period 1970–85 will be in the region of £250 billion.

How are these expenditures to be financed? We cannot at this stage expect to rely to any great extent on local risk capital for specific ventures in the areas of operation of our companies, apart from North America. Although it is interesting to note that the development of North Sea oil has given rise to a number of companies in the United Kingdom and Norway in particular, which have been successful in raising equity money directly for oil exploration, the political environment is of course relatively familiar and the highly speculative investment is a small proportion of the vast volume of more conventional investment in all types of industry. In the international oil scene, exploration and production, which have a high degree of technical risk, are undertaken largely in countries where there is little capital available for speculative oil investment. The finance required is of a long-term nature because of the length of time which it takes for capital investment in oil industry facilities to generate a positive cash flow. This applies also to many of the down-stream facilities of manufacturing and distribution, where most of the capital investment takes place. The money that might become available from producing company governments, following on the "participation" agreements, may make some contribution both up-stream and down-stream and to a limited extent some governments do now devote funds for exploration. For some time to come, however, the only practicable source of capital will be the integrated oil companies, just as they have been the only route by which the public have been willing to invest in the past.

The possibilities of raising additional loan finance are limited. Outside capital has become more important to Group companies in recent years and at the end of September 1972, long-term debt stood at £1,300 million. Ten years ago it was £200 million. The increase represents about 20 per cent. of the capital spending during this ten year period. Borrowing has been heavy over the past three years, but how much more will be borrowed in future must partly depend on the ability of the world's capital markets to channel savings and partly on the constraints on our ability to draw on them.

It is clear that in the future as in the past the bulk of the funds must come from depreciation and retained earnings. Inflation has eaten into margins which, in the Eastern Hemisphere, have been eroded from a level of 53 cents per barrel in 1962 to 34 cents per barrel in 1971. (First National City Bank Energy Memo, October 1972) Margins will have to improve from current levels and this must mean higher prices. If, for market or other reasons (such as Government intervention) prices do not rise, the necessary capital will not be forthcoming and the facilities will not be provided. Before long this will lead to shortages and to consequent price increases with ultimately the same effect as had prices been increased earlier. But this will have involved avoidable economic loss.

68

Before this argument can be accepted fully, it is as well to examine some of the blockages along the channel leading from the point at which savings are generated to the capital markets from which the oil companies will be exhorted to raise more money. The amount available for investment is theoretically the sum total of savings in the broadest sense, whether by individuals, corporations, savings institutions or governments. A large part of these are automatically excluded on structural grounds—for instance those savings retained by corporations for heir own use. Then, of course, the savings are not all suitable for investment in risk-bearing enterprises—hence, despite inflation, the popularity of governmental fixed interest securities. Another limiting characteristic of savings is the period for which they are available—short-term funds cannot be used for permanent financing, even on a revolving basis.

Such blockages are multiplied at the international level. To serve as an international capital market, a domestic capital market must be deep, stable and broad enough to export domestic savings and attract money from abroad. The accessibility of the market to foreign or "multinational" issuers depends on freedom from arbitrary controls and from distinctions as between public and private or resident and non-resident borrowers. Secondly, the remittance of funds to whatever part of the world investments are to be made must be freely allowed. Thirdly, the market must offer institutional flexibility not only in the sense of there being a diverse set of institutions providing the appropriate opportunities to the investor and financial services to the borrower but also in the sense of allowing an efficient secondary market for the notes and obligations incurred which is not dominated by a particular institution or set of institutions.

Measured against such criteria, the domestic capital markets open to the "multinational" borrower rarely match the ideal. New York and London have most of the characteristics and prerequisites of efficient international capital markets. Since the early sixties, however, United States government restrictions, as epitomised by the Interest Equalisation Tax, a measure to increase the cost of borrowing by foreigners, have negated its former role as the exporter of large amounts of capital while access to the London market has been virtually closed by the authorities because of continued balance of payments problems.

A number of European industrial nations have a surfeit of international funds and prima facie have the resources to take on the role of international lender. But this potential role has been subordinated to the need to prevent their economies from being swamped by tidal waves of money which sparked off the realignment of currencies in December 1971 and subsequently. They currently fear that further inflows of reserves causing another up-valuation of their currencies would jeopardise their trading positions in the medium-term at a time when the previous revaluations will really begin to bite. They have therefore taken measures to try to isolate the inflationary effects of burgeoning reserve positions on their domestic economies; and since these measures require the sterilisation of additions to the money supply, country after country has restricted access to domestic bond and securities markets to foreigners. Japan, by contrast, has never allowed access by foreigners to her domestic capital market, though the first tentative steps toward greater freedom recently initiated are to be welcomed.

The restrictions that Shell companies have come up against in practice are numerous. In Germany, the Bundesbank controls the issues of bonds and imposes an obligation to queue, with the constraint that this implies on the borrowing power of Group companies. In 1972, a Shell company made a DM 160 million issue—one of the biggest the market has seen. The German securities market is relatively weak and so dominated by public and institutional borrowers that less than 10 per cent. of funds raised are obtained by private non-financial borrowers. The Swiss market, which owes its leading position to its history of political, economic and currency stability, relies on international capital flows attracted by the privacy and efficiency of its banking system in the absence of a domestic market able to call on the resources of an expansive economy. The relatively small size of issues possible (Group companies raised Sw.fr. 60 million in 1968 and Sw.fr. 80 million in 1971, some $15 and $20 million respectively), the queue system in operation and the need to apply at least one year in advance make for infrequent borrowing opportunities even for a first class borrower. The French market is dominated by the central government which allocates priorities in accordance with "le Plan" and no private foreign loans were floated in France until last year. A succession of small issues have been made in Euro-francs now that exchange control has devolved on a two-tier system rather than on administrative regulations. Amsterdam is a very international market where the Royal Dutch/Shell name has a particular cachet and is characterised by low costs and an efficient secondary market. But it is relatively small, dependent on the inflow of funds from abroad and therefore prone to any suspicion of weakness in the guilder, and closely controlled by the Netherlands Central Bank.

The recourse to the Euro-dollar market might be thought to give the freedom from restrictions that is required. Euro-dollar bonds lay claim to the Euro-title because they are offered for dollars in a market not subject to United States exchange controls and to United States legal restrictions. The justification for having bonds denominated in other European currencies has more to do with the choice of currency of reference and of a tax regime which differs from that governing domestic issues in the same currency. But while the Euro-dollar market offers this freedom, the biggest single sum that companies of the Royal Dutch/Shell Group have been able to raise publicly is $70 million and this has not been exceeded by anybody else.

I have looked at the salient features of each of the main markets, not to suggest that Group Companies have to date borrowed the maximum possible in them, but to suggest the market factors which constrain approaches to borrowing. A realistic assessment of fund-raising possibilities has to recognise effective capital market restrictions. We also run into difficulties concerning the different reporting and prospectus requirements of each Stock Exchange and the differing national legislation governing the financial operations of the markets means that different centres give different ratings and the secondary market lacks depth. For example, the European system is by and large more concerned with the reputation of the issuer and the issuer's advisor than with the formal gradings that are applied by the rating agencies in the U.S.A.

Apart from loan finance, it will no doubt be necessary in the long run to enlarge the equity capital base in order to raise really large sums and to support the financial standing of Group Companies in the money markets. When we come to do this, we have to overcome a number of technical difficulties which arise from the dual Group parentage with Royal Dutch situated in Holland and Shell Transport in the United Kingdom. At present, the shares of Shell Transport are traded at a higher price/earnings ratio than those of Royal Dutch and, if funds were raised from shareholders, the existing 60/40 relationship between the interests of the parent companies would have to be maintained. Furthermore, equity capital is normally an expensive method of financing in terms of the after tax cost of servicing it compared with loan capital. Companies are sometimes urged to adopt more liberal dividend policies, thereby making their shares more attractive and enabling them to finance cash deficits by means of a series of equity issues. Whether or not this is valid, frequent recourse to the equity market by companies whose shares are quoted on a large number of Stock Exchanges would be very expensive in administrative cost, thus wasting the potential advantage in terms of international appeal which one hopes to achieve from a wide-spread shareholding.

I have said that the United Kingdom has not been a suitable market for raising long-term finance for international investment. Quite apart from balance of payments restrictions, the high cost of long-term loans raised in London has been a deterrent to the use of this market. However, the London market is of wider significance to us than just a source of finance and this brings me to my second main theme, the international deployment of our resources. This can be usefully looked at both from the central and the local point of view.

Throughout the history of our organisation, London has been our commercial centre, and financial operations have been concentrated also in London, where an unrivalled range of financial facilities and skills is available. At the end of World War II, when Group companies' overriding problem was to find foreign currency, mainly dollars, for rehabilitation, it was plain that while the United Kingdom economy was badly knocked, the Dutch economy was shattered and could not face even part of this burden. An arrangement was therefore made between the main United Kingdom and Dutch holding companies, with the approval of the two governments, whereby the United Kingdom government assumed responsibility, subject to its own currency regulations, for providing Group companies with the foreign currency they needed, on the understanding that Group central cash resources would, in the main, be centralised in London in sterling.

This arrangement has never led to the frustration of Group capital expenditure plans for lack of finance. A very large degree of freedom has obtained in our relationship with the Treasury, although we have been constrained from time to time to borrow abroad against our better commercial judgement as a consequence of the need to avoid bringing further pressure on sterling during the not infrequent number of occasions on which the Sterling Area balance of payments has been weak.

While the arrangement has circumscribed somewhat our operations in other currencies, and in particular reduced the value of centrally held funds in the £ sterling devaluation of November 1967 and £ sterling "float" in June 1972, it has given us the advantage of access to a flexible money market for the placement of funds. One of the fears often expressed of a multinational enterprise is the supposed ability to bring about such vast speculative movements against a currency that revaluation or devaluation is impossible to resist. Although there is no doubt that "leads and lags" do have a substantial effect on the currency markets, speculation would not only be in many cases illegal but would also be an irresponsible use of scarce resources.

In this connection, we are aware of the advantages of flexible exchange rates which avoid sudden and drastic variations in currency values. We consider it essential, however, that the element of uncertainty in trading transactions which goes with floating rates should be ironed out as far as possible by the existence of an efficient forward currency market.

Looking at the local aspect of financial management, it is vital for the efficient employment of Group Companies' cash resources to maintain full remittability rights, so that funds generated in one function of the integrated industry may be re-cycled for use in another. Any funds surplus to local requirements are as far as possible centralised in London. We do not of course have complete freedom of operation because each Group Company is an independent entity. Remittance of profits in the form of dividends may in some cases be insufficient to absorb a local cash surplus, and for this reason we try to finance companies in the early stages of development or expansion by loans from the holding companies. This then enables repayment to be made when cash reserves of the local company merit it. Even this may not be enough, and in those cases the local company will arrange for the money to be lent formally to the holding companies. Formulation of the financial relationships between companies in this way is not peculiar to multinational enterprises but follows from the necessary emphasis on the separation of corporate entities within each national domain. The precise form chosen may also be influenced by taxation factors, such as the possible different treatment of dividend and interest payments. There will also in many countries be currency problems which will influence financial structures, for example devaluation will be hedged against by minimising the net working capital of an operating company which has to be financed from the centre.

To return to my main theme in conclusion, the problems of managing the finances of a multinational enterprise are clearly not going to get less in the course of this decade, both because of the vast volume of investment capital required and of the need to develop new methods of exploiting the financial resources which are potentially available. We have to be ready to pursue what have until recently been unorthodox methods of finance as well as the traditional sources. However, given the importance of energy to world economic activity, I am confident that the problems can be overcome.

Part III

Multinational corporations and international financial markets

Chapter VI

THE FINANCIAL ROLE OF MULTINATIONAL ENTERPRISES: RECRUITMENT OF CAPITAL

by *W. A. P. Manser*

Definitions

Questions of definitions are first of all important. When considering the recruitment of capital by international company groups, it should be borne in mind that the funds for consideration are either those raised by the subsidiaries themselves, or those transmitted by the parent to the subsidiaries. Capital raised by the parent company for its own internal use is by definition capital employed in the domestic business of the parent's country, and does not come within the purview of the present study. The analysis which follows will therefore be concerned with the capital financing of subsidiaries, either through the latter's local or international efforts, or through the passage of funds to them from the parent company.

Investment capital recruited from sources external to the subsidiary (i.e. from the parent or from the local or international capital market) forms a minor but vital part of the subsidiary's overall financing. This contribution amounts to some 30-40 per cent. of the total sources of funds of subsidiaries, whether these be in developed or developing countries, or whether they be the dependents of parent companies in the United States, the United Kingdom, or in other European countries. This is of course an average figure, and it should be noted that the capital funding of subsidiaries, particularly through the medium of parents' contributions, will be considerably above this average where the subsidiary is newly established.

The stability of the average ratio underlines the essential function of long-term capital input. Capital initiates resource-creating activity, furnishing earnings fairly soon in excess of the capital input: this autonomous generation of funds is sufficient to maintain the stock of assets created by the initial investment, and indeed to contribute significantly towards new assets. Where frequent and substantial additions of assets are required, nevertheless, these internally generated funds are not normally sufficient. Thus where expanding enterprises are concerned, injections of new capital are invariably required The foregoing is no more than a truism, expressing a wellknown principle of financial management of all companies, whether national or international, unitary or multi-divisional.

However, when this principle is applied to the financial management of international corporations, a complication immediately arises. The international multi-company group is distinguished from other company groups solely through the fact that its component members are situated in different countries. The consequence of this for the recruitment of capital is that the subsidiaries of the multi-national company, although registered as national companies of the country in which they operate, none the less are, and are known to be, owned and controlled by a company foreign to that country. The capital recruited by these companies is therefore in principle capital supplied for a foreign user. In an equivalent and complementary way, capital recruited by the parent company in its own country for transmission to its subsidiaries abroad is, again, capital recruited for a foreign user. Thus in all its capital operations, wherever these may be conducted, the international company appears in the role of a foreign concern.

(i) The parent company

This notion requires some amplification. The parent company, raising capital in its domestic capital market, certainly appears as a domestic concern in the eyes of the investors who supply the capital. On the other hand, when it comes to transmit the proceeds of the capital-raising operation to its subsidiaries abroad, it does not so appear to its Government. It is now classed as an exporter of domestic capital, and will incur specific treatment on that score. In a number of countries, including the United States, the United Kingdom, France, and several other Western European countries, quantitative controls are applied to the amount of capital so exported. In the domestic capital market, furthermore, investors—whilst identifying the company as a domestic concern—will be guided in their readiness to furnish capital by their assessment of the prospects of the parent company's foreign affiliates, i.e. by the foreign end-uses of the capital being recruited.

(ii) The subsidiary

In the case of the local recruitment of capital by subsidiaries, it remains true that a number of resident companies, although affiliates of foreign parents, are sufficiently strongly established and familiar members of the host country's business community to be assimilated entirely to the latter in the popular mind. Moreover in some countries, particularly in the developing areas, local affiliates of international companies may rank amongst the largest and most influential members of the local business community. This may be held to give them certain advantages in the raising of capital. Furthermore, where local affiliates are not in themselves particularly prominent, the reputation and financial strength of the parent company will be such that the latter's guarantee will serve to secure the affiliate's borrowing. Thus it might reasonably be held that subsidiaries of international companies, whether locally assimilated or not, and whether locally influential or not, are invariably in a favoured position with regard to the recruitment of local capital.

However, analysis of this proposition discloses a number of important qualifications. In the first place, foreign-owned subsidiaries that have merged into the local national scene will nevertheless retain their separate identity in the eyes of the government of that country, which will have precise knowledge of the proportion of equity held by the foreign parent. Whilst such a subsidiary might therefore receive support from the investors in the private capital market of that country, it will in many cases be subject to government-imposed ceilings on the level of borrowings to which it may resort. A number of governments, having in mind the balance of payments and the domestic capital resources of their countries, allow borrowing only pro rata to the input of new capital by the parent, or in accordance with other similar criteria. The capital markets of most countries are also regulated, either by the public authorities or by a central body representative of the security industry, in such a way as to establish orders of priority for bond issues, or to ensure certain conditions under which equity issues may be made. In either case the issues of nationally-owned companies will tend to receive preference over those of foreign-controlled companies. Finally, in a number of countries, particularly in the developing areas, but also in Western Europe and elsewhere, a large proportion of the loan funds available in the bond market are furnished by state or parastatal institutions, themselves financed either from the public purse or through public savings channels. Given the provenance of these funds, loan advances go frequently in the first instance to borrowers of national origin. It is perhaps worth remarking also that the provision of loan guarantees by parents of subsidiaries lacking adequate standing in their local capital market is not an invariably attractive resource. Such guarantees, although they may not be taken up, and thus engender an effective outflow of funds, nevertheless stand as a contingent liability on the balance sheet of the parent. This therefore constitutes a simultaneous commitment of the funds of, and an increase in the gearing of, the parent, limiting its own recourse to the capital market and providing it with no immediate financial gain. A guarantee is therefore comparable in effect to an actual loan from the parent to the subsidiary, and is not normally undertaken except in circumstances which make it unavoidable.

The conclusions to which the above observations appear to lead is that in the field of capital issues, apparent integration of the subsidiary into the national background of the country in which it is located is of doubtful practical value, since the precedence of its issues in markets regulated or financed by the authorities will be determined in relation to the true facts of its ownership. Where no controls or priorities exist, the fact or otherwise of integration will be immaterial. As regards the competitive size and standing of the subsidiary, these attributes will—questions of control and priority aside—tend to give an advantage. However, the advantage of relative prominence is best exploited in locations where private capital can be freely competed for that is to say in the larger industrialised countries. In these countries, however, affiliates of international companies are by definition less likely to achieve prominence. In those countries where the local subsidiaries may predominate, that is to say in countries of the developing areas, capital markets in which private funds can be freely competed for are sparse or non-existent; capital funds are to a very large extent provided through state or parastatal institutions, which themselves necessarily give preference to nationally-owned enterprises.

It should perhaps be stressed that the foregoing impediments do not apply to the availability of bank credit. In this case, public controls on borrowing do not normally exist; little or no discrimination is exercised against foreign-controlled borrowers, and funds are relatively freely available in most countries. However, the present section is necessarily concerned with long-term capital.

(iii) Conclusions on extra-territoriality

Thus, it appears true to say that in this field, international companies lie under handicaps which are not incurred by multi-company groups operating within the boundaries of single states. The field of capital recruitment might indeed be said to illustrate a double disability familiar to international companies: that of being regarded as nationally based for certain purposes, and, at the same time, extra-territorial for other purposes. Thus the subsidiaries of international companies remain registered, resident companies of the countries in which they are established, subject to the full range of domestic laws and regulations as regards their constitution, tax liabilities, exchange operations, method of conducting business, and so on; at the same time, their extra-territorial origin is taken into account when determining their degree of access to the capital market of the country to whose laws they are subordinated.

Alternative financing

It remains to be seen to what extent international companies are able to obviate the handicaps delineated above. Clearly, there are three broad methods by which international companies might ease their own position. They may firstly reduce the overall reliance of the group on external long-term capital through an intensification of the self-financing, or cash flow, of the group; secondly, they might dilute the foreign character of the subsidiary by increasing the local ownership of its equity capital, thus at one stroke enhancing the subsidiary's ability to borrow, and reducing the parent's need to supply capital across its own country's exchange control; thirdly, the international group might look, outside domestic capital markets, to the international capital market for its funds.

(i) Increased self-financing

The highest attainable level of self-financing, or of cash flow, is the primary objective of all companies. The creation of internal resources is, as remarked upon earlier, the mechanism through which an original capital input is converted into an earnings flow, the accumulation of which, in the medium- to short-term, exceeds this initial investment outlay. The highest attainable level of self-financing, achieved through the medium of maximum dividend and other income payments from the subsidiaries to the parent, is also, as has been mentioned, the primary aim of multi-company groups. Consideration of taxation and exchange risks provide a further incentive to international groups, to direct available subsidiaries' resources into the central funds of the group. Thus on all counts so far examined, international multi-company groups will, regardless of capital recruitment questions, be intent on achieving the highest possible level of self-financing, both within the subsidiary companies themselves, and within the group as a whole. By the same token, the maximum generation of internal resources for deployment to new fixed assets, and consequently the minimum resort to external long-term borrowing, will already be the prevailing rule of action.

As a necessary corollary to the above, it is difficult to envisage how, in contemplation purely of capital market difficulties, international companies could so modify their business arrangements as to increase their level of cash flow. The cash flow of these companies compares closely with that of similarly based domestic companies, and there does not appear to be a margin of potential still to be harnessed. It should be borne in mind that once all latent cash flow has been secured through the appropriate financial procedures, then self-financing remains fundamentally as a function of the industrial and commercial activities of the firm in question. Cash flow will arise basically from the equation between turnover and operating costs; the levels of depreciation and retained earnings from which further investment can be financed will depend on the dividend needs of the company, and of course of the taxation burden imposed upon it from outside. The volume of original cash flow will therefore depend on a variety of industrial, commercial and economic factors; it will be governed by the efficiency of the company in question; by the vigour or otherwise of the industrial branch in which the company is active; and by the level of demand permitted by the public authorities in the economy as a whole. The cash flow of individual companies will, independently of the foregoing factors, vary over the latter's own lifetime; being relatively small at the outset of the company's career, when sales turnover will still be developing; and large at a period of maturity when the company and its product are well-established: the foregoing effect will be particularly true of the element of retained earnings inside the total of cash flow. On the other side of the balance, the degree to which cash flow covers investment needs will depend on the maturity of existing fixed assets, the success of the company in marketing its product, and the prospect for extended sales in the future. Normally, needs and availability can be made to coincide in large measure. Large cash flows will, in most cases, emerge in periods of high economic demand, when future sales are reasonably assured, and further investment is indicated. However, there will be transitional periods where investment needs arise alongside low cash flows.

It will be evident from the foregoing that the predominating factor in the determination of the size of cash flow is the industrial progress of the company, and not an exogenous financial factor such as the state of external capital markets. The international company will thus exert itself, in any event, to maximise its cash flow to the limit of its capacities, and then to see whether desirable expenditure on investment leaves a margin of financing to be covered by external sources. Should such externally available resources prove to be deficient, then it is open to the company to amend its investment plans, or to take such other action as may be possible; but it will not normally be in a position so to adapt its internal structure as to change its cash flow.

(*ii*) Increased minority participation

Shares of the parent

Although the term does not strictly apply to both, "minority participation" will be taken here to mean both the sale of the equity of subsidiary companies to shareholders other than the parent company, and the sale of the shares of the parent company in capital markets other than that of the latter.

The last of these two possibilities should perhaps be considered first. This would consist primarily in the sale of the parent company's shares on the capital markets of many countries, rather than predominantly—as is at present the case—on the capital market of the country of the parent company. Such sales could also be made in the international capital market proper, but this eventually will be considered under Section (*iii*) below. The primary advantage of share issues in other countries would, of course, lie in the parent company's release from exchange control curbs placed by its own Government on the export of capital raised on the domestic market. The international diffusion of the parent company's equity will also have the advantage possibly of easing the parent company's task of capital recruitment, since a low level of Stock Exchange activity in one country might be balanced by greater demand in another. Other advantages would lie in the higher level of international participation in the ultimate control of the company, whilst still avoiding the dilution of the group management's control of its subsidiaries. It should perhaps be remembered, in passing, that the international diffusion of the ownership of existing international companies is in some ways already fairly advanced. The shareholders' register of a number of large international companies already comprises participants of varying nationalities. However, the corresponding shares will have been bought, in the greatest measure, on the national Stock Exchange of the parent company through the medium of capital exported from the participant's own country. The deployment of parent's equity through the medium of local issues in separate countries might represent a more desirable method of achieving the same end.

Three major difficulties appear to lie in the way of the distribution of capital along these lines. In the first place, of course, the existence of exchange controls in the countries of issue presents a significant obstacle. International companies may indeed float new share issues on the Stock Exchanges of individual countries abroad; when, however, they come to the repatriation to the parent country of the proceeds of these issues, they will in most cases encounter exchange control bars to the removal of this capital from the country in which it is recruited. The parent company thus effectively encounters in reverse the same exchange control difficulties which led it to seek to substitute for capital-raising in its own country the recruitment of capital in other countries. Where the parent company raises its capital abroad, then the exchange controls applying there militate with equivalent efficacy against the recirculation of the capital to other parts of the group. Thus it remains broadly speaking true that unless a parent company can devote the proceeds of capital issues in a specific country abroad to its own subsidiary located in the same country, then it will not derive substantial gains from removing the locus of issue from its own country to another. Secondly, the value of the funding practicable by the parent company in any given capital market will be contingent on the size and depth of that market itself. When it is considered that as against a value of $864,000 m. and $200,000 m. for New York and London respectively, the total book value of shares outstanding on the Stock Exchanges of France, Belgium and Italy were $9,400 m., $7,200 m., and $17,400 m. respectively,[1] it might be true to say that only in the first two of the above-quoted countries can a stock market be said to exist which is sufficiently developed to provide an ample reservoir of capital funds. The third and—from the practical point of view—perhaps the main objection to

1. See *OECD Financial Statistics* No. 4, 1971.

the procedure, lies in the fact that dispersed recruitment of equity capital would not, except in the circumstances mentioned above, add to the total capital receipts of the parent company, since the latter would in the absence of issues on foreign stock exchanges normally raise the same amount of equity capital on its home market. The procedure outlined above would represent more a method of diffusing equity issues, than of increasing the amount of equity capital issued by the parent at any given time.

This method being excluded, for the above reasons, from the realm of practical capital-raising by the parents of international companies—at least for the time being—it remains true that the international issue of equity appears to hold out some promise for the future. The procedure, whilst to some extent facilitating the parent's equity capitalisation, would extend international ownership—thus permitting a wider international share both in the ownership and the profits of these companies. As the size and permeability of capital markets in various countries—particularly those of Western Europe— develop, so it may be expected that international companies will increasingly take advantage of the equity capital-raising opportunities so presented.

Shares of the subsidiary

The primary consideration in this instance is group control of the subsidiary. The international company being a multi-company group, the central principle of its structure is that control—where not ownership—of the subsidiaries should be in the hands of the parent company. A situation of 100 per cent. ownership of the subsidiary by the parent guarantees absolute control. Any diminution of the parent's participation necessarily entails a potential loss of control. No clear relationship between ownership ratios and the degree of control can be established. Control of a company can be exercised where the controlling equity participant holds less than 50 per cent. of the shares. A sole shareholding of, say, 30 per cent. or 20 per cent. can, in determined hands—and given no solidarity of views in any equal or greater shareholding percentage of the remaining capital—secure control over the company. Indeed, smaller ownership ratios than this can be postulated. On the other hand, control of a company through a shareholding as thin as that suggested above could in many instances be tenuous; a resolution of the remaining shareholding into unanimous blocks of a size larger than that of the hitherto controlling interest might occur at any time; a block of the remaining shares, sufficiently large to give control, might at any time be sold to a single bidder. Since control is of paramount importance to the parent company, it is unlikely that the latter will allow its ownership to fall below 51 per cent. of the outstanding capital.

Even where control—through a sufficiently high ownership ratio—is secured, a dilution of the parent's equity share may still give rise to some adverse effects. Minority shareholders necessarily have an interest in the income and

84

consequent profits of the subsidiary. Where the ownership of the minority shareholders is diversified, there may be no strong pressures in favour of any given policy diverging from that thought suitable to the interests of the group as a whole. On the other hand, where the minority shareholding is concentrated in few hands, or where the subsidiary has become subject of local attention, this pressure may be substantial. In these instances minority shareholders might call for dividend payments larger than that thought desirable by the multi-company group as a whole. To secure such higher profit distributions, minority shareholders might consequentially call for levels of prices, forms of trade, methods of production, etc., not deemed by the group to be the most suitable in the circumstances. It is of course equally possible that minority shareholders will in all cases find themselves in agreement with the overall policies pursued by the group. However, the emergence of a class of minority shareholders creates a possibility of disagreement that necessarily had not existed hitherto. For this reason again, the optimum long-term interest of the group as a whole will be best secured through the restraint of minority shareholding to the smallest equity ratio possible.

Lastly, as remarked above, the degree to which equity issues may be effected locally depends on the size and depth of the capital market; in countries whose equity securities markets may not have been very substantially developed, opportunities may be relatively restricted.

All in all, therefore, in the light of the foregoing comments, it appears that the recourse of the subsidiary company to local equity capitalisation may in practice be somewhat curtailed; and this conclusion is indeed borne out by such factual data as exists. For American companies local equity acquisitions appear to amount to 1.5 per cent. of total sources of funds in developed countries, and to about 2 per cent. of such sources in developing countries. The Reddaway Report[2] suggests that total minority interests in the sample of subsidiaries taken for the study, amounted on average from 1955 to 1963 to some 13 per cent. The British Department of Trade and Industry[3] shows that of the total net assets of United Kingdom-owned subsidiaries abroad, some 16 per cent. was "attributable to outside shareholders" in 1969; and that for the affiliates in the United Kingdom of foreign parent companies, the total minority ownership amounted to 10 per cent. The United States Department of Commerce[4] indicates that at end 1966, majority-owned affiliates of United States companies abroad (i.e. affiliates where the United States parent company had 50 per cent. or more of the equity) accounted for 87 per cent. of total net worth in manufacturing.

Such joint shareholdings as have arisen appear to have been dictated by a

2. *Op. cit.*, page 239.
3. "Overseas Transactions, 1971"; Tables 35 and 39. *Business Monitor. M4.*
4. *United States Direct Investment Abroad*, 1966.

85

number of practical reasons. Many shared subsidiaries consist of joint ventures, i.e. companies created jointly by two parents of differing specialist abilities for the purpose of establishing a common enterprise, in which these specialities can be pooled. In other cases, a company wishing to enter a given market for the first time may ally itself with an existing company by taking a shareholding in the latter. Government policy frequently prescribes, or induces, the admission of minority interests to foreign-owned subsidiaries. Thus in certain countries, more favoured tax treatment is available for foreign-owned companies having a degree of local share participation. In other countries a given element of local share participation is formally stipulated. In certain broad areas of activity such as mining and plantations, the fact that the investment activity involves the consumption of the natural resources of the host country sometimes leads to circumstances in which an element of local equity ownership is desirable where this is not prescribed by the host government.

On the whole, it appears clear that the acceptance of minority interests has not, in the majority of companies, been actuated by a quest for additional investment capital. Both the numerical data and the range of practical motives outlined above support this conclusion.[5] The admission of minority equity capital does not therefore seem to provide a significant relief to the difficulties encountered by international companies in the recruitment of capital.

(iii) International market

The international market comprises, in reality, a short- and medium-term credit market and a medium- and long-term capital market: the Euro-dollar and Eurocurrency credit markets, and the Eurobond capital market. Since Eurocurrency credits can be rolled over a number of times, they can be used to finance short-term investment projects, or to finance the first phase of longer-term projects. The Eurobond market, consisting as it does of long-term capital available in those currencies which can be lent across frontiers without hindrance, is a ready vehicle for long-term investment projects.

The advantage of the international market lies pre-eminently in the fact that it is a source of funds free of all exchange control restrictions. Euro-dollars necessarily incur no United States exchange controls, and since they take

5. Cf. also the Reddaway Report, page 188: "It was almost always said by companies that minority holdings had not been used as a deliberate source of finance . . ."; Professor Lee Remmers, *op. cit.*, page 271: "Of the many businessmen and bankers who discussed this question with us, it was rare to find one who believed that companies would choose a joint venture for financial reasons alone".

the form of deposits held by banks in American currency, they necessarily fall outside the currency area of other countries. Other Eurocurrencies, such as Euro-sterling and Euro-francs, enjoy the same exchange control freedom, having as non-resident accounts been withdrawn at the outset from the currency area of their own countries. Eurobond funds are by definition free of exchange control. Thus it is possible for a United Kingdom parent company, wishing to finance the investment project of a subsidiary in another country, to obtain funds in the currency of that country through the medium of a Euro-dollar deposit. Since the United Kingdom parent's debt is denominated in dollars for repayment in dollars, no foreign exchange liability other than a contingent one falls upon the United Kingdom sterling area, and this transaction will normally be approved by United Kingdom exchange control. Similarly, no recourse is made to the capital market of the host country, since the investment is financed by the import of the funds derived from the Euro-dollar transaction. Similar reasoning applies to Eurobond operations.

The international market, it will be seen from the above, lends itself particularly well to the solution of the problems attending the recruitment of capital by international companies. The difficulty inherent in the extra-territorial nature of the international companies' capital transactions—seen from the angle either of the parent company or of the subsidiary, is overcome by the simple translation of these transactions into an international arena where national considerations do not apply.

Two broad qualifications have, however, to be attached to the above conclusion. These are that firstly, the international market lends itself primarily to the satisfaction of the capital export requirements of the parent company, rather than to that of the local capital needs of the subsidiary. The international market dispenses with the exchange control barriers applied to the outward movement of capital from given currency areas. It does nothing—outside these particular transactions in themselves—to alleviate the difficulties confronting subsidiaries in the raising of capital in the markets of their host countries. It is true, in principle, that subsidiaries of international companies, unable to obtain locally the capital resources they need, may themselves become direct Euro-dollar or Eurobond borrowers. However, the size of the latter markets is such that parent companies, rather than subsidiaries, are likely to have sufficient access to funds.

Secondly, and as a corollary to the above, the international market remains small in relation either to the national markets which it supplements, or to the investment needs of international companies as a whole. The total Eurocurrency take-up in the period 1964-68 amounted to some $650 m. annually. The total Eurobond take-up amounted to approximately $1,460 m. annually. The two markets together, therefore, offered some $2,000 m. of short- to long-term capital. As against this, the total long-term domestic capital markets of the United States, United Kingdom and E.E.C. combined, in the same period, amounted to some $45,000 m. annually.[6] Total bank credit extended in the domestic markets of the three areas averaged $39,300 m. annually.[7]

As against the $2,000 m. approximately available annually from the Euro-currency and Eurobond markets, the financing requirements of international companies stood at some $7,000 m. annually in 1964–68 for capital exports from parents to their subsidiaries, and some $1,850 m. annually for local long- and short-term borrowing by subsidiaries in the countries where they were operating.

Thus, whether judged in relation to the equivalent facilities offered within domestic markets, or by the latent requirements of international companies, the international credit and capital markets–although they have expanded very rapidly in recent years–do not provide a particularly large reservoir of funds.

Nor should it be thought that international companies are the sole clients of the international market. Other parties, having exhausted the resources of their domestic capital market (for reasons other than those applying to inter-national companies) or seeing other advantages in the use of the international pool of funds, have been active participants; these have included govern-, ments, municipalities, public utilities, nationalised industries and internation-al organisations. These users accounted for over 60 per cent. of total Euro-bond resources. In the Eurocurrency market international companies borrow-ed on average some $650 m. annually in the period 1964-68, as against the annual market turnover of some $3,200 m.–a proportion of some 20 per cent In the Eurobond market international companies borrowed $1,460 m. annually, against the annual market turnover of $3,772 m., or 39 per cent.

None the less, as the above figures imply, the international market remains as a major source of finance for international companies. This is summarised in the following table:

6. Public and private security issues (shares, bonds and debt certificates, but exclud-ing straight loans to companies). Source: OECD, 1971.

7. IMF International Financial Service–Country Tables, line 32c, "Claims on Private Sector" (Year-to-year increase; for USA and United Kingdom 1965-69).

1964–68 (Aggregate)		*$m.*
Total capital transfers from parents to subsidiaries		35,000
Total international financing by parents		10,500
of which:		
Total Eurodollar borrowings by parents	3,200	
Total Eurobond issues by parents	7,300	

As will be seen, 30 per cent. of all capital remitted to subsidiaries was, under this calculation, drawn by the parent companies not from their domestic capital markets, but from the international capital and credit market. Given the share of parents' capital in the total financing of the group—calculated at some 20 per cent. of the total—it follows that the share of Eurocurrency and Eurobond financing in the total sources of funds of international groups as a whole is some 5 per cent.

For the reasons earlier stated, the recourse of subsidiaries to Eurofinancing, where it occurs, cannot be quantified, but if this recourse is at all substantial, then the total share of Eurofinancing in the funds of international groups as a whole will be to that extent increased. It might on the whole be safe to assume that Eurocurrency and Eurobond financing provides some 10 per cent. of the total resources of international groups.

Before leaving the subject of international financing, it is perhaps useful to review briefly the function of a new intermediary recently created by international enterprises to aid in operations in the international money and capital market. The new instrument in question is the international financial company. The need for these companies arises from the fact that the Eurobond market is still supplied in large degree by wealthy individual investors, a prime concern of whose is the avoidance of withholding taxes on the capital and interest repayable to them on their loans. In most industrialised countries such withholding taxes are applied. A number of other countries—amongst whom figure, or have figured, Luxembourg, Netherlands Antilles, and Canada—do not impose such taxes. International companies wishing to raise funds through Eurobonds have therefore frequently created companies in those countries for the sole purpose of making the issues. Their repayments of interest and capital then go to the subscribers free of tax. The immediate financial advantage goes therefore to the subscriber rather than to the international company, although the latter presumes that in so choosing the location of its issue, it will meet with better subscriptions than elsewhere.

To revert finally to the issue of parent company equity in the international market, mentioned at the beginning of the present section, a number of Eurobond issues have also been made convertible into the equity of the parent company. Although this does not introduce a new source of funds—for it is open for the investor in convertible Eurobonds to purchase the parent's equity on the latter's capital market—it does, in providing greater flexibility and lower coupons, add to the attractions of Eurobond issues.

(iv) Conclusions on the international capital market

The recruitment of capital appears to be an area in which international companies will remain under some disadvantage. It should not be supposed from the foregoing that international companies are compelled significantly to curtail their operations on account of these difficulties. Nevertheless, it remains apparent that their operations have to be conducted in face of difficulties which do not arise for multi-company groups operating within the boundaries of single states. The potential relief open to these companies, in the increased permeability of national capital markets, and in the development of the international money and capital markets, can be clearly discerned, but may be slow in materialising.

Chapter VII

MULTINATIONAL COMPANIES AND INTERNATIONAL CAPITAL MARKETS

by *Sylvain Plasschaert*

Introductory remarks

This paper concentrates on the relationship and the interactions between multinational companies and international capital markets. It examines, on the basis of both deductive reasoning and available empirical evidence, whether the multinational corporations are an important factor in the emergence and development of international capital markets; besides, it indicates which types of international capital markets best suit the needs of the multinational corporation.

Throughout the paper, I shall maintain a few assumptions, which allow me to focus on the subject matter, just defined. First, I assume that the internationalization of capital markets is a desirable development. This proposition, admittedly, invites reservations, especially when looked at by national Governments, on account of the possible harmful interferences of international capital flows with national objectives and policies.[1] Looking at welfare in a global, transnational fashion however, the proposition draws support from some solid arguments. Amongst others, border-crossing financial investments are capable of improving investors' welfare[2] and, when unhampered under competitive conditions, they improve the overall efficiency of resource allocation. This assumption allows us to abstract from the reactions of governments to the further internationalization of capital markets—a topic discussed by other speakers at this Seminar. Consequently, I shall look at international capital markets (as defined below) primarily from the vantage point of multinational corporations.

Two further assumptions are that the multinational corporation will con-

1. See Richard N. Cooper, "Towards an International Capital Market?", in C. P. Kindleberger and A. Shonfield (eds.) *North American and Western European Economic Policies*, 1971; also published in John H. Dunning (ed.) *International Investment. Selected Readings*, Penguin Modern Economic Readings, London, 1972. See especially p. 237-40.

2. See Herbert G. Grubel "Internationally Diversified Postfolios. Welfare Gains and Capital Flows", *American Economic Review*, vol. 58, 1968; also in John H. Dunning (ed.) *International Investment . . .* see p. 201-20.

tinue to have huge capital needs and that the authorities should strive to establish capital markets which efficiently cater for those needs. The first assumption, here mentioned, conforms to generally held views; the second one is debatable as other segments of the economy and other social groups may well have priority claims on scarce savings.

At first glance, the title of this paper, may appear self-explanatory and convey the impression that only the relationship between multinational corporations and "the" international capital market *par excellence*, i.e. the Eurobond market is dealt with. On closer inspection, the terms used in the title require clarification. I have less qualms with the *multinational company*. For the purposes of this paper, the existence of one affiliate abroad, engaged in productive activities is a sufficient but necessary condition for labelling a company "multinational": this mechanistic definition, incorporates the feature which most scholars consider essential.

Restricting the meaning of *"capital markets"* to long-term markets (or even only to security markets), conforms to academic traditions in many countries, but would convey an unrealistic picture of the sources of funds available to, and tapped by multinational corporations. I therefore interpret the expression "capital market" in a wider sense and as synonymous with "financial markets".[3] Thus, they encompass long-term, medium-term and short-term credits obtained from banks and financial institutions, as well as other sources of financing, such as private placements with institutional investors. While medium-term and short-term borrowings and transactions are part of this extensive definition, I shall nonetheless be concerned mainly with the long-term needs of multinational corporations.

It is less easy to determine when a financial market becomes *international.* Elsewhere, I contended that "any transaction, one parameter of which lies beyond or crosses given national borders, can be viewed as international".[4] Thus, the purchase on foreign account of shares of a United States company, listed on the New York Stock Exchange, represents an international transaction, although, obviously, a stock market will only become truly international when the proportion of transactions on foreign account becomes sizeable, as when a stock exchange (e.g. Luxembourg) performs mainly an entrepôt function. A bond issue by a United States company on the Swiss domestic market also becomes international, although most of the parameters involved in the issue, such as the currency and the composition of underwriting and selling syndicates, remain eminently Swiss. Fortunately, it has become a common practice to call those issues "foreign issues" and to distinguish them from

3. In France, the "marché des capitaux", usually comprises the short-term "marché de l'argent" and the long-term "marché financier".
4. S. Plasschaert, "A Note on the Major Common Features of Eurofinancial Markets", *Tijdschrift voor Economie*, 1970 IV, p. 421.

"Eurobond issues", with both categories being viewed as sub-species of present-day international bond floatations.[5]

The mechanics of Eurobond issues diverge significantly from those of foreign issues. Eurobond issues have a truly universalistic horizon. Some of the operations, involved in their floating, such as the listing, of necessity are performed in a given city or refer to a specific country. Yet Eurobond issues derive several constituent elements from various jurisdictions, especially from those where they can most efficiently or freely be accomodated; they are devised to appeal to investors in many countries. Contrary to foreign issues, Eurobond floatings are not centrally regulated by a supra-national authority, although they are considerably hampered by the restrictive "peripheral" measures which national authorities may take vis-à-vis resident investors, issuers or intermediating financial institutions.

Looking at financial markets from the viewpoint of the parent company, both foreign and Eurofinancial primary markets are obviously located abroad and constitute foreign and hence "international" sources of funds. The financial resources which the subsidiaries of the multinational corporation may harness for their own uses in local financial markets (as, for example, through borrowings from local banks) should also be viewed as foreign sources—although the subsidiary, legally, has the same nationality as the lending bank. As a matter of fact, unless the concept of the multinational corporation is emptied of its meaning, the subsidiary is an integral part of the multinational corporation-family and the interests of the subsidiary are subordinated to those of the multinational corporation as a whole. In any event, important decisions tend to be taken at the company's headquarters, within the framework of an overall strategy.

The selected aspects of the relationship between the multinational corporation and international capital markets, on which I wish to focus hereafter are:

(a) the impact of financial systems optimization on the need of the multinational corporation for recourse to financial markets.

(b) the typical patterns of financing, both at the level of the multinational corporation-as-a-whole and of the subsidiary and the resulting recourse to financial markets

(c) the role of the multinational corporation in developing the Euro-financial markets

(d) the case for and the trend towards internationalization of the shareholdings in the multinational corporation

(e) finally, the types of financial markets that best serve the needs of the multinational corporation.

5. Ibid., p. 421-24. As noted there, the differences in the internationality of foreign and Eurobond issues correspond to the nuances in the philological meanings of "international".

The effect of systems optimization on outside financing by multinational companies

The proposition that the multinational corporation is capable, on account of its multinationality, of reducing its dependence on financial markets, may sound surprising, considering that investments abroad call for substantial financial resources and cannot be met solely by internally generated funds. Nonetheless, under the assumption of a given, fixed amount of investments carried out by the multinational corporation, when optimizing the potentialities which multinationality affords in the field of financial management, the multinational corporations are in a position to lower their dependence on outside finance.

There exists unambiguous, although scattered evidence, that in recent years, a growing number of multinational corporations are dovetailing the financial management of the various entities of their group, in order to optimize financial results for the multinational corporation-as-a-whole.

Elsewhere, we have discussed a large number of optimizing devices. The objectives of these devices were catalogued as follows:

(i) Minimizing overall tax liabilities
(ii) Transfer pricing
(iii) Speeding up money transfers
(iv) Minimizing intra-multinational corporation transfers
(v) Pooling excess liquidity and facilitating intra-multinational corporation financing
(vi) Facilitating external finance
(vii) Minimizing exchange risk exposure.[6]

There is no need to repeat the detailed analysis given in the article cited, but only to stress the more relevant points. The various devices, however, have in common that they tend to increase profits and, hence, the potential for self-financing of the multinational corporation. To the same extent, they reduce the need for outside financing.

Items (v) and (vi) are more directly related to financial markets. Let us suppose, for example, within a given multinational corporation, that (a), the subsidiary in country A possesses ample liquidity which is neither required for its current operations nor earmarked for investment (b) a sister-subsidiary in country B is cash-hungry and (c) no currency risks in A and B are incurred. If the two subsidiaries are left on their own and given maximum autonomy, the subsidiary in country A will invest the excess-liquidity in the local money-market, whereas the subsidiary in country B will request working capital financing from a local bank. As debit interest rates normally exceed

6. Sylvain Plasschaert. "Emerging Patterns of Financial Management in Multinational Companies", *Economisch en Sociaal Tijdschrift*, December 1971, p. 561-76.

94

credit rates, this approach results in a net opportunity cost for the multinational corporation. This cost can be avoided by channeling the excess-funds from A to B, thus obviating, to the same extent, the need for the latter to borrow in country B. It follows that multinationality allows the multinational corporation to reallocate financial resources that are available and suboptimally used within the multinational corporation. As Professor Robert Stobaugh, Jr. notices "... the subsidiaries can now provide each other with funds. This new dimension increases the financing alternatives geometrically as the number of subsidiaries increases".[7]

Multinationality also improves the chances for obtaining outside financing through the subsidiary and for enjoying comparatively favorable terms on such financings. Each subsidiary, endowed with a distinct legal personality, can act, in principle, as a borrowing vehicle in its local market and transmit the funds thus obtained to a sister-subsidiary in another country. Furthermore, subsidiaries are frequently characterized by low credit ratings on account of running-in problems or an unfavorable debt/equity ratio. In such cases, a subsidiary may have its low credit rating bolstered by the guarantees provided by the parent company or by another seasoned subsidiary in the multinational corporation-family. The network of subsidiaries, therefore, allows the multinational corporation flexibly to mobilize funds and to take advantage of lower borrowing costs and/or the greater availability of funds in a given national financial market.

Admittedly, a uni-national company, conceivably, can also approach foreign financial markets. Some smaller-sized United States companies, for example, and possessing no multinational profile, have floated Eurobonds, for use within the U.S.A. But such companies would not normally have been able to obtain bank credits in Europe, as the banks would not derive any profitable business from a company without local subsidiary.

It is frequently asserted that the subsidiaries of multinational corporations are able to obtain funds, more easily, or at lower cost, in a given national financial market (say, in a European country) than the "native" companies, with resulting harm to the latter. For lack of sufficiently documented studies, it is difficult to assess this assertion. Casual observations lead me to believe that there have been, and still are, cases where local subsidiaries of a multinational corporation reach a superior credit standing than the native competitors. However, generalization seems unwarranted. European bankers have come to evaluate credits to units of the multinational corporation-family in

7. Robert Stobaugh Jr., "Financing Foreign Subsidiaries of U.S.-controlled Multinational Enterprises", *Journal of International Business Studies*, Summer 1970, p. 44. This article foreshadows part of the conclusions to be found in the forthcoming *Money in the Multinational Enterprise; A Study of Financial Policy*, by Sidney Robbins and Robert B. Stobaugh, another volume in the Harvard Multinational Enterprise Series.

terms of the inherent risks, of the guarantees offered and of the attendant generation of banking business. They are no longer unduly awed by a big name; they also came to realize, at an early stage, that the financial optimization approach by a growing number of multinational corporations by-passes the banks and reduces banking profits. This leads them not to neglect the financing needs of native, smaller companies, whenever conditions of stringency impose some credit rationing.

Yet, this attitude does not imply aloofness vis-à-vis the multinational corporation. The very size of financial transactions performed by the subsidiaries of big multinational corporations, the possibility of working one's way towards a share of the financing business initiated by the multinational corporation in the Euro-financial markets, the intensified international competition among the major banks, and, last but not least, the realization that multinational corporations are going to stay and will not shy away from systems optimization have even induced the banking community to accept, or themselves to devise, schemes that reduce banking business and/or profits. As an example, one may cite the compensation between debit and credit interests, charged to or accruing to different subsidiaries of the multinational corporation, to which a bank, with branches in various countries—or engaged in a collaborative venture with foreign banks—may agree.

This analysis warrants the conclusion that integrated financial management within the multinational corporation—whereby the multinational corporation, to some extent, acts as a banker on its own behalf—tends to reduce the need for outside financing, other things being equal. This restrictive effect on the demand for outside finance, however, should not be overrated, as various constraints impede its full realization. First, some impediments are internal to the multinational corporation. Financial systems optimization, while reaping tangible extra-profits, is not without its "hidden" costs, as excessive monitoring and intervention by the parent company tends to damage the morale of the management and to complicate the evaluation of the performance of the subsidiary.[8] Professor Robert Stobaugh Jr. found that the potentialities for systems optimization in the financial field depend on the size and the degree of multinationalization reached by the multinational corporation. He found, with respect to a sample of United States-based multinational corporations, that the small ones typically lacked the international involvement that would warrant the establishment of optimization systems and did not possess financial talent at the parent company, sufficiently versed in the intricacies of international finance. Conversely, the large United States-based multinational corporation "leans towards the system optimization but is too large and complex to implement it", and tends to direct the subsidiary by way of detailed guidelines instead of by imposing specific decisions. In medi-

8. Sylvain Plasschaert, "Emerging Patterns . . .", *op. cit.*, p. 576-79.

um-sized firms—whose profile features total sales of $740 million, foreign sales of $200 million and manufacturing subsidiaries in 14 countries—systems optimization is practised more extensively and purposely.[9] Besides, other constraints on integrated financial management are imposed by the Government in the host-countries. Thus, Australia limits the access of fully-owned foreign subsidiaries to local bank credits. Furthermore, in all national bond markets, flotations on behalf of foreign issuers are subject to approval by the authorities. In most developing countries, severe exchange controls hamper the transfer of funds abroad. And, finally, while systems optimization will normally obviate somewhat the group's need for working capital, it could not possibly meet the financial needs, associated with major investment projects.

So far, the impact of integrated financial management within the multinational corporation on the needs for outside funds, has been analysed under the explicit assumption of fixed financial needs. If we relax this assumption, the proposition that the multinationalization of business has enhanced the worldwide investment ratio (in real terms), appears plausible. As a matter of fact, let us suppose, quite unrealistically, that the waves of foreign direct investments, which we have witnessed in recent years, would not have occurred at all. Under such assumptions, one may plausibly accept the view that the sum of (a) the additional investments which the companies would have been able and willing to undertake in their home-countries and (b) the investments which would have been initiated by native companies in the host-countries would have been far below the value of foreign direct investments which have actually been undertaken by the multinational corporation. As a matter of fact, one may surmise that the opportunities for alternative investments within the home-country would have been somewhat limited, whereas native companies in the host-countries, for lack of complementary factors of production (such as advanced technology and managerial know-how) would not have been able to undertake most of the ventures that have been initiated by foreign-based multinational corporations.

Some comments on the sources of funds for the multinational corporation

In principle, the multinational corporations, with their wide network of subsidiaries, has access to a large number of national financial markets, and to the universalistic Eurofinancial markets as well. The question arises to what extent do multinational corporations rely on outside funds and to which markets will they turn. While some useful insight can be gained through deductive reasoning, only empirical studies are capable of disclosing the ac-

---

9. Robert Stobaugh Jr., "Financing Foreign Subsidiaries . . .", *op. cit.* p. 44-64. The quote appears on p. 53.

tual financial patterns within a multinational corporation. In this section, I attempt to ascertain the impact which the actual financing practices and/or the possible pursuit of optimum financing models by a multinational corporation may have on financial markets.

The sources of finance for a multinational corporation can be rubricated, according to a geographical criterion, into domestic and foreign sources: alternatively or in parallel fashion, one distinguishes between internally generated funds (within the company) and outside financing (with the company approaching financial markets). In discussing financial patterns, however, one should state which viewpoint is adopted. As a matter of fact, what appears as internal or outside financing depends on whether one views the multinational corporation as-a-whole or, on the contrary, looks at a subsidiary in isolation. Equity underwritten by the parent company in the subsidiary or advances to the latter constitute outside financing to the subsidiary; when looked at by the multinational corporation as-a-whole, they only represent an internal reshuffling of funds that are part and parcel of the pool of financing resources, available within the group. In other words, intra-multinational corporation financial flows are consolidated when the multinational corporation is viewed in a global way.

Optimizing behavior of the multinational corporation, obviously, would consist in tapping the financial resourses where they are cheapest (duly recognizing the opportunity cost of internally generated resources) and directing them to the units within the multinational corporation-group, where they are most needed and/or can most profitably be put to use. Thus, the relative cost-of-capital of various sources emerges as a major criterion of financing decisions within the multinational corporation.[10]

One would expect a multinational corporation to mobilize, to a large extent, funds on the financial markets of the home-country. As a matter of fact, many multinational corporations are headquartered in industrial countries with large and sophisticated financial markets. This may not be quite true for multinational corporations based in small countries like Switzerland,

---

10. The cost-of-capital approach is also used for capital budgeting purposes. Apart from controversies about the proper way to measure the cost of different types of capital, the many complicating factors surrounding multinational business render it difficult to devise operational yardsticks. It should come as no surprise that empirical studies have generally found that, as noticed in one source, "financial considerations are pertinent to the *how to* rather than to the *whether to* finance a foreign investment". See, Judd Polk, Irene W. Meister and Lawrence Veit, *U.S. Production Abroad and the Balance of Payments*, National Industrial Conference Board, New York, 1966, p. 108, also reprinted in *Readings in International Financial Management*, ed. Arthur I. Stonehill, Pacific Palisades 1970. See also, in the same collection of Readings, Arthur I. Stonehill and Leonard Nathanson "Capital Budgeting and the Multinational Company", which first appeared in the *California Management Review*, Summer 1968, p. 38-54.

the Netherlands and Sweden, but it certainly applies to the U.S.A., and, to a smaller extent, to the United Kingdom, Germany and Japan. On such markets, normally, over the longer run (i.e. abstracting from differential cyclical movements in the interest rate level) funds will be obtainable in comparatively large amounts and at low cost. Besides, borrowings are supported by the credit standing of the parent company.

In fact, however, no maximum use appears to be made of the facilities of the home-country financial markets. The available evidence, some of which is mentioned below, clearly indicates that, on the contrary, multinational corporations seek, to a large extent, host-country financing for their subsidiaries. This, of course, is partly attributable to institutional constraints and to imperfections in international financial flows; the measures taken in the United States in 1965 and reinforced in 1968 and tending to restrict the outflow of funds for real investments abroad, provide a conspicuous example of such constraints.

But institutional factors are not the only determinants of the bias for host-country financing. Already, the Polk-Meister-Veit enquiry, conducted in 1961-63, indicated that, generally speaking, multinational corporations tend to give preference to foreign borrowing, even at a higher cost (within limits).[11] Apart from the fact that borrowing by the subsidiary is sometimes considered, rightly or wrongly, to favour responsible management in the subsidiary, the desire to hedge against foreign exchange risks provides the main rationale of this preference for foreign outside financing. By balancing liabilities and assets, in the same currency, the exchange risk, as measured in terms of the domestic currency (of the parent company and of the majority of the shareholders) is effectively neutralized. This device is particularly useful in host-countries experiencing frequent devaluations and rapid inflation, as in some South-American countries.

But is the exchange risk concept, as traditionally defined, still relevant to the present-day multinational corporation and especially to those who are deeply immersed in foreign operations and are increasingly adopting a cosmopolitan outlook and perimeter? In my view, a negative answer is in order. As is generally acknowledged, the recent monetary upheavals, especially the ones that led to the second dollar devaluation on February 12, 1973, would not have occurred without the huge shifts of funds out of the United States dollar into currencies that were viewed as strong. There exists scattered, but convincing evidence that United States holders of United States dollars, and among them United States based multinational corporations, did not hesitate to convert dollar balances into, say, DM-assets and/or to borrow dollars for

---

11. Polk-Meister-Veit, *op. cit.*, p. 93, 102. Also reprinted, as a separate chapter in the Stonehill Readings.

conversion into strong currencies.[12] In other words, United States based multinational corporations did not behave in a "patriotic" way, and wavered in their allegiance to the "domestic" currency.

Business circles claim that such actions reflect the desire to hedge against currency losses and that they are defensive in nature and serve sound business objectives. In practice, however, the tenuous borderline between defensive hedging and aggressive speculation seems to have been frequently overstepped, as can be inferred from the substantial short positions taken in dollars.[13]

Thus, multinational corporations apparently are increasingly considering "money as a commodity", in which they deal not only to avoid currency losses but also to reap profits resulting from shifts in currency positions. Hence, the tactics of many multinational corporations are predicated rather on the concept of currency *uncertainties* than on the traditional one of currency *risks*. The home-country currency is no longer the sole—and solid—yardstick, even if the shareholders of the parent company are remunerated in that currency. This trend towards "de-nationalization" of the currency framework of the multinational corporation is bound to accelerate as a growing number of companies are going multinational and as financial management within the multinational corporation reaches higher levels of sophistication.[14]

Motives, other than comparative cost-of-capital considerations and currency uncertainties also influence the domestic/foreign financing mix for the global multinational corporation. The availability of capital resources in given markets, at times, becomes a more important consideration than (within limits) its cost. It is known, for example, that several multinational corporations have gone to the Eurobond market, ahead of actual needs, in order to benefit from the temporarily good reception to issues. Besides, a multinational corporation may need to establish its creditworthiness in a credit market, not previously entered into. Thus, on foreign and international public bond

---

12. See, for example, the analysis in *World Financial Markets*, Morgan Guaranty Trust, February 23, 1973, p. 1-2. The need to unwind short dollar positions was one of the determinants driving up short-term Euro-dollar rates in February 1973.

13. One may wonder whether the short-run gains of speculators may not be nullified, in the longer run, by the harm inflicted on business by the disruptions in the international payments system and by the countervailing measures which governments are apt to take in response to currency crises. This may be even more the case, as the views about parity changes may not have been based on underlying economic fundamentals but be inferred from rumors that rapidly escalate into a self-reinforcing "conventional wisdom".

14. One senses the "de-nationalisation" of the currency framework within multinational corporations, when one contrasts recent behavior on the exchange markets with the implicit reference to the "strong" domestic currency, that is used in recent text books, dealing with international business finance, as in David B. Zenoff and Jack Zwick, *International Financial Management*, Englewood Cliffs, 1969.

markets, a relatively unknown company will normally have to offer a slightly higher yield to investors, at least initially, than its intrinsic strength would justify.

So far, we have implicitly assumed that capital flows between transactors located in different jurisdictions were free and only influenced by considerations of cost, currency uncertainties, availability and accessibility. In the real world, many additional policy variables that are also subject to frequent changes add immensely to the "complexity of international financing structures and flows which differ from case to case in endless variety".[15] Among the variables, one may mention exchange controls and restrictions on the outflow of dividends or other income; the tax treatment of income and capital flows; discrimination with regard to the access of foreign companies, or their local subsidiaries, to local financial markets. Furthermore, a general concept of the multinational company covers a wide variety of enterprises that differ in such respects as the degree of multinational exposure and vertical integration, their business philosophy and the specific location of their foreign subsidiaries. At best, therefore, one may recognize some practices that are used fairly commonly as well as behavioral patterns, which empirical research shows to be characteristic for a particular category of multinational corporation.

Studies-in-depth are rare as yet. The Stobaugh paper, investigating the financing patterns of the *global multinational corporation,* found that large (United States based) multinational corporations tend to use a wide variety of financial sources; the latter include credits obtained from local non-bank institutions, issues on foreign financial markets and on the Eurobond market. Conversely, small multinational corporations tend to use relatively few sources of finance. This appears attributable as much to a small unsophisticated financial staff as to limited accessibility to foreign or international markets, where the name and the fame of a company matter.[16]

I would like to summarize two fairly recent careful studies about the financing pattern of *subsidiaries* in a *given country.* Brooke and Remmers investigated the sources of finance of 115 subsidiaries located in the *United Kingdom,* of which 90 belonged to United States based multinational corporations and the remainder to European multinational corporations. They arrived at the picture, given by Table I.

The predominant part of financing is seen to stem from host-country sources, with the cash flow generated within the subsidiary providing the bulk of that host-country's financing. Thus, funds from the home-country are limited and provided largely in the form of advances by the parent company

15. Polk-Meister-Veit, *op. cit.* in note 10, p. 102.
16. Stobaugh, *op. cit.,* p. 51 and 55.

Table I

Sources of finance for 125 foreign subsidiaries in the United Kingdom, 1960–1967 (in percentages)[17]

	115 Subsidiaries	90 United States subsidiaries	25 European subsidiaries
Foreign	*19.3*	*8.8*	*28.0*
issued capital	7.5 %	4.4 %	8.6 %
intra-company liabilities	11.8	4.4	19.4
Host-Country	*80.6*	*91.4*	*72.1*
liquid assets	2.2	2.2	2.2
long-term loans	7.5	7.5	8.6
bank-credit	11.8	11.8	11.8
retained earnings and depreciation allowances	59.1	69.9	49.5

to the subsidiary, rather than by way of equity participations. It follows that subsidiaries tend to be thinly capitalized, although, from an economic point of view, the loans by the parent company to the subsidiary are akin to equity funds, especially when put in a subordinated position vis-à-vis other debt items of the subsidiary.

The authors noticed that the return flow of dividends to the parent company was over 1.5 times the inflow of funds from the parent or other affiliated companies (and nearly 3.5 times for the United States-subsidiary). The subsidiaries were also found to rely on local borrowing of all types for slightly over 19 per cent. of their combined total assets in 1967—a ratio, which is similar to the one displayed by listed United Kingdom companies in the same year. Local borrowing was obtained mainly in short-term form. The authors also found evidence of stepped-up borrowing activity in times of sterling weakness. Local long-term financing was comparatively less important than that of United Kingdom listed companies. This is explained both by the reluctance of host-country authorities to grant authorization for long-term

17. Source: as inferred from figure II.2 on page 155 of Michael Z. Brooke and H. Lee Remmers, *The Strategy of Multinational Enterprises*, Longman, 1970. p. 155. The subtotals do not exactly add because of the approximate character of the measurement and because of rounding. Appendix II of the Brooke-Remmers study contains a mass of data for individual subsidiaries, covered in the sample.

financing to subsidiaries of foreign companies and by the fact that many subsidiaries were rather unknown to local financial institutions.

The table also suggests that the United States subgroup of companies was more thinly capitalized than the European subgroup and obtained less funds from the parent company and affiliated companies. This difference is presumably only partly due to the United States Balance-of-Payments measures (since 1965), but should also be related to the significantly higher profitability ratio of the group of American subsidiaries compared to the European subgroup.[18]

Another thorough and highly representative study covers foreign industrial investments in *Belgium*. The approach adopted consisted in dividing the series of 1968-values into quartiles. By and large, the findings are similar to those of the Brooke-Remmers study. Only 17 per cent. of the subsidiaries derived more than 75 per cent. of the funds needed for *net* investment purposes from within the multinational corporation; almost two-thirds of all subsidiaries obtain less than 25 per cent. of financing from that source; the percentage, however, is significantly larger for subsidiaries of EEC-based multinational corporations (excluding, at that time, the United Kingdom, Ireland and Denmark) than of American subsidiaries. Self-financing by the subsidiaries was found to contribute the major part of financing. Substantial recourse to the Belgian financial market—mainly by way of so-called long-term "investment credits" from financial institutions, which frequently benefit from interest-rate rebates granted by the Government—only occurred with a limited percentage of subsidiaries; here, the frequency was higher for subsidiaries of United States companies. Equity funds were comparatively lower in United States subsidiaries than in European, and especially in German subsidiaries. However, this is partly attributable to the recency of a large part of direct investment by United States based companies in Belgium.[19]

One should be careful in drawing undue generalizations from the above-mentioned studies. The amount of empirical evidence is still limited; furthermore, the conclusions drawn from the data used may already be partly obsolete as, in the meantime, the multinational corporations may have altered their financing philosophy and behaviour. More particularly, the trend towards integrated financial management seems to have accelerated in recent years. This sequence, normally, can be expected to entail a somewhat higher proportion of intra-multinational corporation financing for the subsidiaries than the studies suggest.

Yet, the studies mentioned allow a few general impressions. Internally

---

18. *Ibid*, p. 309.
19. D. Van den Bulcke, assisted by J. De Sloovere, E. Van de Walle and K. Kongs-Steel, *De Buitenlandse Ondernemingen in de Belgische Industrie*, Ghent 1971, especially Chapter XIII. This study has since been translated into French.

generated funds remain the mainstay of financing: this implies that the "pooling approach" (whereby all resources within a subsidiary are repatriated to the parent company and redistributed by the latter) is less prevalent than one would expect, when remembering the advantages which, in principle, the multinational corporation may derive from centralized financial management. As already suggested, practical and tax considerations stand in the way of extensive roundabout reshuffling within the multinational corporation; this is particularly the case whenever the subsidiary itself needs funds for expansion. The importance of self-financing becomes even more obvious when both financing needs and sources are put on a *gross* basis: with increasing capital deepening in modern industry, depreciation allowances are bound to represent a growing percentage of total sources of funds for gross investment. All in all however, both intramultinational corporation financing on behalf of subsidiaries and recourse by the latter to the host-country financial markets, are by no means negligible, although basically, the subsidiaries remain financially largely independent from the multinational corporation-group.

The multinational companies and the Euro-financial markets

Data about the *Eurobond* market proper, shown in Table II for the period 1965-72, indicate that out of a cumulative total of $23.8 billion of gross offerings, $14.9 billion or 62.8 per cent. were issued by private companies. Although several cases are known where United States companies have used the proceeds within the U.S.A., one may safely assume that the overwhelming part of the corporate issues have been floated by multinational corporations.

No comprehensive data are available about borrowings in the *Eurocurrency* markets.[20] Available partial evidence proves that medium-term loans have been very substantial and have exceeded, in most recent years, the gross amount of funds mobilised through the bond market. As tombstones bear witness, multinational corporations have figured eminently among the borrowers. More recently, however, governments and government-sponsored companies in developing countries have become comparatively more important on the demand side of the market.

The high percentage of borrowings on account of multinational corporations in both Eurofinancial markets, suggests, *prima facie*, that the rapid growth of those markets would not have occurred without the multinational corporations approaching the markets—as they actually did, almost in droves.

Of course, both markets would not have expanded as much as they did, in

---

20. According to the *Financial Times*, March, 5, 1973, at a recent conference in London, W. F. Howell of Manufacturers Trust put the total volume of medium-term credits outstanding at the end of 1972 at somewhere between $30 billion to $50 billion.

the absence of the United States Balance of Payments measures. One may surmise that, if access to the New York capital market had remained unencumbered for foreign issuers, the attempts by European bankers to develop an international issue market, which were made already prior to 1963, would at best have resulted in a fairly small bond issue market, that would have been parallel and second to national security markets. As a matter of fact, the traditional borrowers on international markets, such as the Scandinavian countries, would not have been deflected from the New York bond market. European savings institutions, which were reportedly already buying a substantial portion of the foreign issues in New York, would further have been directed to the New York Bond market, thereby conveying, to a large extent, an entrepôt function to the latter.

Thus, after 1965, the Eurobond market naturally attracted the United States based multinational corporations. But the successful launching of their issues implies that the additional demand by United States based multinational corporations also elicited a sufficient response on the supply side. In other words, we should explain not only why multinational corporations came to the emerging primary market "in Europe" [21] but also why European investors were willing to buy the bonds issued.

These United States based multinational corporations, obviously, had no other choice, if they wanted to expand overseas—the more that local European markets were not capable of mobilizing sufficient capital or were not easily accessible. Their use of the Eurobond market was certainly not motivated by the efficiency of that market. As a matter of fact, the size of a Eurobond issue was typically smaller than on the United States bond market. The yield to be offered and the issue costs were higher; investors' response was largely untried and whimsical; in order to ensure sufficient absorption, special inducements, such as medium-term bonds (the 5-year notes) or the convertibility feature had to be offered at times. As the years went on, however, these initial handicaps abated somewhat as the Eurobond market gained strength.

Besides, dollar-denominated Eurobond issues can be arranged quickly. Contrary to issues on domestic markets, they are not centrally controlled by the financial authorities. The multinational corporations also find here a source of funds that could be used for global purposes, i.e., "wherever the central authority in the group wants to invest them",[22] a freedom of manoeuvre not always open to other sources. In this connection, it must be

21. Since Japanese and Middle Eastern funds have become important elements on the supply side, the expression "Euro-" has become even less appropriate than previously.

22. A. W. Clements, "The International Money and Bond Markets—A Borrower's Eye View", *Euromoney*, May 1972, p. 8.

recalled that the trend towards more centralized financial management, discussed in section II, enhances the scope for global-use funds.

Soon, non-American multinational corporations (and, among them, several of the European giants) also came to the issue markets, as did a flurry of United States companies, which, by American standards were smaller-sized and were not well-known to the investing public, not even to the bankers in Europe.

The Eurobond market has significantly broadened and internationalized the horizons of European investors and of their bankers-advisers, as well. The spectrum of investment opportunities was significantly broadened. Soon lists of Eurobonds outstanding featured many of the most prestigious company names. The latter, frequently got a better credit rating—as inferred by the differentials in yields offered—than Governments or public-sector entities. New, hitherto largely unknown instruments, such as the convertible Eurobonds, were devised and, at times, got an enthusiastic reception. For all practical purposes, coupons could be encashed free of withholding tax. Several formulas, such as the European-Unit-of-Account and currency option clauses have been introduced to minimize currency risks . . . although, paradoxically, over the same period 1965-72, the dollar segment, in which 66.6 per cent. of the aggregate amount have been issued, was going to suffer the greatest degree of depreciation.

Substantial amounts have been invested in Eurobonds, both straight and convertible ones. It is not feasible to ascertain whether these investments have been compensating for disinvestments in national security markets; or to compute which part of the funds now placed in Eurobonds would otherwise have moved to those national security markets. Investors, for example, may have switched from investments in shares on the New York Stock Exchange into Euro-convertibles. The significant widening of investment vistas which the Eurobond market brought about, however, leads me to submit that, although some degree of substitution may have occurred, the overall net effect of the Eurobond market has been to increase the percentage of savings, that were invested in securities.[23] This wider investment horizon may also have increased somewhat the macro-economic savings rate in European countries. This claim, however, cannot easily be substantiated and the resulting shift in the savings/consumption ratio has been, if anything, quite limited.

Multinational corporations also appear to have been a significant factor in the growth of the Eurocurrency pool, which has now grown to around $85 billion. As a matter of fact, multinational corporations figure prominently both on the demand and supply (for capital) sides. Many multinational corpo-

23. The same opinion is expressed by Robert L. Genillard, "European Capital Markets—Unification or Internationalization?" Talk at the Royal Institute of International Affairs, May, 18, 1967, mimeographed, p. 13.

rations, and among them most prestigious ones, have borrowed short- and medium-term. This, at times, has driven up interest rates and drawn fresh resources into the Euro-dollar market (e.g. through conversion of non-dollar assets into Euro-dollar deposits). The attraction of Euro-dollar borrowing derives from the speed with which the transactions could be arranged and the large amounts that could be mobilized. Lately, the maturity of the loans has also tended to lengthen. On the supply side, multinational corporations have been important holders of Eurocurrency deposits.[24]

One may mention in passing, that some of the financial technology developed on the Eurobond and Eurocurrency markets, has been adopted on domestic capital markets. This sequence is exemplified by the following two cases. First, on the Belgian issue market, convertible bond issues are no longer exceptional: since their legal status was liberalized in 1962, seven issues were floated in the 1965-68 period and eleven in 1969-72. The spread of the convertible bond vehicle is not a mere coincidence, but may be partly linked to the acquaintance with the convertible instrument, which the Eurobond issues brought about. Second, the Unit-of-Account principle was recently adopted for a Government bond issue on the French bond market.

Multinationalizing the shareholdings in multinational companies

Multinational corporations employ people in several countries; the production in their foreign subsidiaries and sales abroad may reach a high percentage of total output and turnover; yet, with rare exceptions, the shares of the multinational corporations belong overwhelmingly to residents of the home-country. It is frequently claimed, that the multinationalization of shareholders is the next inevitable step in the development of the multinational corporation and that multinational corporations should aim at the international spread of shareholders.

Several arguments are advanced in supporting the need for multinational ownership of multinational corporations. First, widening the circle of the actual and potential stockholders enhances the ability of a company to raise equity in primary markets. In this connection, it is worth recalling that huge future capital needs are generally forecast for the multinational corporation and that, while, as already explained, local borrowing by the subsidiaries

---

24. One additional, and possibly substantial impact of multinational corporation on the enlargement of the Eurocurrency pool, would stem from the role of the multinational corporation in the credit-multiplier process, whereby loans extended to multinational corporation by the "Eurocurrency banking system" create deposits. Whether credit-creation occurs in the Eurocurrency markets and, especially, what its quantitative importance is, remains the object of controversy as are many other aspects of the Eurocurrency markets.

makes sense for the multinational corporation, there are limits to the leverage the multinational corporations could sustain. Hence a stronger equity base, through reinvested earnings and capital increases, eventually becomes necessary. Besides, distribution of stock with the local investing public shapes a better image of the company as a "good citizen" of the host-country, thus allaying some of the tensions between multinational corporations and host-countries. Yassukovich, for example, stresses that unless multinational corporations achieve multinational ownership "they will increasingly be identified with economic colonialism by public opinion".[25] The charge would be made that residents of the host-countries are not allowed to share in the profits earned by the subsidiaries. There are also cases, where the host-country government imposes local majority, or at least minority, holdings in the subsidiary; these participations, however, in developing countries are usually taken up by local industrialists or public entities and are not distributed among the general investing public. Finally, there is something illogical about a company, which views and plans its operations worldwide and refrains from broadening the circle of its stockholders.

I would agree that the trend towards more international shareholdings, already discernible, naturally follows in the wake of the international spread of production and marketing by the multinational corporations. Already the multinational corporations and their bankers are searching for ways to achieve a more international pattern of ownership. Multinational corporations have an obvious interest in spreading the ownership pattern, considering their foreseeable needs for equity capital. I seriously doubt, however, whether the internationalization of ownership really is capable of substantially reducing tensions with the host governments, as is commonly claimed.

This scepticism derives mainly from two observations. First, in modern companies with shares widely distributed, decision-making powers are in fact not located with the stockholders but with the top-managers—although shareholders are, theoretically, the owners of the company and possess legal prerogatives to influence corporate decisions and the composition of the board of directors. The multinational spread of share holdings would further consummate the divorce between management and shareholders. Therefore, the multinationalization of the top-management echelons in the parent company appears of more importance than the "de-nationalizing" of the legal ownership.[26] Second, such attempts at multinationalizing the shareholders of the

25. Stanislas M. Yassukovich, "The Prospects for Euro-Equities", Address at *Financial Times* Conference, February 20, 1973, p. 7.

26. Although the importance of the nationality of top-managers should not be exaggerated. Managers tend to develop a loyalty to the multinational corporation, whereas the aims of the multinational corporation and of the home-country are frequently at odds, as discussed, with respect to United States–based multinational corporation by Raymond Vernon, in *Sovereignty at Bay* . . ., p. 205-15. It is also striking that many

parent company will, for a long time to come, be strongly opposed by Governments. A few years ago, for example, Belgium, an otherwise liberal country with respect to foreign investments, took legislative action to thwart the attempted take-over of one of its star companies, viz. Petrofina. Nestlé, while deriving about 95 per cent. of its turnover from operations abroad has a large number of foreign shareholders, but has stated, as a matter of policy, that the majority of the shares must remain in Swiss hands.[27] Could one imagine the United States Government, business circles or trade unions agreeing to the transfer of the majority of the shares of a giant multinational corporation into foreign hands?

One should add that cross-participations between different countries are likely to reduce the tensions connected with the ownership pattern of multinational corporations. Such cross-shareholdings already occur, to quite some extent, between the U.S.A. and Western Europe. Transactions on European account on the New York Stock Exchange are by no means negligible, whereas United States investors also own part of the shares of major European companies. In such circumstances, the grievance that the domestic economy is dominated by foreign-owned multinational corporations, becomes less convincing. In developing countries, however, the situation is generally different. The lack of reciprocity in the investment flows—both direct and in the form of portfolio investments—between the capital-importing and the capital-exporting country and obvious differences in economic and political power between the two, feed suspicions and resentments. Joint ventures, therefore, may well ease tensions. Several governments impose joint ventures, frequently with the local interests in a majority position. The complex subject of joint ventures cannot be dealt with in this paper. But one may observe that (a) partial, or even majority control by local shareholders does not involve control over the parent company—where the major strategic decisions are taken; (b) the frequently conflicting aims of the parent company and the host-country shareholders as, for example, with respect to the dividend pay-out ratio, tend to cause friction; (c) the local participations are generally held by industrialists or government institutions and are not distributed among the general investing public—except in countries, like Brasil, where security markets are developing, and where the public sale of stock in the local subsidiary is intended to contribute towards building up a viable capital market; (d) it is difficult to assign an appropriate value to a subsidiary, whenever the latter is part and parcel of the multinational corporation-system and cannot be conceived independently as, for example, when the subsidiary

---

multinational corporation executives have become exposed to several cultures or are of multinational extraction and seem to have lost the sense of belonging to a single country.

27. "How Nestlé revives its money-losers", *Business Week*, Jan. 27, 1973. p. 46.

109

manufactures components that are subsequently fitted into the end-product of the multinational corporation.

Many steps have been taken in recent years by multinational corporations and the international banking community to internationalize shareholdings and widen primary distributions of shares.[28] Governments, despite their commitment to the free international movement of capital, have been notoriously aloof with respect to such developments. A discussion at the technical level, of the various devices introduced, would be out of place in this paper. Let me only make a few comments on the type of international equity markets, which appear most suited to the needs of multinational corporations.

A thriving, broad and diversified *secondary* market is a technical prerequisite for a well-functioning primary market. There already exists a sizeable degree of international investment in shares between, say, the U.S.A. and Europe. Besides, several measures were taken to more adequately link investors with foreign stock exchanges; one may mention the various types of depository receipts and the listings of multinational corporations on foreign exchanges. These steps are useful, although, when the markets are of greatly different size, the flow-back phenomenon[29] seriously reduces their merits. Apart from freedom of capital movements and appropriate technicalities, the main prerequisite for interconnected secondary markets appears to be the prevalence of an international horizon with a large number of investors. This, I would deem, has now already been achieved to quite an extent. As argued above, in this respect, the emergence of the Eurobond market has been of prime importance. The professionalization of portfolio management, with individuals increasingly entrusting the management of their portfolios to financial institutions and specialists strengthens this trend.

In Europe, there have been few attempts at simultaneously tapping fresh resources for equity investments in the various national markets, thereby submitting to the regulations in each of these markets. The Solvay *primary* issue (which was combined with a secondary offer) (1968) stands as a lone example. As explained by one of the technicians involved in the management of the issue, the great diversity of legal systems in the EEC-countries (as, for example, with respect to shareholders' preemptive rights) greatly hinder such approaches.[30] Harmonization of the legal systems in the EEC-area is a pre-

28. For a bewildering list, which also highlights the abuse of the term "Euro-equities", see Barry Phelps, "Euro-Equities", *Euromoney*, July 1971, p. 39-42. See also "Prospects for an International Equity Market", *Multinational Business*, The Economist Intelligence Unit, December 1972, p. 37-45.

29. This problem is stressed by Stanislas M. Yassukovich, *op. cit.*, p. 3. Listings on local stock exchanges, however, seem to accomodate odd-lot investors, as explained by H. G. Hooft, "Why Continental Depository Receipts work", *Euromoney*, October 1972, p. 75-76.

30. Etienne Bairiot, "Les émissions de titres de sociétés en Europe et aux Etats-

requisite before the large savings potential in the EEC-countries can be mobilized in a convenient way, by way of simultaneous equity issues.[31]

Other attempts at mobilizing equity capital have adopted Eurobond tactics whereby primary offerings are launched from a "tax haven", thus side-stepping stringent national regulations, whereby the securities are placed in several countries through an international syndicate. The offerings of shares of the ill-fated I.O.S. Management Company, falls in this category, as do, in a way, a few issues of convertible preferred stock.

Euro-convertibles are the major type of equity-linked securities that have been floated according to Eurobond mechanics. They have provided the multinational corporations with substantial funds and, in the 1965-72 period, represented 22.7 per cent. of all issues on the Eurobond market. (See Table II).

But they exhibit some peculiarities, which do not make them the most appropriate instrument for raising equity capital. First, according to textbook logic, companies, when floating convertibles, intend to have the bonds ultimately transformed into equity. On the Eurobond market, however, it appears that, generally, this aim was not primarily pursued and will only partly be fulfilled. As a matter of fact, multinational corporations seem to have chosen the convertible road mainly, because, in given periods, this formula evoked a better response from investors than straight bonds. In other words, issuers of Euro-convertibles have been motivated more by the availability of funds than by the desire to achieve a broader equity base. The increase in equity funds for a big multinational corporation that would ensue if all Euro-convertibles were tendered for conversion would anyhow remain minimal. Besides, individual purchasers—who dominate the Eurobond issue market—have typically viewed Euro-convertibles as bond instruments. They rather preferred to keep the bonds in convertible form and to reap capital gains by selling the convertible bonds instead of effecting conversion into shares.[32]

One other method would consist in floating shares of a holding company, with the latter comprising the multinational corporation-interests in a given geographical area. The small "Euro-medico" issue in 1970 may be cited as an example (although it represented rather an international issue for a company, which, as yet, had its assets almost exclusively in a single country and, accord-

Unis", paper submitted at a conference at the Université Libre de Bruxelles, Nov. 1968, mimeographed, 42 p.

31. The Ente Nazionale di Energia Elettrica-issues (1965) provides a similar example of a pluri-national issue in the bond sector. But differences in bond rates in the various countries involved, render such operations difficult.

32. For other interesting comparisons between United States convertibles and Euro-convertibles, see J. M. Hessels and M. Mendelson, "Converteerbare Amerikaanse and Euro-obligaties: een Vergelijking", Bank- en Effectenbedrijf, Jan1972.

Table II

Selected data on issue activity in international issue markets, 1965–1972

(in millions of United States dollars)

	1965	1966	1967	1968	1969	1970	1971	1972	cumulative 1965-1972
Eurobonds	*1041*	*1142*	*2002*	*3573*	*3156*	*2966*	*3642*	*6320*	*23842*
of which									
· United States private companies	358	439	562	2096	1005	741	1098	1977	8276
· other private companies	319	376	575	603	817	1065	1113	1759	6613
· all private companies	677	815	1137	2699	1822	1806	2217	3716	14889
(percentages of Total)	(65.0)	(71.4)	(56.8)	(75.5)	(57.7)	(60.9)	(60.9)	(58.8)	(62.4)
· in United States dollar	726	921	1780	2554	1723	1775	2221	3893	15889
(percentages of Total)	(69.7)	(80.6)	(88.9)	(71.5)	(54.6)	(59.8)	(61.0)	(61.6)	(66.6)
· convertible bonds	110	242	260	1910	1131	238	295	1220	5406
(percentages of Total)	(10.6)	(21.2)	(13.0)	(53.7)	(35.8)	(8.0)	(8.1)	(19.3)	(22.7)
Foreign bonds	*376*	*378*	*403*	*1135*	*827*	*378*	*1538*	*2060*	*7095*
of which									
· by private companies	99	95	113	195	351	138	412	560	*1963*
· in Swiss franc	78	94	153	238	196	193	669	815	*2436*
· convertible bonds	10	—	—	—	66	—	30	—	*106*
Total international bonds	*1417*	*1520*	*2405*	*4708*	*3983*	*3344*	*5180*	*8380*	*30937*

Source: *World Financial Markets*, Morgan Guaranty Trust, several issues

ingly, cannot really be called multinational). IBM-Europe is rumoured to envisage a similar issue. Such a device would spread ownership in the same area, in which productive assets are located. It would create, say, a more "European" image for the company. Apart from the staggering technical difficulties to be faced in canvassing the issue, there are some additional pitfalls. Of necessity, the balance sheet of the regional holding would differ from the consolidated balance sheet of the multinational corporation-as-a-whole and investors would tend to value the two types of stocks differently. Besides, the regional holding would still remain part of and controlled by the worldwide multinational corporation. Furthermore, the countries, where the shares are marketed, would not necessarily coincide with those where the productive facilities are located. And, as is the case with the Euro-financial markets, the concept here discussed implies a continued fragmentation of national savings markets in Europe.

Towards large integrated security markets?

So far, it was found that multinational corporations have significantly contributed to a much higher degree of interconnectedness between investors and borrowers, located in various countries. It also became obvious, that the term "internationalisation" (of financial markets) covers a great variety of links between countries.

The emergence and the rapid growth of the Euro-financial markets have been a major development. This international and potentially worldwide market, has been substituted for the large United States market, which, previous to 1963, was largely serving the world's needs. The Eurobond and Eurocurrency markets have served the multinational corporations well and provided them with substantial funds for global uses. They have shown remarkable resiliency and withstood the many currency crises of recent years.

However, both in terms of the needs of big multinational corporations and of the efficiency of capital markets, Euro-capital markets are only a "second-best" solution. These markets remain beset by several structural weaknesses. Although issuers and the managing banks, on the whole, have displayed a healthy sense of self-discipline, disclosure standards have not always been adequate. A few issues should never have been floated, as they were utterly speculative and sold to investors who were not sufficiently aware of the serious risks involved.[33] The information given to investors is also hampered by regulations imposed by the authorities in some of the countries where the bonds are placed. Although secondary, over-the-counter markets have greatly

33. Names are given by Nicolas J. Baer in "Problems of the Eurobond Market", *Euromoney*, January 1971, p. 21-22.

113

improved, the after-issue flow of information remains inadequate.[34] Finally, the degree of sophistication of investors—mainly individuals—although improving, remains rather weak. This leads to investment decisions which are not sufficiently based on objective analysis.[35]

In a world with capital-hungry multinational corporations, first-best solutions would emerge when national capital markets become integrated within a wide geographical area endowed with a large savings potential and sophisticated financial mechanics. Two such areas may emerge. If promises are held, present balance-of-payments measures in the U.S.A. will be discarded progressively, starting in 1975. United States companies would then be able to export freely the capital funds floated on the United States securities market, instead of having to turn to foreign capital markets. The abrogation of the Interest Equalization Tax would imply that United States investors could henceforth purchase non-American securities.

This development would prove of tremendous importance in integrating the presently segregated domestic United States and Eurobond markets into one large issue market, which, for lack of a better expression, I call an "Atlantic" bond market. As a matter of fact, some of the parameters in the two markets are already uniform while the differences with respect to other features could easily be reconciled, with the possible exception of the tax aspect. The United States dollar already is the main denomination currency in the Eurobond market. Underwriting and selling syndicates are already internationalized and comprise both United States and European institutions.

Bond issues on the United States market are subject to exacting Securities and Exchange Commission disclosure rules, whereas Eurobond issuers are largely free to determine themselves the extent and quality of disclosure. In the new situation, created by the ending of United States capital export controls, issuers on the Eurobond market would tend, in my view, voluntarily to upgrade the disclosure standards and to approximate Securities and Exchange Commission criteria: otherwise, the issues would connote a lower quality. Equally, issue costs on Eurobond flotations, which exceed those on bond issues in the U.S.A. would tend to decline, thereby reinforcing a development which is already discernible. One major problem would be the tax aspect—one which, in itself, is capable of effectively segmenting capital markets. United States issuers, adopting now well entrenched mechanics on the Eurobond market, would naturally be enticed to float through a Curaçao or Luxembourg "launching pad" financing vehicle, thereby avoiding United States-withholding at the source. It is doubtful whether this logical conse-

34. As stressed by Yassukovich, *op. cit.*, p. 5.

35. For a further discussion of the operational inadequacies and of the limitations to be integrative power of the Eurobond market, see Morris Mendelson, "The Eurobond and Capital Market Integration", *The Journal of Finance*, March 1972, p. 110-26.

quence of the abrogation of the Interest Equalization Tax, would be acceptable to the United States Government, at least as far as United States investors are concerned. [36] All in all the analysis here attempted leads me to the conclusion that, provided the tax problem can be solved satisfactorily, market forces and the ingenuity of intermediating banks would soon lay the foundations for an unprecedented, vast and truly Atlantic bond issue market, in which the Eurobond market would soon merge with the United States domestic bond market.

The other welcome development would consist in the unification of the national capital markets with the EEC. The direction and the outcome of this development are clear and probably irreversible; the pace of implementation, however, is bound to be slow. An EEC-capital market would enable an efficient transformation of savings. As in the Atlantic market, big multinational corporations would be able to mobilize large amounts of capital, including equity. At the final stage, the capital markets of EEC-countries would become integrated, or, more precisely, the integrative process would result in a single capital market as part of a full-fledged economic union. To reach this final stage, however, one single EEC-currency should have emerged or, at least, the various currencies tightly knit together at fixed rates or within a minimal band of permissible fluctuations.

36. It is interesting to note that, in 1972 a change in United States legislation permitted United States companies to approach directly the Eurobond market, without setting up, for tax purposes, a Curaçao or Delaware "launching-pad" financial subsidiary. Also a few days ago, the Securities and Exchange Commission submitted to the United States Congress a proposal whereby off-shore mutual funds could be brought under Securities and Exchange Commission-supervision without losing their tax-free status. Of course, the two measures are intended to prop the United States balance-of-payments and United States-investors cannot benefit from them, as long as the Interest Equalisation Tax applies.

Part IV

Financial institutions and the growth of multinational corporations

Chapter VIII

FINANCIAL INSTITUTIONS AND THE GROWTH OF
MULTINATIONAL CORPORATIONS *

by *Jack Hendley*

One can define multinational companies in several different ways. For the
purposes of this paper, it is convenient to adopt a wide definition, because
many of the particular problems which they present to financial institutions
are common to most large undertakings operating internationally. Indeed,
some of the relevant considerations apply to large companies generally, even
if their operations are confined to this country. Accordingly, in this context
multinational companies are regarded as any companies which operate in
more than one country—in a United Kingdom context this means both in the
United Kingdom and at least one other country; generally the term "operating" will involve having international markets, as well as international investments in production facilities. Sometimes the United Kingdom institution is
the parent body, operating elsewhere through branches or subsidiaries. Often,
however, it is a subsidiary or associated company, the parent institution being
located elsewhere, probably in the United States, since this is the centre—
insofar as one can describe such undertakings as having a centre—of many
multinational companies. Thus, this definition covers a variety of different
type of company, one major distinction being whether the United Kingdom
company is the parent or a subsidiary.

In the main, I shall be using a fairly narrow definition of financial institutions, referring chiefly to banks, and in particular the London clearing banks,
this being where my own experience lies. However, the clearing banks today
comprise not only the original parent institution, but all the various other
institutions which are associated with them in their group organisations. Like
commercial banks in many other countries, the London clearing banks no
longer confine themselves as much as they did in the past to providing short-
term finance; they provide a wide variety of different types of finance, appropriate to the needs of their customers, either directly through the parent
institution or through subsidiary and associated companies. As explained in
more detail below, they do this not only on a national but an international
basis. Indeed, financial institutions, particularly banks, are often themselves
multinational companies.

Multinational companies are by no means uniform in the structure of their organisation. If a company is operating in only one other country, its structure may be relatively simple. Where it is operating in a considerable number of countries, it may adopt any one of several different basic types of structure—for instance, organisation on a geographical or on a product basis. Its structure may be changed, not only because of its own experience and development, but because of a growing body of general experience of multinational organisation. For most organisations, purposes and problems change and develop rapidly these days, calling for changes in the structure of the organisation. Multinational companies are no exception to this; indeed, they are perhaps more liable than simpler organisations to overhauls of their structure. One of the problems which this poses to outside financial institutions, such as banks, is that it is not always as clear as it is with domestic customers just where financial decisions are taken within the organisation. In some, the various operating divisions may have a considerable degree of autonomy; in others, central control is tight, particularly of cash flows and financial management generally, though not necessarily in detail. Even if the structure is clear today, the points of decision-taking may be altered from time to time. Thus, a major problem for financial institutions is to know how the requirements of their multinational customers can be clearly identified.

You will see from what I have said above that there is no clearly-defined group of organisations which can be described as multinational and distinguished from all other types of company. Indeed, some analysts try to distinguish various types of undertaking—such as the national firm with foreign operations, the international corporation and the multinational corporation—depending upon such matters as the extent to which not only operations but also ownership and control are spread around the world. Differences in these respects may, indeed, make for vital differences in their financial affairs, but I do not think that in practice one can draw any hard and fast distinctions which would be useful for the purpose of this paper. Because of this, I shall not attempt to sort out any hard facts or firm figures concerning them. Nobody questions that, on any definition, they are large, both individually and collectively, and growing exceptionally rapidly. The approach in this paper is to look at them first of all from the point of view of a single financial institution in a single country. Here, naturally, it is the viewpoint of a British banker that I shall be adopting. The analysis might be different if I were adopting the position of a banker in some other country, and I shall try to indicate what the nature of such differences might be. Then I shall say something about the international development of banks and other financial institutions, and how this relates to the growth of multinational companies.

In many respects, the banking business of multinational companies may be little different from that of other companies, particular other large companies. This is specially so if one is dealing only with a single company which is the national subsidiary of a multinational group centred elsewhere, and so one is not the main banker to the group. The great bulk of work will be familiar routine work concerned with maintaining their current banking accounts. In other words, multinational companies are both depositors with banks and borrowers from them, in much the same way as other customers; they may have more complex requirements also, which are discussed further below. They are also more likely than most companies to use many ancillary banking services, particularly those connected with international financial transactions, but these are not necessarily different in principle from similar transactions for other customers. In Britain, they may use more than one main bank, but so do many other large companies which are not international; thus this presents complications, but familiar ones which are not unique to multinational companies. However, they will also have banking relationships with banks abroad and in Britain at least this may complicate their domestic banking, since approaching 250 overseas and foreign banks have branches in London. In particular, multinational companies centred on the United States may have a major banking account with a London branch of their main bank in the United States. Indeed, until recently this was the staple business of United States banks in London. The Monopolies Commission[1] found that, at the end of 1967, subsidiaries or branches in Britain of American companies accounted for two-fifths of the sterling deposits of American banks in London, and four-fifths of their sterling advances; both proportions had been falling, and are probably substantially lower today.

If a bank is lending to a multinational company on a secured basis, no special problems need be involved. Increasingly, however, banks are tending to lend on an unsecured basis, on an assessment of the company's financial position and in particular of its cash flows. Multinational corporations commonly have a good credit rating; this not only enables them to obtain favourable interest rates, but may also help them to obtain unsecured lending facilities. This gives rise to some complications when lending to a group of companies, and in particular to a multinational group. Not only is their cash flow liable to be affected by special considerations, referred to below, but banks need some familiarity with the finances of the whole group. In particular, they need to know something of the degree and nature of the financial responsibility of the parent for the liabilities of the subsidiary—both the formal obligations and an assessment of any additional responsibility which might be undertaken in practice if the national company were in financial difficulties. We have seen in Britain in the past few years that large undertakings which are household names may nevertheless get into such a position from time to time. Assump-

1. The Monopolies Commission: *Barclays Bank Ltd., Lloyds Bank Ltd. and Martins Bank Ltd.—a report on the proposed merger.* July 1968 (H.C.P.319).

tions which have hitherto been implicitly held, that the national government would not permit such an undertaking to fail, need to be rigidly assessed. To quote an example from the international field, most of the large motor manufacturers in Britain are subsidiaries of United States parents. A year or two ago, when business conditions were creating difficulties for some motor manufacturers in Britain, their parents in the United States were sometimes experiencing similar problems.

Multinational companies may have within their organisation special financial bodies which assist them in their cash flow management and financial control generally, as well as in the raising of funds. One such arrangement is an international finance corporation subsidiary, this being the body which raises funds on the Eurobond market; these may be set up specially when the corporation wishes to go to the market. Some multinationals have finance companies which provide something akin to a factoring service to their various subsidiaries; they refinance the debtors of the operating companies and themselves collect the debts. Others may have a central clearing system for inter-company payments; this reduces cash flows across national boundaries and their need for associated bank services, thus cutting costs and rationalising cash flows.

This is not to say that they may not move funds around quite substantially in accordance with their financing needs. They may indeed do so quite frequently and in substantial sums. To the extent that they meet the cash shortages of some parts of their organisation from the temporary surpluses of other parts, they are, in effect, meeting their own banking needs, since one of the main functions of banks and other financial intermediaries is to garner surplus funds where they become available, and channel them to where they are needed. Multinational companies may also move funds in response to interest rate differentials, so as to obtain the best rate of return on surplus balances. They may also move them from one country to another in accordance with their view of possible future exchange rate movements. In such movements, the distinction between good financial management and speculation is not easy to define.

Thus, the movements on bank accounts of multinationals, both credit and debit accounts, may take place for reasons quite other than those with which the banks are familiar in respect of the great bulk of their customers. There are many imperfections and irrationalities in financial markets, both within particular countries and internationally, and multinationals are well placed to know of these and to take advantage of them. Banks, too, should know the financial markets, but they do not, of course, have a comprehensive picture of the day-to-day financial position of multinational groups, and so are not in a position necessarily to understand the purposes of the particular selection of transactions which they see passing through their own books.

In Britain, the variety and complexity of our financial markets are as great

122

as anywhere in the world. As we have seen, multinationals may place their surplus funds with the banks or anywhere else in the various money markets. Thus, the banks need to be flexible and competitive in their interest rate policy. Before September 1971, when the London clearing banks abandoned the agreements under which they offered uniform rates on deposits and agreed to a rather looser uniformity on lending rates, they were increasingly unable to attract the credit balances of multinational companies—and, indeed, of other big companies—against competition from other banks and other financial intermediaries within Britain, let alone internationally. The solution to this was found by forming special deposit-taking subsidiaries to operate freely and competitively in the various money markets. This was not a complete solution, however, because money market rates were particularly volatile, compared with the stability of clearing bank rates, which were linked to Bank rate set by the Bank of England. At times, when money market rates rose sharply, the structure of rates became so distorted that companies were able to draw upon their agreed overdraft limits with the clearing banks and lend the money in the market at a higher rate of interest. At times, they might even be borrowing from one part of a bank group and lending the money back to another part of the same group at a profit.

Since September 1971, the clearing banks have been competing actively and directly as regards interest rates; their lending rates are linked to base rates determined by themselves and, although various banks have arranged their deposit-taking in differing ways, all are able to quote competitive rates for deposits. Even so, situations have arisen, if only temporarily, in which market rates rose sharply and it would have been possible for multinationals to borrow from the clearing banks for relending in the market unless base rates were promptly raised. Experience suggests that, under the new system, market rates are more volatile than before and base rates may have to be moved more frequently than hitherto, if we are to avoid the kind of distortions which give multinationals and other large companies the opportunities for making profits from the rigidities of the market. Thus, to some extent, such companies are effectively placing pressure upon the banks, through the market, to make adjustments which they might not otherwise wish to make. For instance, the needs of the great run of our customers might be better served if our rates of interest, both charged and allowed, did not change quite so frequently.

The use of bank overdraft limits for speculative purposes or taking advantage of interest rates differentials is a dubious one. When arranging such overdraft limits, it is usually desirable to have the purposes drawn fairly widely and in any case the banker cannot distinguish the purpose of any particular transaction on an account. Possibly, it might be desirable to introduce some understandings as to what is and is not a legitimate use of a credit facility. This, however, would be difficult to monitor and enforce. Compared with most other businesses, banks are marketing a relatively undifferentiated range of services; customer loyalty to a particular bank is noticeably lower among multinational companies than among customers generally. Some kind of a market solution would seem preferable.

The irrationalities of financial markets internationally are no less great than those within Britain. In theory, if interest rates are comparatively low in a particular country, multinationals and others will move funds out and the resulting credit stringency will raise interest rates and attract funds back again. It need not be stressed here that this version does not adequately describe and explain short-term international capital flows today. Thus, the banks and other financial institutions in some countries, such as Britain, may be faced with a sudden and large outflow of funds and those in other countries, such as Germany, with a similar inflow. Credit balances of multinationals must be regarded as volatile and liable to influences which do not affect the great run of deposits. If the irrationalities of the international monetary system can be overcome, and if the United States dismantles its controls on capital movements as it is now proposing, relative rates of interest will become of much greater importance, giving banks potentially more control over such balances.

Most of the above is concerned with multinationals as holders of large liquid balances, for which financial institutions are competing. But their rate of capital development makes their need for finance also great, so that while some are large lenders, others are large borrowers—or, more generally, require to turn to the various financial markets for substantial funds, possibly to be provided in a number of different forms. Here we must consider financial institutions generally, not only banks. In some countries, such as Britain, financial markets are diversified, and while, as described above, the British banks are diversifying into groups aiming to provide all forms of finance, they remain keenly aware of their traditional position, which sees the requirements of lenders as quite different from—potentially in conflict with—those of risk-bearers, such as equity holders. In some European countries, by contrast, industry has long depended upon the banks as the main providers of most forms of finance, including equity.

Some financial problems arise from the sheer size, complexity and geographical spread of the operations of multinational companies. Banks have developed their own methods of appraising the finances of customers, which are suitable for most purposes, and branch managers get to know a fair amount about technical aspects of industries which are prevalent in their area. However, these methods are inadequate for dealing with multinationals. For instance it may be necessary for banks and other financial institutions to employ industrial specialists in some of the fields in which multinationals operate—either their own staff specially trained or experienced men brought in from the industries concerned. The oil industry is an obvious example

124

where such expertise may be necessary for adequate appraisal of both technological and economic factors.

Again, multinationals will commonly prepare their financial plans on a global basis for several years ahead, particularly for capital financing for new developments. For these, they may require very large sums, possibly beyond the resources of any one bank or financial institution in the country where development is to be situated. They may require these large sums to be made available in different parts of the world, and possibly in different currencies. The mixture of different forms of finance, and the timing of its provision, must have a degree of flexibility to take account of the market situation, though it will be planned in advance as far as possible; bank borrowing may be an integral part but it will probably also be the residual part, or at least the flexible part to bridge over a period when circumstances in longer-term markets may be unpropitious. All this will comprise a complex financial package which in turn is only one part of the plans which have to be worked out in considerable detail before projects are approved.

Financial markets have developed to meet these kinds of needs. Indeed, such needs have been a major spur to developments which were already occurring. One such development is the Eurobond market. Eurocurrencies—both dollars and other currencies—have grown in magnitude rapidly in recent years and have effectively provided a means of cutting through some of the restrictions affecting national currencies, both in the short—and long—term markets. Thus many multinational companies have formed international finance subsidiaries, which issue bonds on this market, often convertible at specified later dates into the equity of the parent company. These issues are commonly sponsored by a number of banks of various kinds, both commercial and investment banks. Depending upon the nature of the bank and the degree of freedom permitted to it by its national laws, they may also take up and hold such securities as investments, so that the needs of the multinational are effectively being met by an international consortium of banks. Considerable technical developments have taken place to enable a secondary market to be formed in such securities, though there may still be room for further improvement. Medium-term loans in Eurocurrencies, often provided through consortium banks, are another technique which experience suggests may provide a useful contribution to the needs of multinationals.

The issuing of Eurobonds is an example of the way in which the financial needs of multinationals are increasingly being met by groups of banks and financial institutions. This is happening not only at the international level but—in Britain at least—also at the national level. For some years past each of the clearing banks, which previously confined themselves largely to short-term finance, has been developing a much wider range of lending services, partly through the parent bank but more usually through subsidiary and associated undertakings. Indeed, each of the clearing banks is now the parent of a financial group through which most of the financial needs of any of its customers can be met. Nor is this process yet necessarily at an end. The Bank of England recently announced very substantial relaxations in its rules regulating participations by clearing banks in merchant banks and this may well lead to closer associations of a kind which will facilitate the provision of finance to multinationals. At the same time, the rules concerning participations by foreign banks in British banks were eased and this may assist the development of multinational bank groups or looser multinational associations of banks.

Thus multinationalisation of banks is a trend which has been going on for some years past. As far as British banks were concerned, it was partly a development in thinking internationally and partly an answer to the development of the E.E.C., whether Britain joined or not, as well as a means of meeting the needs of any company which might require banking services in more than one country.

To illustrate this kind of development let me mention some of the international connections of the Midland Bank; a similar story could be told by other British banks and by many European banks. About ten years ago, we formed the first of the new form of multinational banks, by associating with three Commonwealth banks to form a joint subsidiary mainly for financing Commonwealth development. At about the same time, we formed a looser association with three large European banks, to which two others have since been added. This group has various subsidiaries both in Europe and in other parts of the world and through them or in other ways we are participating in banks or finance corporations in several other areas of the world including the United States, Latin America, Asia and the Pacific area. The forms of organisation and the forms of finance provided are very varied and it cannot yet be said that we provide a comprehensive world-wide financial service. But it would be difficult for a multinational corporation to set up operations anywhere where there is no Midland Bank connection and where some part of its financial needs, at least, cannot be met by us.

It is possible that the kind of approach described above may not prove adequate in the future—indeed may not be adequate at the moment for banks which wish to retain or attract more of the business of multinational companies. It is not easy to give any figures, even if one were to select any particular definition of a multinational company. However, it is clear that they are already large in relation to national economies and to international trade generally. Thus, any major bank will find that a substantial proportion of its domestic business, and perhaps an even larger part of its international business, is conducted with multinational company customers. Moreover, since the business of multinationals is growing relatively fast, the proportion of total banking business which they represent has no doubt been rising and can be expected to continue to rise. Accordingly, any major bank must ensure that its services are at least adequate to meet this challenge and this may call for changes in the structure of their organisation.

It may be that financial markets are more internationalised than the banks which operate in them. Many banks still tend to think primarily in terms of operating in their own countries—where the great bulk of their customers by number are to be found—rather than in global terms, and often their organisation is on a regional basis within that country. Similarly, to the extent that they operate overseas, either directly through branches or through subsidiaries, there is a tendency to organise activities in terms of geographical areas. Investment banks, particularly British merchant banks, may have a stronger tradition than commercial banks of thinking in international terms and their organisations are small enough to be readily adapted, but the resources they command are correspondingly smaller and inadequate to this situation.

The geographical kind of structure may not be well suited to the financial needs of multinational companies, however suitable it may be for other purposes. The characteristics of their needs are their large size, the multiplicity of currencies and places in which they are required, and the complex mixture of different types of finance. Banks are not likely to rush to make fundamental changes in the structure of their organisation to meet requirements which can be dealt with adequately by ad hoc methods of liaison. However, they may increasingly have to think in terms of functions on a global basis, rather than of geographical areas. The tendency of multinational companies to divide their business among many banks militates against this. However, let us assume for the moment that a particular bank has—or is seeking to obtain—the whole or the great bulk of the banking business of a particular multinational company. It might be desirable for the affairs of that multinational group to be dealt with comprehensively at a central point by one officer or group of officers, rather than being split among a number of officers in different places, possibly of different though associated banks, whose activities may not be easy to co-ordinate and who may not all be adequately informed. As noted above, multinationals tend to use bankers whose services meet their requirements, rather than be affected by ties of sentiment and loyalty; if banks need this business, they must be prepared to take whatever steps are necessary to handle it efficiently.

In this respect, United States banks have some significant advantages. It is not only that more multinationals have their origins in the United States than in any other country, and so are already more closely linked with United States banks. The restrictions on the geographical spread, within the United States, of the activities of any one bank have driven some of the largest to think in terms of international development for some years past. Thus, some of them already have a network of overseas branches of the parent bank, which is accordingly more truly a multinational bank than the consortium banks and other forms of banking association to which European banks, in particular, have resorted. Consortium banks should at least be thinking in terms of developing the kind of mutual arrangements which some of us have already introduced, whereby one national bank can make all the necessary arrangements for credit to be provided, to one of its customers, in another country by its associated bank in that country.

Apart from the Eurocurrency and Eurobond markets, national capital markets still tend to be too limited and insular to meet the needs of multinational companies. Among other differences, the ratio of equity capital to debt of national companies tends to vary between countries, depending upon the traditional structure of their national capital markets. For instance, the proportion of equity in total capital is relatively high in the United Kingdom. Again, a few countries—notably the United Kingdom and the United States—have large and diversified capital markets with various types of financial institution operating in them. Others, particularly some European markets, tend to be dominated by finance provided through banks and other financial institutions, which effectively arrange various types of finance. These distinctions are perhaps tending to break down; for instance, in Britain, the provision of long-term and equity finance through such institutions as insurance companies and pension funds is now of major importance. These limitations and differences of national capital markets do not measure up to the global requirements of multinational companies. The need for truly multinational banks, capable of meeting all their requirements, is growing.

Chapter IX

FINANCIAL AND MONETARY ASPECTS OF DEVELOPING
MULTINATIONAL ENTERPRISES

by *Patrice de Vallée*

There are different categories and various stages in the development of multinational enterprises:
—A continued expansion of well-established multinational companies in oil,
computers, tractors, automobiles, etc. . . .
—Internationalization of companies previously confined within national markets.
—Generalization of international development strategies followed by enterprises in certain oligopolistic industries (e.g. food and pharmaceuticals). In
such industries some enterprises are considered by other firms as endowed
with leadership characteristics, and therefore models to be imitated and followed.
—The induced establishment abroad of suppliers, subcontractors, and suppliers of services which follow their domestic clients abroad, often because
they fear that they may lose their clients nationally if they do not follow
them internationally, to their more enterprising competitors.

The development of the first generation multinational enterprises (the major
oil companies, IBM, General Motors, etc.) which took place between 1950
and 1960, did not rely heavily on the resources of multinational financial
institutions abroad. These expanding multinational companies usually had at
their disposal substantial internally supplied funds; in addition, given their
sound balance sheets and the size of their resources, these companies had
little difficulty in raising funds locally. This situation led to a close working
relationship with foreign local banks. Thus the role of international financial
institutions was neither very large nor crucial.
    Multinational companies tend to work with multinational banks because
of identical national origin (usually American) and because of the more comprehensive world-wide network offered by American banks than by banks of
other nationalities. But it would be a mistake to think of the development
abroad of the large multinational (IBM, ESSO, GM, etc.) as having depended
on American banks, their credits, their branch networks and their services.
    Perhaps the opposite is true.
    One may ask whether these American banks—which have been praised for

their dynamism and their importance in the development of Europe—have not played more an induced than a primary role in this development. It was perhaps more a case of following their clients abroad rather than preceding them.

American banks, which did not have assured sources of foreign local deposits, found it difficult to accomodate the local financing needs of their clients while foreign local lending institutions provided the security of access to a stable deposit base.

The major weakness of American banks abroad is the weakness of their local deposit base, which results from their limited number of branches and from the fact that their clients are predominantly American companies which are net borrowers.

The mandatory recourse by European branches of American banks to different national money markets for a substantial portion of their treasury needs could not satisfy their clients that these banks would be able to renew or increase their lines of credit or short-term advances, let alone to refinance their medium-term credits.

The activity of multinational banks was considerably modified with the appearance of a "new generation" of multinational companies.

One may relate this phase in the development of multinational companies, and especially of the American ones, to the Rome Treaty, access to external convertibility for a number of European currencies, limited growth in the U.S.A. under the Eisenhower administration, and finally the realization by American companies that there were interesting opportunities offered by the Common Market with its potential expansion beyond the six original member countries.

This second generation of multinational companies required the services of financial institutions, which were truly international.

These new multinational enterprises made much larger demands on foreign banks and particularly on the international banks of their own countries. For a European bank, the risks presented by a more or less well known American company still remain somewhat vague. The evaluation of these risks becomes even more difficult when a company is established in Europe—as is nearly always the case—with a weak capital structure, a high level of debt, expectations of losses òn initial activities and a reluctance on the part of the parent company to provide a guarantee for the benefit of its subsidiary.

Indeed, these companies (and here we are generally referring to American companies) were usually set up with a small capital base, substantial advances from the parent company and some facilities from local banks. The insufficiency of these financial resources in relation to financial requirements

130

(normal start-up losses in the first years, investments and working capital needs) forced these companies to turn to the only financial institutions which could meet their needs for local credits in foreign currencies. Such credits were usually out of proportion in relation to the capital of the subsidiary, and were obtained largely because of some guarantees given by the parent company to the Head office of an American bank. It then instructed its local branch to extend credit to the companies' foreign subsidiary.

These American banks were in a better position to judge the risks involved since they were able to place the European operations of the subsidiary into the context of a worldwide relationship existing between the bank and the company. They were also able to accept that a "Monkey letter" or quasi-guarantee replace the formal guarantee that was usually required by foreign banks. A "Monkey letter" could be considered by a United States bank as equivalent to a guarantee, but was phrased in such a way that the company did not feel obliged to mention this guarantee as a contingent liability in its annual report.

Finally, the emergence of the Euro-dollar market, and later on of other Eurocurrencies, which accompanied the relaxing of national regulations concerning borrowing in foreign currencies, enabled American banks in Europe to refinance their borrowing from a broader source which had more of the characteristics of a true money, or rather multimoney market.

This extension of credits by American banks in Europe enabled European subsidiaries of United States companies to expand much faster than if they had had only to rely on credits from national banks.

The counterpart to these features was that the quality of the loan portfolios of these American banks in Europe was such as to be a cause of concern to any auditor: bank debt represented a multiple of net worth and there were cases of negative cash flows. Granting such loans was only justified by the relationship between the Head offices of the bank and of the company.

American banks have therefore helped the international expansion of American enterprises by enabling the foreign subsidiaries of United States companies to utilize the credit—ratings of their Head offices through a transfer of guarantees.

The growth of banks which have become, by choice or necessity, multinational involved profound changes in their traditional arrangements of dealing with the international problems of the clients through correspondent banks.

Basically, banks are subject to numerous and pressing request from their clients who demand:
—a presence in a number of countries
—local financing
—international financing
—money transfers.

Besides these demands for traditional services, companies also required certain other services: advice relating to the entry into foreign countries, investment services and foreign exchange facilities.

Traditionally, banks had referred their clients to their correspondent banks in foreign countries. This recourse to a network of correspondent banks rapidly proved ineffective, with all the defects associated with a system of distant indirect relationships.

Of the top three American banks, First National City Bank and Bank of America adopted a worldwide strategy, with a wide network of branches throughout the world. Chase Manhattan Bank was slower to react in gradually extending its network, and followed in certain countries a policy of minority or 50-50 joint participations, which offered less services to clients than 100 per cent. controlled subsidiaries or branches.

It is probable that the future expansion of international transactions will produce an increase in the number of multinational banking facilities in the world and this will take the form of opening new branches.

In that period, one has seen the growth of the consortium banking phenomenon (SFE, ECIB, ORION, etc.). This development was in no way just an attempt to patch up existing relationships between correspondent banks, but rather a more fundamental effort to overcome certain weaknesses. These weaknesses may be of the following kinds:

—Regulatory:	Exchange controls; Credit controls;
—Timing:	Credit restrictions;
—Dimensional:	Limitations on maximum lending permitted;
—Political:	Relations between states;
—Professional:	More or less perfect knowledge of countries, industrial sectors and financial practices;
—Administrative:	Lending policies;
—Geographical:	Absence of local branches.

In this respect, ORION (at the same time, a merchant bank and a bank for medium-term credits and for multinational services) can be seen as a successful example of this type of institution. The secret of its success lies, perhaps, in its resemblance to the Common Market, with its three levels of control:

1. Heads of State (the chairmen of the six participating banks) who meet on the occasion of the IMF meeting;

2. Council of Ministers, consisting of the representatives of each of the six banks, who look after the interests of their own banks, define the policies that will be acceptable to each bank, decide what activities will be left to the individual banks and what to ORION, and finally co-ordinate their joint activities;

3. Executive Committee, i.e. the bankers who constitute ORION and who,

within the framework of well defined policies and with the certainty that effective arbitration procedures exist to deal with cases of conflict, ultimately account for the acknowledged success of ORION.

It is possible that in the future the kind of solution adopted by ORION will be more favoured than other less well structured and well defined solutions such as some loose associations between foreign banks.

The proliferation of agreements between banks and joint ventures—sometimes redundant and conflicting—is anyway such that one may easily foresee a dissolution of some of the existing agreements.

Returning to our short historical retrospect, we may take the liberty to forecast some of the broad tendencies to come: the expansion of multinational companies and financial institutions has considerably altered the rules of the game. Some of the more remarkable of the international bankers (e.g. White Weld) have strongly contributed to these changes. Other traditional banks, such as the First National City Bank, have also brought in innovations. But this upheavel of markets, of credit instruments and of habits were accepted only with some difficulty by the majority of the so-called international banks.

Let us not forget that American banks were reluctant to venture into the Euro-dollar market ten years ago. This reluctance could be explained by banks' traditional reluctance to enter unregulated money markets, the absence of a central record of liabilities, imperfect knowledge of the total indebtedness of multinational enterprises, confusion between the lending and the foreign exchange aspects of some transactions, the lack of faithfulness in relationships, the gradual narrowing of spreads and the easier access of enterprises to money markets—all features which characterize the Euro-dollars phenomenon.

One can understand the reluctance and even the hostility on the part of bankers at that time to participate in this event which, for reasons outlined above and because of the importance, not only of the amounts at stake but also of the participants, involved serious upheavals in the rules of the financial game.

This survey should urge us to be modest. What could we have answered or foreseen ten years ago if we had been faced with the question put to us today: financial establishments and growth of multinational enterprises?

Could we have foreseen the large flows of funds that we all now know and estimates of some 90 billion Euro-dollars and of 268 billion dollars short-term assets held by multinational companies?

On the other hand, it would have been relatively easy to have foreseen the growth of American banks abroad, given the particularly imitative nature of

133

oligopolistic competition, which typifies the behaviour of American banks. In such a context, what can we predict?

It is neither evident nor certain that the growth of multinational financial institutions is necessarily linked to the development of multinational companies, as may be suggested by the title of this paper. To suppose so would not take into account the type of clientele constituted by States which have recourse, directly or via quasi-governmental institutions, to financial establishments for syndicated loans, project financing, for financing of imports, or private placements. It would also underestimate the actual tendency of banks established abroad to find and attract local clients and sources of deposits. Finally, it would ignore the fact that multinational companies are not necessarily always interesting clients for the banks from the point of view of profitability.

For some years, one can has seen certain tendencies which have reduced the profits that these banks make from their operations with their multinational clients;

—systems of cash management and international money mobilization policies advertized by the banks themselves and the application to financial flows of the principles of "financial hydraulics", has considerably reduced the volume of "float" at the disposal of the banks;

—treasurers of multinational companies have become much more aware of the possibilities to make better use of the services which the banks are eagerly competing with each other to offer them;

—the generalisation of the practice of "floating rates" linked to the rates on the Euro-dollar market, plus a margin, with a resulting progressive tightening of profit margins;

—lastly, a number of foreign banks in London—too large a number in fact— are, to ensure their presence in London, prepared to grant loans without reference to profit margins, provided the spread on such transactions covers their operating and overhead costs.

This narrowing of margins poses a serious problem for American banks because they are subject to two constraints: the first being the return on invested capital, which influences the performance of their share on the stock exchange; the second being the leverage ratio (ratio of liabilities to net worth) which should not go unchecked.

For some years—years characterized by uncertainty and instability in the international monetary system—the treasurers of multinational companies have been more and more concerned with problems of exchange rates and money management.

The expansion of international activities and the consequential multidirectional and multicurrency flows, and the barriers imposed by exchange con-

134

trols and the corresponding separations between national systems of financial institutions, means that a co-ordinated global approach is necessary towards the financial problems of these companies, rather than a country by country approach.

Multinational banks have offered to multinational companies of varying sizes, multi-purpose/multi-currency/multi-country lines of credit, including leasing and factoring and also facilities for the management of their international funds.

One may ask oneself whether these banks knew how to and have in practice been able so far to deal with their own exchange and currency problems and allowed their clients to benefit from such a service for which multinational enterprises have, excluding the very large companies, a great need.

Let us try to summarize the role that could be played by a bank in assisting its clients to formulate a truly integrated concept of the financial management of a multinational enterprise. This management involves:

1. *Carrying out permanent arbitrage operations*
(in principle successful) with the funds of the Group, with its implicit and explicit global foreign exchange position, both present and future, and taking exchange positions between:
a) currencies (forward cover or lack thereof)
b) Rates (different currencies and same currencies in different markets)
c) Maturities (borrowing or lending, short- or long-term).

2. *Centralizing activities in a central agency*
a) of the internal flows of the Group or at best of the knowledge of the actual or projected timing of such flows (in and out);
b) of information on the financial markets (rates) and spot and forward exchange markets (premium, discounts);
c) of internal decisions (internal rates of reference) within the Group;
d) of general policies and day-to-day decisions;
e) of placements;
f) of relations with banks (lines of credit, movements).

3. *Behaving, not only as Treasurer, but also as Banker and Financier of the Group*, by
a) arbitraging between funding and financing;
b) drawing short-term (generally cheaper) on long-term lines of credit.

4. *Managing the various elements of a worldwide financing policy through arbitrage operations between countries and currencies* of
a) Inventories;
b) Receivables;
c) Suppliers.

135

Multinational banks, even those which have the largest international clients and the greatest volume of exchange transactions, are—paradoxically—little equipped to render these services.

The weakness of these banks in this area may lie in the cultural isolation of exchange brokers with their exotically incomprehensible language for the non-initiated; with the insufficient training of bankers in foreign exchange matters; with the poor understanding by bankers of the concept of internal flows of companies (while a bank has no real internal flows of its own); and finally with the isolation of economists who are often far away from the practices of foreign exchange-traders, the financing requirements of the enterprise, and the subtle alchemy of bankers' dealings.

The future for banks and bankers depends upon their ability to bring together a team of experts possessing the qualities necessary today for dealing with complex realities. Such an approach requires that the bankers' talents should be complemented by the intellectual approach of economists, the daily professionalism of foreign exchange traders and the treasurers' experience in managing company's funds.

Chapter X

FINANCIAL INSTITUTIONS AND THE GROWTH OF MULTINATIONAL
CORPORATIONS— AN AMERICAN POINT OF VIEW

by *Donald W. Vollmer*

Multinationalism and international banking

Can banks be considered multinational?

Academicians, business leaders and politicians have given us a variety of
definitions of what is meant by "multinational". Michael Z. Brooke and
H. Lee Remmers in their book *The Strategy of Multinational Enterprise* offer
us a very broad definition. They say a multinational company "is any firm
which performs its main operation, either manufacturing or the provision of
services in at least two countries". Christopher Tugendhat, a Member of
Parliament in Britain, in his book *The Multinationals* on the other hand
appears to exclude banks when he defines for his purposes multinational
corporations as being those "very large manufacturing companies with especially far-flung interests".

The *Daily Telegraph* attributes the following definition to Hawker Sidde-
ley's Sir Arnold Hall: "a multinational corporation is an American registered
company manufacturing its products where labour is cheapest, and channeling its profits to another country where taxation is lowest or preferably
non-existent".

May I give you our work-a-day definition? In Bank of America we have
defined a multinational enterprise as being: *an essentially private business
organization which conducts its operations through direct investment abroad
and which aims to harness its resources to achieve global objectives without
regard to national boundaries.*

The term "multinational" has normally been used rather differently when
applied to banks. In the past few years a number of banks have been established that have been generically referred to as "multinational banks". For
example, the May 1971 issue of the British journal *The Banker* has an article
entitled, "New Model Multinational Bank". The article described the triple
alliance of Commerzbank, Credit Lyonnais, and Banco di Roma. The label is
used when discussing the Orion Group, a joint venture involving the Westdeutsche Landesbank Girozentrale, the Royal Bank of Canada, National Westminster, Chase Manhattan, Mitsubishi, and Credito Italiano. What these banks
have in common is that they are *owned* by organizations of different nation-

alities. Their operations are not necessarily multinational in the sense that the word has been normally used by politicians, business commentators and academicians.

We believe Bank of America is multinational *through its operations* in the same way that Shell, I.B.M., Nestlé, Unilever, and other well known international enterprises are multinational. There are several other major international banks which could equally lay claim to the multinational label, e.g. First National City Bank (which advertises it is the world's "largest international bank"), Barclays Bank Group (with over 1,600 branches in 41 countries), Bank of Tokyo ("leaders in international banking since 1880" with 72 branches and 20 representatives in 37 countries), etc.

Norman Macrae, deputy editor of the *Economist* in his survey "The Future of International Business" felt that banks had been left out of too many compilations.

Andrew F. Brimmer, member of the Board of Governors of the United States Federal Reserve System, in his December 1972 article "Multinational Banks and the Management of Monetary Policy in the United States" classified 20 American banks as being "multinational". Foreign deposits, as a per cent. of total deposits of these "multinational" banks, varied from 12 per cent. up to 47 per cent. Each bank had one or more branch offices in foreign countries. More than half of the "multinational" banks had business loan holdings which amounted to more than 60 per cent. of their total loans.

It has been said that perhaps banking was the *first* of the multinational enterprises. Didn't the Rothschilds and, in the fifteenth century the Fuggers, from Augsburg, finance ventures in practically every country of Europe almost without regard to which country was fighting whom?

To me, a world-wide network of overseas branches is a primary requirement for becoming a multinational bank. Perhaps a brief review of the history of overseas branch banking might illustrate how banks became a part of the multinational phenomenon.

Because of the publicity American overseas investment has invoked in the past decade, one may forget that only in recent years have United States banks generally become more significant participants in international banking.

Internationalization of American banking

Regarding United States overseas banking, Ray Westerfield in an early text, *Money, Credit and Banking*, wrote: "The failure of our banks to develop foreign branches lies not in want of legal authority, but in the fact that our banks, like our industrialists turned their full attention to the United States interior and left the international business to the British and others who were skilled and long-experienced in that line. With the American invasion of for-

138

eign markets after 1900, our manufacturers missed the support which British, German and other exporters got from their banks".

At the beginning of the 20th century, England had 32 so called "colonial banks" with head offices in London and 2,104 branches overseas. France had 18 so-called colonial banks in Paris with 104 overseas branches, while Germany had 70 overseas branches and Holland followed with 68 foreign branches.

While the first United States branch bank established overseas dates back to 1887 there were only a handful of United States Banks overseas at the turn of the century. In 1926 the total number of United States banking institutions having any operations overseas had actually dropped from a high of 20 in 1920 to 12 institutions. By 1933 the figure had fallen to 8 institutions, a direct expression of the lack of confidence in the international economic situation.

Even as recently as 1954, only a few United States banks had overseas branches and offices. Of a total world figure of approximately 1,250 overseas banking offices, United States banks accounted for 112 compared with 500 for the United Kingdom, 376 for continental Europe (mostly Holland) and 118 for Canada. Most United States banks continued to rely on correspondent relationships with foreign institutions. A United States Federal Reserve study summarized the situation by noting that while the United States and the United Kingdom each accounted for roughly 15 per cent. of world trade in 1954, United States banks had only about 10 per cent. of the total of overseas establishments, while the United Kingdom accounted for 40 per cent. of all foreign banking offices.

The establishment of American overseas branches began to pick up in the late 1950s. In 1960 8 United States banks had 131 branches abroad. By the end of 1965 there were 188 overseas branches held by 13 American banks. By the end of 1968, 27 banks operated 340 overseas branches. On June 30, 1972, 106 American banks had established 558 foreign branches (many of these banks had only one, or possible two, branches, primarily in London and Nassau).

Total assets of American foreign branches were roughly $3.5 billion in 1960–$7.5 billion in 1965–$35 billion by September 1969–to almost $70 billion at the end of June 1972.

Reasons for the tremendous growth of American banks' international operations since 1946

Speaking generally, American banks were in many ways forced into international finance, i.e., "trade follows the flag". After the war, countries everywhere looked to the United States for finance–first tapping the United States bond market and then when that source was effectively closed (by The Interest Equalisation Tax in 1964) by taking loans from the big commercial banks. When this source was also effectively closed by mid 1965, by the Federal Reserve's Voluntary Foreign Credit Restraint programme, the banks' international departments were put to work overseas via foreign branches.

The Euro-dollar was a key factor in causing American banks to internationalize their operations.

The October 1972 issue of the *Federal Reserve Bulletin* reports: ". . . the pace of expansion in the activities of foreign branches of United States banks has been influenced by the rapid growth in the Euro-dollar market". The article went on to explain how most of the American overseas branches set up in the past decade, were initially for tapping the Euro-dollar market. Because of the controls over bank and non-bank capital outflows from the United States, banks had to move abroad to continue, and to expand, their international business.

Regulation Q and United States money market conditions also helped to introduce some previously non-committed banks to international banking. During the 1966 and 1969 United States "credit crunches", there were strong incentives for United States banks to borrow abroad to offset run-offs in domestic certificates of deposit (which because of regulation Q were at uncompetitive interest rates). The banks primarily borrowed from their long established or recently established foreign branches (mostly in London).

Federal Reserve statistics show what happened. In mid-1965 foreign branches of United States banks supplied a net amount of $0.5 billion to their head offices. By September 1966, the net amount supplied was more than $2.5 billion. In October 1969, when the United States "credit crunch" reached its peak, net foreign branch claims on head offices stood at almost $15 billion. Today such claims approximate $1.5 billion.

What happened? As conditions in the United States money markets became more relaxed, the funds returned from the head offices. The old-timers and the newcomers began lending the dollars to non-bank users. The Federal Reserve reports that by June 1972 more than one-half of the branch claims on *non*-bank borrowers were dollar dominated, whereas in 1965 more than two-thirds of their claims had been non-dollar dominated.

As trade tends to follow the flag, most banks tended to follow the lead of their clients in developing international operations. American banks expanded their international services to meet the demands of their existing commercial customers who were increasingly looking overseas for markets. Banks failing to respond to their customers international banking needs found that these customers soon moved *both* their domestic and international banking to the rapidly emerging international banks. A look at the market potential of just servicing American companies shows what is involved.

According to *Business Week*, some 3400 American firms "have built a stake in around 23,000 businesses abroad, including more than 8,000 producing affiliates".

Raymond Vernon in his book *Sovereignty at Bay* reports that America's 500 largest firms owned about 2,500 manufacturing subsidiaries, and that 187 of these firms (each of which had established subsidiaries in six or more countries) owned more than 2,000 of them.

The banking laws of the United States certainly played a significant role in making American banks more attentive to overseas markets. In Europe it is normal for a bank to have branches all over their own country. In the United States branch banking is confined to a city, a region within a state, or at the most to an entire state. To the big commercial banks in New York City (until only very recently limited to branches in the metropolitan area) international banking was a golden opportunity. For example, one major New York bank in 1960 had only 75 overseas branches and offices in 29 countries. Today this same bank has 310 overseas branches and offices in 60 countries (including affiliates, 90 countries). While figures going back say 10 years are not readily available, as of June 30, 1972 many of the large New York City banks' foreign deposits were a third or more of total deposits.

London—the overseas branch explosion in microcosm

The November 1972 issue of *The Banker* reports that there were 202 foreign owned banks from 53 countries directly represented through a branch or office in London. Of the 202, 50 come from the U.S.A.; 19 from Japan, followed by Italy and Switzerland with 12 each.

The great rush of American banks to London came during the previously described Euro-dollar era, i.e., 1965-1971. The market has changed. The September 23, 1972 *Economist* survey on "The City" comments: "Since the heydays of 1968-69, the growth of the Eurocurrency markets as a whole has slowed down; the proportion of dollars in those markets has diminished; the share of the business done by London has become smaller; and, to cap it all, the proportion of that London business done by the colony of American banks in the City may have contracted." "For these American banks in London in a position to exploit them, the new opportunities of the (sterling) credit revolution may have come just in time. *The salad days of their Euro-dollar business could be over.*"

Bank of America's international growth

Bank of America at the end of the Second World War had one overseas branch, a branch located in London which was established in 1931. The branch was the result of the Bank buying into the business of the British Italian Banking Corporation Limited. Offices of Bank of Italy, Bank of America and Bancitaly Corporation—all affiliated institutions at that time—were already doing business in London in 1928.

In 1954, we accounted for 10 of the 112 American overseas offices, or only about 9 per cent. of the United States total. However, by 1968 we accounted for 85 offices or about 23 per cent. of the total of United States offices overseas, (excluding the offices of our subsidiary, Banca d'America e d'Italia which itself had 85 offices located around Italy).

Today Bank of America has 100 overseas branches, 10 representative offices, 81 subsidiaries and affiliates in 77 countries and territories. Bank of America probably accounts for roughly one-third of all United States banking overseas offices. This takes on added significance when one realizes that 106 different American banks now have some form of banking office located overseas.

Bank of America, which was founded 67 years ago, is today the world's largest private bank with total resources as of December 31, 1972 of almost $40.9 billion, deposits of approximately $35 billion and loans of $19 billion.

What has involvement in international business meant for the Bank of America? In 1945, when we had only one overseas office, total resources were approximately $6 billion and deposits $5 billion. It would be inaccurate to imply that Bank of America's growth has been primarily from international expansion. Growth has primarily been the result of the Bank's location in California, now a state of approximately 20 million people. (Japanese and European banks, recognizing the business potential of California and the Pacific Basin areas, have been quick to open branches and subsidiaries in California, e.g., the Barclays Group has over 23 branches and Bank of Tokyo 13 offices). Most importantly, for Californian banks, Californian law allows state-wide branch banking. While not the oldest bank in California, Bank of America today has over 1,000 branches in California. The closest California bank to Bank of America for ranking by total resources was 32nd in a recent world ranking of banks.

Nevertheless, as our overseas branch figures suggest, international banking has been one of the major ingredients in our growth. In 1972, Bank of America's international resources exceeded $12 billion, or roughly 30 per cent. of total resources, and were a substantial contributor to total earnings of $192 million.

The Bank had approximately 49,000 employees world-wide. Total overseas staff is approximately 7,000 of which only 320 are United States citizens. As further evidence of Bank of America's multinationality, it is important to note that most of our overseas official staff in non-American. Additionally, many of the key senior positions in our International Banking Department are staffed by persons born and trained outside the United States.

142

While I do not know off-hand the various citizenships of our fourteen Regional Vice Presidents posted around the globe, I do believe only four or five were born in the United States.

In a recent article on the trends of international banking, the Chief Executive of our International Banking Department, Executive Vice President C.M. van Vlierden, spoke of banks becoming more *geocentric*, i.e., employees, regardless of nationality, will be encouraged to identify with the world-wide goals of the global bank. Geocentricism will further demand that all key positions in international banking be open to the best people, regardless of nationality. Staff-wise, I would offer that Bank of America is the world's most internationalized, largest private financial institution.

Multinational corporate banking

In 1970 Bank of America established a Multinational Division. The following assumptions led to the establishment of the Division: The emergence of the multinational type of enterprise will be the *most important* institutional change in international business during the next quarter century; the international production of goods and services, rather than traditional export/import trade, being the main focus of these world businesses. We further assumed that these businesses should account for the majority of the world's output of goods and services by the year 2000.

The above assumptions are well on their way to being realized. Recently, an article in the *London Sunday Times* reported that total sales of foreign subsidiaries of all nationalities are $100 billion *greater* than the total value of world exports.

The Bank's Multinational Division was given world-wide responsibilities for developing a *global* relationship with a designated list of multinational enterprises, American and non-American based. Specifically, the Division develops and manages the global strategy for achieving Bank of America's objectives with these clients.

Determining the multinational clients and prospects

To determine which companies could be best served by the Multinational Division, particular attention was given to the number of countries in which the company had operations. The more countries we both operated in, the greater the potential benefits of our service to the company and to the Bank. For example, one of my clients has significant operations in 33 of the 77 countries in which we have banking offices. Another operates in 64 countries. On the other hand, a major *Fortune* "500" company operating in only two or three of our overseas serving areas might be more suitably assisted by the Bank's United States National Division. Other such criteria were utilized to select the truly multinational enterprises. Using such criteria you can readily guess that the number of companies followed by the Multinational Division is rather small. They tend to be companies that are shown in the *Fortune* "500" of United States firms and in the *Fortune* "200" of foreign firms.

Organizing for multinational corporate banking

The Division is headed by a Senior Vice President located in our San Francisco Headquarters. He reports to the Chief Executive Officer for International Banking, who in turn reports to the Bank's President and Chief Executive.

In his book *The Multinationals*, Christopher Tugendhat refers to the multinationals' head offices as being the "brain and nerve centre" while the sub sidiaries are the "limbs carrying out approved tasks". If I may use Tugendhat's analogy, our organizational structure was specifically established to give optimum service to *both* the brain and the limbs.

A number of senior officers of the Multinational Division, referred to internally as multinational account managers, are individually assigned a given number of clients. These account managers are located strategically around the world, in order to be in close proximity to an assigned client's head office, i.e. the "brain and nerve centre". For example, the London multinational account managers are assigned only United Kingdom headquartered multinational enterprises.

The Multinational Division office in Tokyo has similar global account managers, as do the offices in Paris, Chicago, Brussels, Frankfurt, Los Angeles, San Francisco and New York City; all responsible for the assigned multinational companies headquartered in their serving area.

The multinational account manager is Bank of America's "Man-on-the-Spot" for the multinationals. As such he is directly responsible to the Senior Vice President of the Multinational Division for the world-wide relationship of the assigned multinational companies headquartered in his geographic area. He has credit authority and depending on the amount of the credit, approves or recommends all credit transactions involving his clients.

Providing multinational corporate banking

The multinational men-on-the-spot are expected effectively to utilize the Bank's global complex of financial services. The only way this can be successfully done is for the multinational account manager to work through the Bank's world-wide organization of branches, subsidiaries and affiliates, and other head office divisions.

Should one of the Bank's branches in India be approached for a credit facility by a subsidiary of one of the assigned British multinational companies, the London multinational officer is involved. If he should feel it appropriate, he would initiate similar discussions with the pertinent financial officer in the company's head office. Thus both the "brain and nerve centre" and the analogous "limb" receive a co-ordinated response to the subsidiary's request.

On the other hand, some of our clients don't want credit to be discussed locally until the financing need has been first cleared in their head office. Contact by the relevant multinational officer with the company's head office can then be especially useful to an alert Bank of America branch or merchant bank manager who feels there is an excellent opportunity to develop local business, say in France, but who in the past has been turned away by the company's local people because of the need for their head office's clearance.

A Frankfurt based multinational acount manager might find it useful to make joint calls with the local branch manager on a client's local subsidiary, say in France or the United Kingdom. We have found that local executives appreciate having the opportunity to talk with a person already familiar with their head office structure.

Making multinational corporate banking work

To make such a system work, the multinational account manager must know as much as possible about the Bank's full complex of financial services. He is equally expected to have a detailed knowledge of the client's world-wide relationship with the Bank. Fortunately, the computer can help. We have a management information system that will give us various global statistics by bank serving unit, and geographic region.

Such information is also indispensable when soliciting banking services from the multinational treasurer. The treasurer or finance officer wants to feel that he is dealing with an organization *that acts as one bank*, not a far flung organization of independently acting branches, subsidiaries and affiliates. Understandably, a multinational finance officer has little patience with the bank that fails to take into account the overall bank relationship when local banking decisions are being made with his subsidiaries around the globe. Local custom and regulations permitting, Bank of America aims to consider the overseas units of a multinational client as being an *integral part of one economic entity*.

The Bank's multinational approach takes us well beyond being merely a supplier of local financing and substantial financing for the parent. Our primary aim is to provide the multinationals with the most efficient and economical banking services obtainable in *each* of the countries in which we both

145

operate. As finance is progressively centralized by international companies, such local attention becomes particularly beneficial, i.e. the treasurer's office can take advantage of the knowledge and economics of scale implicit in our world-wide network.

Likewise, by reason of our geographic spread, we share with the multinational company the advantage of being able to reduce some of the economic and political uncertainties of relying on only one market. This enables us to consider risks which other banks, less well situated, cannot entertain. We also have the opportunity to bring to our multinational clients the experience we have gained by being exposed to a variety of economic and financial situations and problems around the globe.

Recognizing that it is essential for a bank to treat the overseas operations of a multinational client as one economic unit, you may wonder how we keep our Bank officers informed of a client's activities. Each of the assigned multinationals has a marketing dossier prepared on it within the Bank. The dossier gives one such information as the names of key corporate contacts around the world, a short company history, discussion of significant organizational aspects such as the geographic distribution of sales and profits, summarized financial statements, a relationship evaluation, a detailed schedule of global credit commitments, outstandings and deposits by location. Additionally, brief marketing comments by location, including the name of the Bank's own contact officers responsible for developing the local relationships, are found in the dossier. The dossier is kept current and is distributed periodically to all units around the world on a need-to-know basis.

Another key management tool, is the quarterly Global Marketing Plan which establishes objectives for the quarter and the specific plans for implementing the objectives. Objectives are given specific target dates within the quarter. Should any of the objectives not be implemented they are carried forward into the next quarter. The objectives set are realistic aims for the time period. For example, one of my objectives may be to hold a meeting on a given date, to become better acquainted with a client's head office financial decision making network, or to familarize myself with a client's overseas inter-company cash flow. The plan is sent to all officers receiving the marketing dossier.

The multinational account manager is responsible for ensuring that all of his colleagues are kept properly informed on the divisional strategy and latest developments regarding the assigned multinational corporations. The advantage for the client is thay he need approach only *one* key banking officer for world-wide banking assistance and access to Bank of America's complete array of financial services.

How do other American banks serve the multinational corporation?

To my knowledge no other American bank (or even non-American bank) has established a *specific* division, with key staff located strategically around the globe, to serve only multinational enterprises.

One major New York bank has established in its head office a special liaison group that attempts to identify multinational corporate business development opportunities. The intelligence is then brought to the attention of the bank officer best able to cope with the situation. The officer responsible for responding to the situation can be either overseas or in the United States.

Another bank has a designated multinational group, again located only in the head office. The group attempts directly to solicit business from multinational enterprises. While I do not know for sure, I would suspect such an approach, because of geographical considerations, results in this particular bank's multinational officers working mostly with American headquartered multinationals which are in close proximity to the group.

One major American Bank is establishing around the globe local corporate banking divisions. For example, in London (where the idea apparently originated), the banking activities of Citibank are divided into three major divisions: The Corporate Banking Division, The Retail Banking Division, and the Treasury/Administration Division. The Corporate Banking Division is subdivided by industry, e.g. petroleum/chemicals, transportation, consumer products, engineering (which ranges from cars through electronics), mining and metallurgy, and financial institutions. The three Divisions are highly specialized concentrating on their markets, i.e. the corporate banker does not get involved with personal loans while the Retail Division is busy attracting the business of individuals through their "money shops" etc.

The great increase in consortia and merchant banking activities of United States banks in London in the past three to four years is certainly aimed at serving amongst others, the multinational corporations. Going through a table in the November 1972 issue of *The Banker*, I was able to identify 16 different merchant banking/consortia banking institutions with significant American ownership; all could claim they can provide banking services to multinational enterprises. (Add these "newcomers" to the traditional array of 28 London merchant banks, plus United States investment banking activities, plus the 5 clearers, plus over 202 foreign commercial banks, etc., and one can see why the City is considered overbanked!)

Both Bank of America and Citibank have London based merchant banks. Chase Manhattan joined National Westminster, the Royal Bank of Canada, Westdeutsche Landesbank Girozentrale, Credito Italiano and Mitsubishi to form the Orion Group, also performing merchant banking operations. Morgan Guaranty owns 32 per cent. of Morgan Grenfell & Co. The London Multinational Bank Limited is 50 per cent. owned by two American banks, etc. etc.

One observer of the London banking scene wondered whether perhaps there were not more merchant banks than merchant bank*ers*. At any rate, the struggle for reasonable profitability for all the merchant banks could get tougher.

The same is true for the commercial banks. The cost of operating in London is high and some foreign banks are reportedly having a difficult time to cover even their overheads (in fact some look upon their London office as a form of institutional advertising). The joke in London is that no American bank wants to be the *first* to close up shop, but a lot would be pleased to be second.

Some trends in international banking

London as an international centre

One American banker when commenting on how American banks look at London, said some consider it the "flagship" of their international operations, while others view the City as an "outpost in an alien and foreign world".

My feeling is that the major American banks will continue in the next decade to have an important presence in London. Some of the newcomers will undoubtedly quietly withdraw. Whether London has the same relative importance to the major American banks' international operations, that it had in the past decade, depends primarily on the vitality of the Eurocurrency markets; most especially the Euro-dollar market. The viability of these markets is very much dependent on the ultimate structure of the international monetary system, now being so industriously designed by the authorities.

A strengthened dollar should allow the United States authorities to more or less eliminate the various controls that closed off the United States in the 1960's as a source of international funds. The extensive international banking apparatus, built up primarily in New York City after the Second World War, has been lying rather dormant the past decade. From a management, financial, and political point of view, there are strong incentives to re-establish New York City's prominence as a major international financial centre. This could well mean that a lot of the competent and ambitious bankers now located in Europe will be returning to New York, to once again exploit a centre which has the financial capability to raise more funds quickly and efficiently than any other existing centre. The jet and trans-atlantic telephone calls will help keep them in touch with their existing contacts.

The aim of the European Common Market countries to operate their currencies around a system of narrow margins while at the same time enjoying their independence on domestic monetary and economic policies has resulted in the member countries imposing restrictions and controls on capital movements amongst themselves and against the outside world. Such a situation effectively eliminates the advantages of a Eurocurrency market. Domestic banking markets become important, not Eurocurrency centres.

The major American international banks, if they are to build on the international business of the past decade, will have to strengthen greatly their ability to compete in local markets with *local* funds. Competition between indigenous and foreign banks can only increase (unless local banking lobbies and the authorities become protectionist and try to exclude competition, a step which must be considered a move backwards for any given economy). Several American banks are already actively cultivating retail business, e.g. "money shops", branches in shopping centres, etc.

United States banks, because of the need to be able to compete more successfully in local markets will be strengthening their existing branch facilities (more retail banking tied into computorized administration centres?) and developing closer ties with non-dollar currency banks through joint ventures and membership in consortiums.

The emerging "supermarkets" of finance

There is a strong trend under way in America for banks to diversify into financial services, both domestically and internationally, that heretofore were considered unrelated to commercial banking, i.e. the "supermarket" concept of banking.

In my discussions with one particular major bank's management regarding their rather significant overall growth in profitability compared to their competitors in the past decade, I received the comment: "We asked ourselves what business we were in. Our conclusion and subsequent response: we were in business to provide *financial services*. Many of our competitors are still focusing on providing banking services." By banking services they meant basically taking deposits, making loans and moving funds.

The "supermarket" services, sometimes also called "near-banking" services, include computor related services such as financial planning and forecasting, merger and acquisition advice, foreign exchange exposure management, factoring, leasing, pension fund management, etc.

One particular "near-banking" service that should become increasingly important to multinational corporations is transborder leasing. For example, a multinational leasing company of a major international bank could find for a United Kingdom company Swiss funds to be used in leasing United States equipment to a German company operating in Italy. The advantage to the United Kingdom client would be that the arrangements would be handled by *one* leasing company for at least the same financial costs if independently arranged (multinationally arranged deals should be cheaper, because of intelligence network inherent in a global leasing company).

149

Broadening competition

As American commercial bankers were beginning to realize that diversification could mean market growth and greater profitability, the rather domestically orientated large American *investment* banks were also re-examining their markets. The profitability of international banking caught their attention. Now there is increasing competition in the overseas markets between *both* the American commercial banks (and their merchant banks), the American investment banks, the traditional United Kingdom merchant banks, the German universal banks, the Banque d'Affaires, etc. The specific market: multinational corporations and Governments. The competition has recently been joined by the major Japanese banks and security houses; making finance no longer a predominantly western domain. Hopefully, this trend towards greater competition between financial intermediaries will continue.

However, clouding any favourable scenario of a further increase in beneficial competition is the distinct possibility that the retrogressive forces of protectionism and neo-isolationism, whether by individual countries or by *economic blocks*, could return us to a world of economic nationalism similar to that of the 1930s—a development which would be to no one country's long-term advantage.

From short-term to medium-term to long-term . . .

Bankers are becoming more tolerant (if not yet completely comfortable) with lending money on longer terms. The successful Euro-markets practice of pricing credits on a floating rate basis, which eliminated the interest risk for borrower and lender, undoubtedly contributed to the trend towards longer maturities. Improved methods in bank liability management (funding operations) have also enabled banks to take longer maturities. But the main force leading to longer terms has undoubtedly been competition. When I arrived in London three years ago, the maturity horizon was 3-5 years. As loan opportunities became scarcer, 7 year loans appeared; then 10 year loans . . .

Now some Japanese banks provide private placement facilities of millions of dollars for 10-15 years at *fixed* interest rates.

While terms lenthened, interest margins declined.

If you cannot make a profit on loans and deposits, perhaps there are profits in operating costs . . .

Many American banks are increasingly focusing their attention on the "paper flow", the "back-room problem", etc. as a way of improving their services and increasing profits. While a bank's cost of funds depend primarily on market conditions, administrative costs can be controlled. Now the bright managers can find equally challenging and rewarding positions in bank operations, not just in loan officer careers, the traditional road to the top in American banks.

150

One major New York bank, for example, has announced that it intends to keep its operations expense flat over the next five years. The executive given the job of keeping costs flat is a M.I.T. trained graduate engineer in his early thirties. His position is one of the top executive assignments in his bank.

Paper flow problems are now treated by banks as production problems: gólden opportunities, not inherent burdens.

Banking competition will ensure that the customer benefits through better service and lower prices.

Some current issues of multinational corporate banking

Foreign exchange advice

One of the main services expected from an international bank should be timely foreign exchange advice. The multinational bank's world-wide intelligence network gives it special capabilities in following international currency developments.

Customers appreciate hearing their banker's views on interest rate trends—forecasting changes in currency relationships is a logical extension of such financial counselling. However, I feel the international banker, through no fault of his own, faces a dilemma if he considers giving foreign currency advice to his clients. Could the banker's responsibilities to government and to his commercial clients be at cross-purposes?

You may recall the hectic Wednesday morning in May 1971, when the Bundesbank bought over $1 billion in the first half hour just before it finally closed its windows to dollar sellers. After the D.Mark floated, I read that the treasurer of a major international firm shortly before the float had been agonizing over the decision when to sell $250 million from United States operations to the Bundesbank. Was he a speculator? I believe he was a treasurer facing a difficult *commercial* decision on how to maintain the value of the assets under his control. What especially intrigued me about this story was the magnitude of the transaction. Should anyone be surprised that the Bundesbank could receive over $1 billion in a half hour's time?

When the Italian authorities in January 1973 introduced the two-tier market for the Lira, Bank of Italy statistics indicated that the exaggerated changes in trade leads and lags had been a principal cause of the sustained capital outflow. For the first ten months of 1972 on a payments basis, Italy had a trade deficit of appoximately Lire 1.1 billion. However, on the basis of Customs figures the deficit was only Lire 282 million. According to the Financial Times, the difference of Lire 873 million was "above normal and believed to reflect massive prepayments for imports".

In the Fall of 1972 the treasurer of a major and, by all criteria, a very sophisticated multinational corporation reported that he had been "caught

151

off guard" by the sterling "float". Through their extensive global subsidiary network, the company had obtained the opinions of various major European banks and corporations about the strength of the pound. The consensus was there was little risk in being long in sterling, i.e. hedging action was heavily influenced by the politics of the "snake in the tunnel". The company's management felt this was sufficient intelligence and decided that there was no need to cover. They subsequently learned, to their regret, that they should have also determined the attitudes of major United States international corporations. Apparently the United States firms, because they were further away from the European political scene, were more concerned with economic reality rather than political postulates. This particular company has several billion dollars a year in commercially related foreign exchange flows. What happens when such companies improve their intelligence network?

Recently the United States Tariff Commission published a study which claims that private international institutions at the end of 1971 held $268 billion in short-term assets. The Commission claimed that the above volume of funds was about twice as much as the funds controlled by all central banks and international monetary authorities at that time.

The popular attitude has been to blame recurring currency crises on international banks and corporations. However, I believe one could make a strong case that the international banks and corporations *react* to economic imbalances rather than *cause* them. Isn't the problem that the international monetary system is woefully behind the times? The system is biased towards meeting nationalist aims.

A monetary system that recognizes the inevitable evolution towards the internationalization of production and the concomitant trend to a world wide parity in national standards of living is essential. A monetary and banking system based primarily on nationalistic considerations is out of step with the economic reality that human enterprise is now treating the world as one market.

Too many respected economists and other observers of the rapidly changing world economic structure have made convincing arguments recommending a system of flexible exchange rates for me not to fall in line with their views. Such flexibility is consistent with freer trade and a vigorous expansion of foreign trade and investment. (There are certainly difficult *political* considerations regarding the future role of private enterprise in the internationalization of production. However, on the economic front I am convinced that multinational institutions have been a positive economic force towards a more open and equitable world society.)

As Secretary Shulze remarked before the I.M.F. on September 26, 1972 "The pursuit of the common welfare through more open trade is threatened by an ancient and recurring fallacy. Surpluses in payments are too often regarded as a symbol of success and of good management rather than as a

152

measure of the goods and services provided from a nation's output without current return".

I hope you will excuse me for the above detour (and editorializing) but until the international monetary system serves as a true international economic catalysis, international banks such as my own may face a difficult predicament. In an atmosphere of border controls and a rigid exchange rate system, could the multinational banks perhaps become the international currency "storm warning" centres? If this happens the astute corporate treasurer need pay little heed to the economic rationale behind an international bank's exchange advice; but a great deal of attention to determining who else is listening to X bank's advice? Perhaps the decision makers will then have to agonize over the problem of determining which global communication network is the most influential . . . However, the preferred solution must be to foster an environment hospitable to the creation of more multinational banks and more multinational corporations, and an international currency system suitable to the 20th and 21st century, i.e. an environment that leads to a freer flow of goods, services, people, capital and ideas.

Is the internationalizing of banking a constructive social phenomenon?

Not only are the major banks *individually* becoming financially stronger; their ability to marshal resources internationally has greatly increased through joint ventures, cross-border unions, consortiums, etc.

To Professor Perlmutter (in his article, "The Multinational Firm and the Future"), such "world banking systems to service the financial needs of world-wide firms" seem inevitable.

Will the treasurers of multinational corporations, because of the magnitude of finance needed and because of the financial complexities of managing a world-wide operation, need to rely more and more on the services of the multinational banks; banking networks offering complete "in-house" service efficiently in virtually all of the client's countries of operations?

J.K. Galbraith in his book *American Capitalism* wrote: "As the banker, as a symbol of economic power, passed into the shadows, his place was taken over by the great industrial corporations". Because money is homogeneous (the flow can be restricted but the ultimate impact is the same regardless of currency), the evolving multinational banking systems could well financially match or surpass the largest of industrial multinationals.

What will be the social role of the emerging multinational banks?

153

Presently, the essential element of any "world-wide banking system" is a network of overseas banking branches. Some banks, in addition to having a global network of branches, are now busy establishing a network of international merchant banks. I believe such networks will remain, in the foreseeable future, as an essential ingredient but will be greatly rationalized through computorization and telecommunication advances.

How useful is a branch network to a multinational treasurer? Paul Ferris in *The Money Men of Europe* writes that he was told by a senior finance officer of a major multinational "that a lot of the talk about international giants of industry needing international giants of banking was rubbish". Ferris quotes the senior finance officer as saying: "The multinational company has to spread its favours, partly because of its size, partly to make itself politically agreeable to as many countries as possible, and so it uses dozens of banks". "As an international organization you can only operate as a *good careful citizen*".

Is the above a prevalent attitude? At a multinational banking seminar, the treasurer of an equally large multinational company said: "The world-wide branch network of an international bank can be an extremely effective treasury tool for us. It is our normal policy to maximise banking competition by using both indigenous and international banks."

Is the issue really one of "good citizenship", as is implied in the first finance officer's comments? With justification, he believes his firm has a unique product or service to offer the various host countries. Why can't the branch(es) of the multinational bank equally serve a useful economic function?

Just recently, while soliciting the business of an overseas subsidiary of one major multinational, we discovered that the local bank took almost two weeks to transfer remittances from the host country to the company's main bank in the United Kingdom. We found we could reduce the transfer time to about two days. An account was opened with us for transferring funds. A few weeks later the local bank agreed to become competitive and transfer funds equally as efficiently, but strongly urged that the account with us be closed. Our account was closed. While we lost the local business, the multinational company now receives more efficient banking services in that country. However, because we are multinational, the customer tried us in another country, this time on a local financing transaction. In the latter country the local bank failed to respond to the competitive challenge, and now we both share the banking. The relationship with this particular multinational firm was virtually nil several years ago. Now we are one of its main international bankers. Like so many firms, the company finds it makes sense to use *both* indigenous and international banks—competition can be a wonderful force!

154

Can anyone seriously doubt whether the internationalization of banking, whether by European, Japanese or American banks, has made banking more efficient, more competitive? Isn't this also being "a good citizen"?

Borrower's financial statements, "Cash-Flow" forecasts, guaranteeing subsidiary bank debt, and other such "Red Tape"... (at least in some treasurer's view)

About a year ago a wholly owned subsidiary of a major company sought a multi-million dollar loan from one of our overseas branches. The local subsidiary had a highly leveraged (geared) debt/worth ratio. The parent company, believing the group's reputation was sufficient for our purposes, was unwilling to guarantee the subsidiary's loan. In effect, we were being asked to make available depositors funds in lieu of shareholders funds.

Another company's subsidiary sought credit from us, but said the subsidiary's balance sheet was unavailable ("no other bank required the subsidiary's financial statements"). Again, we were being asked to lend on the reputation of the group.

Many of you are familiar with the reasoning behind some corporation treasurers' reluctance to provide the "red tape" which prudent banks must request; i.e. our company would "never let their bankers down", "It is a relationship of trust", "we could not afford to damage our credit standing", etc.

Two points especially interest me. First, there are a few treasurers who seem to forget trust goes both ways. They want the banker to have faith in the moral responsibleness of the company's management, and yet they will not entrust the banker with the company's financial statements.

More seriously, the rather general "relationship of trust" may be causing bankers and treasurers to engage in some unsound financial practices from their's and society's point of view. Because of competitive factors, treasurers of major companies have been able to obtain finance without providing the borrower's balance sheets, used depositors funds where equity funds properly belong, forced rates lower than the risk warrants, etc. I do not fault the treasurer—in his shoes I would probably attempt to do the same thing.

However, are we both perhaps unwittingly contributing to an atmosphere of financial imprudence which may eventually result in rather significant financial imbroglios? What happens when the directors have a different opinion from the treasurer on the company's moral obligation to its bankers? What about shareholders' attitudes? What happens when the treasurer is gone?

Recently, the chief finance officer of one of our major multinational clients told me he was equally disturbed about the unwritten "credit understandings" the overseas companies and the parent had with its many bankers. The top management and directors of his company firmly believed that they had a moral obligation to stand behind *all* the bank obligations of the group's wholly owned companies. Over the years this "commitment" had crystalized the company's bankers' minds.

What in fact was happening was that the banks felt rather "risk free" on obligations which the holding company was no longer in a position to underwrite because of a rapidly changing *political* environment. On the other hand, the banks were charging affiliates (where the company had minority shareholdings, but effective control) "very high rates", relative to what the multinational parent would itself pay, in cases where for *commercial* reasons, the multinational firm had strong incentives to keep the borrower(s) viable. In neither situation did reality correspond with the "understood" objectives of the multinational company's management.

Wouldn't the corporate treasurer's, the banker's, and society's interests be better served by a greater exchange of financial information between corporations and financial intermediaries, and more preciseness in credit relationships?

Part V

*Multinational corporations and national
monetary and financial policies*

Chapter XI

MULTINATIONAL ENTERPRISES AND DOMESTIC CAPITAL FORMATION

by *John H. Dunning*

I. *Introduction*

This paper will be mainly concerned with the impact of multinational enterprises[1] on the generation of real capital formation and on the application of macro-economic policy in countries which are hosts to their affiliates.

We have chosen to focus attention on the capital formation of multinational enterprises for two reasons. The first is that the long-term economic effects of multinational enterprises derive from their control of *all* the resources in their possession, irrespective of how these are sourced.[2] In the last decade, the proportion of net capital formation of American affiliates in both Canada and Europe financed from direct investment inflows has steadily fallen and is now around 40 per cent. and 25 per cent. respectively; in the period 1957/60, the proportion of plant and equipment expenditures by US foreign manufacturing affiliates financed by savings from the US was 35 per cent., by 1967/70 it had fallen to 22 per cent.* However much foreign direct investment may act as a catalyst to the recipient country's capital formation, and whatever the short-term significance of financial flows for the balance of payments may be, the last twenty years of increasing capital controls (Cairncross, 1973) have coincided with a steady growth of the foreign activities of multinational enterprises[3]. This suggests that their real distinctiveness

---

1. Defined simply as an enterprise which owns and controls income generating assets in more than one country.

2. Polk (1971) defines international production as "production in which management and financing provided by one country (or countries) work together with factors of production of other countries" or "production emanating from foreign direct investment".

3. Polk (1971) has estimated that in 1970, output financed by foreign direct investment, i.e., the foreign production of multinational enterprises accounted for about 15 per cent. of gross world production and is currently increasing at the rate of 8 per cent. a year—twice the rate of growth of the non-international production.

---

* Since this paper was written, a report by the United States Tariff Commission has been published which gives details of the financing of investment by United States affiliates' activities 1966 and 1970. These are presented in Table 1.

Table 1
Estimated fund flow of United States-owned multinational corporation affiliates abroad 1966-1970 (cumulative)

	(Amounts in billions of dollars) Amounts			Percent of total sources/uses		
	All industries	All manufacturing	Other	All industries	All manufacturing	Other
Sources of Funds:						
Depreciation, depletion, and related charges	26.0	13.9	12.1	20	26	16
Net income of affiliates after taxes	42.1	14.8	27.3	32	27	36
Net affiliate borrowing outside the United States[1]	34.1	18.7	15.4	26	35	20
Net capital flow from parents to affiliates	21.3	6.5	14.8	16	12	20
Unallocated[2]	6.2	-0-	6.2	6	-0-	8
Total sources	129.7	53.9	75.8	100	100	100
Uses of funds:						
Investment in new plant and equipment	51.2	24.8	26.4	39	46	35
Remittances of dividends and[3] branch profits to parents	21.3	6.1	15.2	16	11	20
Increase in non-fixed assets	57.2	23.0	34.2	44	43	45
Total uses	129.7	53.9	75.8	100	100	100

to host countries lies in the "foreignness" not of their capital, but of other resources, including managerial control.

The second reason is allied to the first. If there is a single feature which marks out direct from portfolio capital flows, it is that the former is almost always part of a package of income-generating assets made available to the borrowing country, while the latter simply consists of loanable funds or savings. Indeed, it is the other ingredients of the package (technology, management, entrepreneurship, access to markets, etc.) which makes direct investment so welcome to host countries, and enables foreign affiliates to compete effectively with indigenous firms. This being so, there is much to be said for adopting Irving Fisher's interpretation of capital as any income-generating assets, and investments as anything which augments these assets.[4] When related to the activities of multinational enterprises, capital then consists of all forms of assets which are capable of generating a flow of income; *inter alia*, these include the stock of material assets, of productive knowledge and of human skills. Again, while the way in which the latter two components are financed may be important in analysing their effects on the economy in which

4. See also Johnson (1968).

NOTES AND SOURCES FOR CASH FLOW TABLE (Table 1)

Notes:
(1) Net of borrowings used to liquidate liabilities to foreigners, and excluding foreign borrowing by parents.

(2) A principal item here consists of sales, retirements and similar disposals of fixed assets—the remaining component of internally-generated funds besides retained earnings and depreciation/depletion charges. The cumulative value of this item, comparable to the $6.2 billion "unallocated" amount shown, is conservatively estimated at $4.0 billion. Allocation of this amount has not been made because data are not available for its two components: sales of fixed assets, the net proceeds of which should have appeared in the income statements as extraordinary income (non-operating income); and ordinary write-offs (retirements), which are not reflected in net income. The former of these components, to the extent that it has importance, already is reflected in the "net income" source of funds. The latter, however, cannot be specifically identified and allocated.

(3) Excludes estimated interest remittances to parents. While relevant for measuring balance of payments flows, interest remittances are entered as costs in income statements, with the result that these remittances should already be reflected in the "net income" source of funds above, as deductions from that source.

Sources: United States Tariff Commission *'Implications of multinational firms for World trade and investment and for US trade and labor'* United States Government Printing Office, Washington, 1973.

Based on data for 1966 and 1970 supplied by United States Department of Commerce, Bureau of Economic Analysis, International Investment Division; and supplemented by information from *Survey of Current Business*, September 1971 and October 1971.

they are used—e.g. whether management expertise is imported or locally supplied—it is the total capital formation with which we shall be concerned.

The paper proceeds in the following way. Section II outlines the distinctive characteristics of multinational enterprises (or their affiliates), compared with (a) other generators of international capital flows, (b) national enterprises which are multi-plant, or engage in international activities abroad not involving a capital stake and (c) indigenous companies which compete with the affiliates of multinational enterprises in host countries. Section III examines how far these distinctive characteristics help explain the contribution of multinational enterprises to investment flows and capital formation in host countries. Section IV discusses the effects of government policy in host countries on the capital formation of affiliates of multinational enterprises. Section V is concerned with some broad macro-economic implications and with the consequences of the activities of multinational enterprises in three areas of particular interest to national and international economic policy.

II. *The multinational enterprise: its distinctive features*

Like a multi-plant national enterprise, the multinational enterprise owns income generating assets in more than one location: unlike it, it owns these in different sovereign states. Like a national firm engaged in international trade, it buys and sells goods and services across national boundaries; unlike it, its activities involve a capital stake, and much of its trade is not between independent economic agents at arms length prices, but between different parts of the same enterprise, at prices which will best serve the enterprises' interests. The behaviour and performance of its affiliates are likely to be different from those of indigenous firms, partly because, since they are part of a larger enterprise domiciled in another country, they are likely to be truncated,[5] and partly, since they are part of an international network of activities, the opportunities for specialisation and nationalisation are that much greater.[6]

Although it might be argued that these differences with national enterprises are ones of degree rather than of kind, and largely reflect the fact that the world is divided into a number of sovereign states, they do confer a certain distinctiveness on the multinational enterprise, and its affiliates. The

5. A truncated firm has been defined as "one which does not carry out all the functions—from the original research required through to all aspects of marketing—necessary for developing, producing and marketing its goods" (Gray, 1973, p. 405).

6. These opportunities may also be available to home based multinational enterprises. Similarly, the principle of truncation applies to all branch operations of a multi-plant firm, whether it is an multinational enterprise or not.

extent and character of this distinctiveness[7] will vary according to the industry(ies) and country(ies) in which it operates and its organisational logistics. But wherever it occurs, the response of multinational enterprises and their affiliates to the economic environment, or changes in that environment, will be, to some extent, different from that of other firms.

Because of this, and also because part of the output generated by affiliates in one country will accrue to the residents of other countries, both the international allocation of resources and the distribution of output will be affected. Since the operating objectives of affiliates will be geared to those of the enterprises of which they are part, rather than those of their adopted countries in which they operate, clashes with host governments over some aspects of their behaviour will inevitably occur. These clashes will be the greater, *inter alia*, the more a country pursues a policy of economic nationalism, the more the activities of multinational enterprises are the result of market imperfections, e.g., barriers to trade in goods, over- or under-valued exchange rates, and the greater the differences in incentives and/or penalties exerted by countries, which cause multinational enterprises to shift resources, or claims to resources, from one country to another.

Like trade, free capital movements, particularly when accompanied by productive knowledge and access to markets, will tend to raise the level of world output, wherever market conditions are competitive. The main costs are those which arise from the reallocation of resources to changing demand and supply conditions, i.e., disturbance costs, and the possible adverse effects on the distribution of income (both within and between countries). Within a nation state, instabilities and inequities caused by national firms operating in different parts of the country can, at least, be partly mitigated by the appropriate national fiscal or monetary policies. There is no institution which can perform this kind of rôle in an international context.[8]

The effect on international capital flows and capital formation of multinational enterprises will also depend on their organisational and financial strategies. There are many of these which could be pursued (Perlmutter, 1969) but, for the purpose of this paper, we shall simply distinguish between enterprises which treat their affiliates as *independent* operating units, in which there is a minimum of intra-group trade in either goods or services, and those in which the affiliates are *interdependent* units, geared to a global production and marketing policy, and between which (and the parent company) there may be a good deal of buying and selling.

---

7. Most of the literature tends to stress the advantages of distinctiveness (see particularly the Gray and Tariff Commission reports, *op. cit.*) but in some cases multinational enterprises or their affiliates may be at an operating disadvantage cf. national enterprises or indigenous firms, e.g., with respect to access to local capital markets (see, e.g. Manser, 1973).

8. See p. 182 for an extension of this argument.

163

We conclude. The distinctiveness of the multinational enterprise as an economic phenomenon arises because it owns and uses income generating assets in different nation states; its special impact on the world economy follows from this, and its ability to acquire and exploit both resources and markets better than can national firms. Its unique contribution to the countries in which it invests arises from this flexibility and the foreign technology, capital and management it makes available. At the same time, the behaviour of its affiliates will be geared to the goals of the parent company; this may mean, in some cases, their operations will be deliberately limited in scope and potential, or simply be a replica of those of the parent company (Gray, 1973), the social cost of which to host countries e.g., in terms of reduced opportunities for local resources, may be considerable. At the same time, the contribution of multinational enterprises, or their affiliates, may be strongly influenced by the policies pursued by national governments, and cannot be properly assessed without also considering what would have occurred in their absence.

III. *The determinants of capital formation by multinational enterprises and their affiliates*

There are various approaches one could adopt to this subject, and which one chooses largely depends on the precise question one is seeking to answer. The first approach we shall consider in this paper is that of the international economist who is primarily interested in capital *flows*. Here one takes the standard models of international *portfolio* capital flows, which relate the supply of funds to interest-rate differentials (or changes in interest rates) or to the yields of real investment (or changes in yields), both appropriately discounted for risk, and then attempts to see how far these can explain the supply of direct investment by multinational enterprises or capital formation of multinational enterprises.[9] The answer is that, very often, they cannot, partly because the value of a direct investment is assessed by its long term contribution to the investing enterprise *as a whole*, of which the earnings of a particular affiliate may be an unimportant part, e.g. as in the case of some horizontally and vertically integrated investments, and partly because one of the basic determinants of foreign direct investment is the expectancy that affiliates can perform better than indigenous companies in host countries. This suggests that while long-term portfolio capital will normally move across national boundaries to those sectors in the borrowing country, which have a higher yield than their counterparts in the lending country, direct investment

9. For a discussion of alternative theories of international capital movements, see W.H. Branson and R.D. Hill. *Capital movements in the OECD area: an econometric analysis*, OECD, 1971.

will flow to those sectors of the host country in which the *investing* country has an *overall* competitive advantage, but which can produce or partly produce goods more cheaply than can the investing country. Much of the work of economists concerned with direct investment has been directed to identifying and evaluating the form of these advantages and the reasons for them. We shall return to this point later.

The second approach is more micro-oriented and stems from the theory of investment behaviour of *firms*. There are two variants of this approach. The first, which represents the main stream of research to date, has been to extend models of the domestic investment behavior of firms to explain either the capital formation of the affiliates of multinational enterprises or that part of it financed by the investing firm.[10] Almost all the empirical work has been based upon data of the plant and equipment expenditure of United States affiliates abroad, or that part of their total investment financed from United States sources, including the reinvested profits of the affiliates. The second variant has had very little attention in the literature. It concerns the extent to which models of investment behaviour by indigenous firms can be used to explain the behaviour of investment by foreign affiliates in similar industries.

(a) *The capital formation of multinational enterprises*

Broadly speaking, there have been two groups of the first type of study—the *investing* country approach. The first is illustrated by the work of Stevens (1969 and 1971), Severn (1971) and Popkin (1965) and other writers.[11] Severn, for example, used a neoclassical, two country, model (the United States and the rest of the world) to explain both differences in the specification of domestic and foreign investment functions of firms, and the distribution of corporate funds between home and foreign uses. He concluded that subject to a liquidity constraint, the accelerator type models gave the best answers in both cases. He also found that multinational enterprises allocated funds without reference to national boundaries and that, eliminating factors common to both foreign and domestic investment, the two were at least partially substitutable for each other and inter-related through the financing mechanism. Popkin, in his study of United States manufacturing affiliates (1965), also asserted that the relative profit rates and other financial variables were more important than market structure and technological variables in explaining variations in their investment behaviour. Stevens (1971), using similar data, and an extension of the Modigliani-Miller (1954) theorem,

10. Sometimes, too, comparisons are made between multinational enterprises and firms only engaged in domestic activities. See Vaupel (1971).
11. These are summarised in a more recent paper by Stevens (1973). See, too, J.H. Dunning (1973b) from which the following two paragraphs are derived.

derived equations which, *inter alia*, related plant and equipment expenditure to the maximisation of the market value of firms, and also financial flows to the same goal and that of exchange loss minimisation. He found that all equations explaind past data quite well.

Most of the research just mentioned accepts that there are certain determinants of the foreign capital formation of multinational enterprises which are unique to such firms, and the second group of studies has attempted to identify these to explain the growth of United States direct investment in Western Europe since the mid-1950s. The writings of Bandera and White (1968), d'Arge (1970), Scaperlanda (1967), Wallis (1968), Scaperlanda and Mauer (1969) and Krause (1968) are examples of this approach. Most of these, using either time series or cross sectional data, relate either absolute values of United States investment (or capital stake) to profit rates, size of markets, growth of markets, tariff rates and some kind of trend and/or slope shifting variable; the Bandera and White study included an international liquidity variable. The cross-sectional studies very clearly show that the capital stake of United States affiliates has risen most in those countries which have recorded fastest rates of growth of G.N.P., with profitability and other variables, including tariffs, the formation of the E.E.C. being of secondary importance.[12, 13] The time series data lend support to these conclusions particularly when the capital stake is taken as the dependent variable (Bandera and White, 1968). Again, in all cases, the market variable showed up better than the profit rate.

As an explanation of the distribution of investment by multinational enterprises between home and foreign activities where these are *independent* of each other, these studies are generally acceptable; where, however, their activities are *interdependent* they are less convincing. This is because they tend both to assume the goals of affiliates are synonomous with those of the investing firms, and to focus attention on the income stream of the former, rather than that of the latter of which they are part. The profit variable is a key example. Assuming the aim of investment by multinational enterprises is to maximise their post-tax profits, it does not follow this objective will be achieved by maximising profits of each and every affiliate. There are three obvious reasons for this. The first is that where tax rates are different between countries, a £'s worth of income earned in a high tax country is worth less than the same income earned in a low tax country. The second is wherever the activities of one part of the multinational enterprise affect the profits earned by another part, the profits of the first part will understate or

12. A exception is that of Krause (1968) who argues that there is some relationship between indices of plant and equipment expenditure by United States firms in the EEC in different industries and the common external tariff.

13. On the impact of the EEC opinions differ somewhat: compare, for example, the approach of Scaperlanda (1967) and d'Arge (1969).

overstate its contribution to the group; export-replacing investment is a case in point. The third is that profits may inadequately measure the worthwhileness of affiliates, such as where investment leads to the feedback of technical knowhow, or gives access to markets and/or raw materials, or where income is remitted in other forms, e.g., interest, royalities, fees, etc. or via intra-group transactions at above or below arms length prices.

These possibilities are most obvious in the case of horizontally or vertically integrated multinational enterprises as they have more opportunity for shifting income to the place from where it is earned to where it is taxed the least. Investment by United States companies in Taiwan to supply the United States market with TV sets is not motivated by the size of the Taiwan market; this is no less true of the vertical specialisation by IBM in the European market or the auto companies in the Latin American market. But, in principle, the issue arises not primarily because a firm is multinational but because it is multi-plant, and it is difficult to identify goals of plants without reference to those of the firm of which they are part.

The above discussion suggests that the determinants of capital flows or capital formation is as much a question of location theory as corporate investment theory. For while the latter may help to establish the *level* of investment (for this is primarily a question of the marginal efficiency of capital, related to size of market and structure of input prices and productivity), the former is necessary to explain where that investment is located, i.e., its geographical distribution.[14]

(b) *The capital formation of the affiliates of the multinational enterprises*

This brings us to the second variant of the approach to micro-investment studies. From the viewpoint of the policy of *host* countries towards foreign investment, it is less important to know the differences in the factors influencing the behaviour of multinational enterprises at home and abroad, or between multinational enterprises and indigenous firms in *investing* countries, as those which influence the behaviour of affiliates of the multinational enterprises in host countries with those of their indigenous competitors.

Received theory suggests that the level of real corporate investment is a function of the cost and availability of loanable funds and the marginal efficiency of capital. In turn, the marginal efficiency of capital is determined, *inter alia*, by the productivity of the investing firms, the prices of inputs, other than loanable funds, and the market for the products the investment helps to produce. Similarly, changes in capital stock will be governed by the sensitivity of investment to changes in the values of these variables,

14. Indeed, the techniques to appraise alternative investment projects can easily be applied to appraise the same investment project in alternative locations.

and the extent of these changes. Host governments, through their ability to affect both the conditions under which loanable funds are supplied and the marginal efficiency of capital of firms, e.g., by fiscal or exchange rate policy, can obviously influence capital formation and its financing.

But to what extent is the marginal efficiency of capital of affiliates of multinational enterprises or the price they have to pay for loanable funds likely to be different from that of indigenous firms? Even a cursory examination of the literature reveals that not only is production financed by direct foreign investment rising more rapidly than the increase in world output and trade (Polk, 1971), but this production has certain characteristics.

Vaupel (1971) has shown that, relative to national enterprises, multinational enterprises tend to concentrate in research intensive industries, in those with diversified product structures and above average advertising budgets, and in those which export an above average proportion of their output. Similarly, relative to indigenous firms, the affiliates of multinational enterprises tend to be most active in these same industries, particularly where the locational advantages of production favour the host country. In a recent study of American affiliates in forty United Kingdom industries, it was found that their participation ratios[15] varied from 89.5 per cent. to 0.3 per cent. around an average of 12.9 per cent. (Dunning, 1973(a)). In general, the higher the ratio, the greater the distinctive advantages of the affiliates relative to indigenous firms. Such advantages might take various forms; a better product; superior technology or management; access to inputs at lower (or subsidised) prices, and so on. The ability to acquire loanable funds both from other parts of the organisation or from external markets, sometimes at lower interest rates, may also be important.[16] The market for the goods produced by affiliates may be wider than that of domestic companies, although this will partly depend on the extent to which they are allowed to exploit these markets by their parent companies. Where barriers to trade are negligible or where it is more efficient to supply the market from elsewhere, the opportunity cost of a local investment may be high; where barriers are high, and production advantages favour the host country, local production will be preferred to imports.

The extent and share of capital formation in a particular country or industry by multinational enterprises, then, depends first on their comparative advantage (vis à vis indigenous firms) in acquiring those inputs (including knowledge) necessary to produce the output in question, and second on the comparative advantage of their affiliates in that country (vis à vis their parent companies or other affiliates) to undertake the production or part of the production process. These conditions also explain the growth of such invest-

15. Defined as the share of the gross output a particular industry accounted for by United States affiliates.
16. Because of the truncated activities of the affiliates.

ment, although as the participation of foreign firms increases, so will the barriers to entry facing indigenous firms.

The level of capital formation by multinational enterprises in any one country will also be related to the *type* of operations which it is desired to exploit. Even for an multinational enterprise operating independent affiliates, the choice is usually not between producing the whole of the output of a product from one location or another, but between producing an increase in output from one location or another. It is the capital formation necessary to produce this extra output which is in question, and this, unless costs are sharply increasing, will be less than the capital formation per unit of product, because of certain fixed costs, incurred on behalf of the group, which are located elsewhere, usually at the group's headquarters. On the other hand, a multinational enterprise might choose to locate part of its group capital formation, e.g., R & D, in one of its foreign affiliates. Several United States firms, for example, have centralised their European administrative and R & D activities in a single European country.

In between, there will be a whole spectrum of activities which will be determined by locational factors and the logistics of the multinational enterprise. An interdependent multinational enterprise which specialises vertically or horizontally will engage in the capital formation appropriate to that activity to which it is best suited. These activities will not necessarily be substitutes for imports. They will be conducted on the ordinary principles of location theory—i.e., given the level of demand, a profit maximising firm will choose a location which will minimise total costs. *Inter alia*, this would suggest that multinational enterprises should concentrate labour intensive activities in areas of labour availability and/or low labour costs, and high capital intensive activities in areas of capital availability, and/or low capital costs. The extent of Government pressure on the activities of firms, and movement costs including tariffs, and competitor's behaviour may also be significant. But the evidence on the location of production and other activities of multinational enterprises does seem to support this proposition.

The effects of capital formation by the affiliates of multinational enterprises on particular industrial sectors has not received much attention in the literature, but one would suppose that these are not very different from those of the national multi-plant firm in a regional context. In general, one would expect a rather more concentrated output, in terms of ownership of assets, than would have occurred in their absence; this concentration tends to be associated with a greater capital intensity and more opportunity for the territorial specialisation of product and processes. In response to a situation which reflects the free play of market resources, the mobility of capital leads to higher efficiency; where it is the result of imperfections, e.g., import controls, non-tariff barriers, differential taxes, etc., this need not be the case.

169

IV. *Capital formation of multinational enterprises and Government policy*

Having outlined some of the main factors which will determine the share of capital formation in particular countries or industries accounted for by affiliates of foreign multinational enterprises, we now consider the extent to which their response to changes in the value of these factors will be different from that of indigenous firms. To narrow our discussion, we shall focus attention on three areas of any host government's policy, viz., monetary, fiscal and exchange rate policy, and we shall further distinguish between two effects of a change in policy, the first being the initial responsiveness of affiliates and the second the effect on their competitive position.

Since we have suggested that affiliates of multinational enterprises *do* possess distinctive characteristics vis à vis indigenous firms, there is a strong presumption that their reactions to changes in policies affecting their investment behaviour will be different. But in what way? Will they be more or less responsive to e.g. movements in interest rates, changes in corporation tax, regional subsidies, capital grants and so on? Let us consider these questions in relation to four major ways in which affiliates of multinational enterprises differ from indigenous firms, after normalising for structural differences, e.g., capacity utilisation, size and industrial composition, these are:

(1) their activities will be determined by what is best not for themselves but for the enterprise of which they are part;

(2) their operations will almost certainly be truncated to some degree or another;

(3) they have access to the resources, notably knowledge and managerial expertise, well beyond those which they can generate themselves, and usually at lower or subsidised cost; and

(4) because they operate in different national markets, their opportunities for sourcing inputs, location of production units, and access to markets are that much greater, as are those for moving resources across national boundaries *within* the firm.

With these points in mind, consider, first, the possible effects on the capital formation of affiliates of multinational enterprises of an increase in the rate of interest on loanable funds in the host country. Will they react more or less noticeably than indigenous firms? It is difficult to give a generalised answer, as there are forces working in both directions. On the one hand, affiliates may find it easier than indigenous firms to obtain capital from other sources outside the host country (e.g., from their parent companies or the Euro-dollar market). This suggests that while they will be *more* interest responsive in their demand for loanable funds from sources, in the host country they will be *less* interest responsive in their capital formation. Their sensitivity will also be less where the elasticity of substitution between their capital and other inputs is less than that of indigenous firms (and there is reason to

170

suppose this may be so in capital-intensive industries) or the elasticity of demand for their finished products is lower. In this latter case, it is the nature of the export market which is crucial; here, one might suppose that because of their specialised character, intra-group exports would have a relatively inelastic demand, while independent exports might be more or less responsive, depending on the structure of the markets served.

On the other hand, what of the opportunities for supplying the market from alternative locations? A rise in domestic interest rates in one country, adds to the cost of production in that country relative to elsewhere. This obviously reduces the attraction of the first country as a locational base. An indigenous company may have little option but to produce in that country a foreign based multinational enterprise may be less constrained. Where capital is mobile across the exchanges, it is unlikely to use this option; where this is not the case or affiliates adopt an "every tub on its own bottom" type financial policy, then a capital intensive firm, faced with a high elasticity of demand for its finished product may well respond to an increase in interest rates by switching its investment elsewhere, in which case the policy will be more effective than in the case of indigenous firms.

Depending on the balance of these forces, affiliates of multinational enterprises are likely to increase or lower their market share of capital formation relatively to indigenous companies. Our impression is that in the United Kingdom at least, they have strengthened their competitive position, mainly due to the greater opportunities to obtain capital from other sources, at times of domestic credit restraint, and that on other grounds, too, their interest sensitivity (in respect of capital formation) is less than that of indigenous firms.

Table 2 illustrates some possible effects of other types of domestic policy measures intended either to induce or curtail the level of capital spending or to affect its pattern. Most of these operate through making it more or less costly for firms to borrow money; but some operate, indirectly, through their effect on the demand for the finished product. Exchange rate changes, in general, have had wider purposes in view.

How far will affiliates of multinational enterprises react differently to such changes, compared with indigenous firms? The incidence of a change in corporation tax cannot easily be shifted by indigenous firms; but by various devices (e.g. by transfer price manipulation, including prices charged for services of intra-group transactions) affiliates may be able to shift the earnings of pre-tax income from the higher tax country to elsewhere where tax rates are lower.[17] Alternatively, they may be better placed to convert their equity into debt capital. On the other hand, since net profits after tax have now been

17. Effectively by increasing costs in the high tax country and increasing revenue elsewhere in the system.

Table 2

Response of affiliates of multinational enterprises, relative to those of indigenous firms, to selected changes in policy on capital spending

	Elasticity of substitution		Location of new investment	Likely effect on total costs	Elasticity of demand for product		Net effect on distinctive advantage (vis à vis indigenous firms)
	Capital from other sources	Other factor inputs			Intra-group trade (cf. all exports)	Others	
(a) Monetary policy							
Increase in rate of interest	More, leading to less effect on capital formation	?	more	less	less	?	more
Reduction in availability of credit	"	less	more	less	less	less	more
(b) Fiscal policy							
Increase in corporation tax	no effect		more	?	less	?	?
Increase in consumer credit (in UK)	no effect	more	?	?	no effect	?	?
Increase in investment allowances	no effect	more	more	more	less	?	more
(c) Exchange rate policy							
Pre devaluation	more	more	more	?	more	?	more
Post devaluation	more	more	more	less	less	?	less

172

reduced relative to those which might be earned in other locations, an affiliate might be tempted to shift new investment (or even existing investment) elsewhere.[18]

This same flexibility makes affiliates more sensitive to changes in investment incentives of one kind or another; several surveys (McCleese, 1972; Forsyth, 1973; Dunning and Yannapoulos, 1973) have emphasised the importance of financial inducements by countries, or regions within countries, as important factors influencing the location of United States manufacturing affiliates to supply markets in Western Europe, and to the extent that the options open to multinational enterprises are more than those available to national firms, one would expect a greater sensivity to such inducements. This would certainly seem to have been believed by some of the less prosperous regions in Europe in recent years, who have made extensive use of fiscal incentives to attract new United States capital, though whether this has had very much effect on the total amount of United States investment in Europe, is doubtful. The claim has been made that Europe has been subsidising United States investors to do what they would have been doing in any case! To the extent that affiliates tend to be more capital intensive than indigenous firms, capital grants will benefit them more; on the other hand, regional employment premiums may have the opposite effect.

Efforts to stimulate or retard investment by operating on consumers' expenditure may also have discriminatory effects. As a group, multinational enterprises tend to supply products with a higher income elasticity of demand, and there is some evidence that their profits are more susceptible to cyclical fluctuations than those of indigenous companies. On the other hand, since they often export a higher proportion of their output (Dunning, 1973 (a); Hirsch, 1973) an increase in domestic spending will have rather less effect. The effect on capital spending of an exchange rate change may be less marked than with indigenous firms, as a fairly substantial percentage of both imports and exports of affiliates tend to be intragroup, and hence price inelastic. Moreover, multinational enterprises tend to operate in oligopolistic markets where prices are often insensitive and where world markets are divided between individual affiliates the opportunities of any one affiliate for exploiting competitive advantage might be blunted. At the same time, this inelasticity would emphasise that affiliates, particularly those of integrated concerns, are *more* susceptible to changes in economic conditions *outside* the host country, including policy changes of other governments, than are indigenous firms.

We conclude. The level and structure of capital formation of affiliates in particular industries in host countries will be different from that of indige-- nous firms for various reasons, which are partly to do with their competitive-

18. There is some evidence to suggest that corporate tax rates do affect the geographical location of investments (see Mellors, 1973).

ness, partly to do with the nature of their operations, and partly to do with their greater opportunities (or those of the group of which they are part) for moving goods and services (including capital and entrepreneurship) across national boundaries. These factors explain why the shape of investment functions will differ from those of indigenous firms and that the nature and/or extent of this difference will depend on the type of policy instruments introduced. Some of the macro-implications of these differences will be explored in the final section of this paper.

V. *Macro-economic implications*

The *total* capital formation of a country depends very much on the national economic management policy pursued by the Government. But clearly, multinational enterprises do have some impact on the formation and direction of this policy and its success. This they can do in two ways. First, by the way in which their capital is financed and, in particular, the extent to which it is obtained from outside the country of expenditure. Second, by the indirect or multiplier effects of capital formation by multinational enterprises on the capital formation of suppliers, competitors and customers.

Once again, there are no generalised answers to these questions. Apart from the extent to which there is capacity of capital and labour at the time the initial investment is being made, whether capital formation by multinational enterprises augment a country's stock of capital will vary with circumstances. Most import substituting production will increase the demand for indigenous capital goods as the new output need not replace domestic output; by contrast, if inward investment, however financed, is spent on imports of equipment, domestic capital formation may be less than it might be. The implications of an investment to finance a take-over are different from those of setting up a 'green field' venture; an investment to supply a completely new product will have a different effect than one to replace an existing product. According to how capital is sourced and spent, the implications for planned savings and planned investment will be different.

Such data as are available from a variety of case studies suggest multinational enterprises and their affiliates are strongly concentrated in capital intensive industries; that in these industries, their affiliates' operations tend to be more capital intensive than those of indigenous firms; and that, initially, their products neither replace imports nor are destined for markets that otherwise would be served by other parts of the organisation. The proportion of imports of capital equipment varies between industries, but it is not noticeably higher than that of indigenous firms. On the other hand, the import of human and knowledge capital is almost certainly greater than that of indigenous firms.

174

Concerning the influence on the *supply* of capital, we have already said that only a small proportion of the capital formation of (United States) multinational enterprises is funded from capital imports; the greater part is self-financed through depreciation and profits. The balance is borrowed locally or internationally, noticeably from the Euro-dollar market. In terms of the *demand* for funds, the impact is fairly small, but this may have repercussions. Multinational enterprises have almost certainly increased the demand for indigenous knowledge or human skills in the countries in which they operate and, in some cases, this has affected the price for such inputs. As to the spillover effects of the presence of multinational enterprises on capital formation, much depends on the proportion of purchases bought locally and the extent to which capacity is being used efficiently. Competitors are stimulated wherever foreign firms bring higher price, technical or scale efficiency. These effects will be spread over time, as indeed will be the 'technological' multiplier effect (Quinn, 1968). This reinforces the normal Keynesian multiplier effect and results from the improvement in productivity made possible by new innovations.

The other main effect on other capital formation arises from the character of the operations of affiliates of multinational enterprises. Here the argument is sometimes put that multinational enterprises do not create income generating assets of the right kind and that they may even reduce a country's ability to create income for itself, by forcing it to rent capital. This is directed particularly to knowledge capital. There are two versions of this contention. One is that foreign firms somehow prevent host countries from developing their true economic potential; this is a variant of the infant industry argument, but arises out of the monopoly power which multinational enterprises are said to possess over (de novo) local competitors. It suggests that the system for the dissemination of knowledge is not that which maximises dynamic comparative advantage. The second version is based on the assertion that either the country does not get a fair distribution of the output created by the operations of multinational enterprises, or it prefers to be in control of its income-generating ability, even if this should result in a lower income than it might earn as a hirer of capital.

VI. *The effects of capital formation*

There are certain features about capital flows of multinational enterprises common to those of all capital movements. In a world free of imperfections, capital movements between independent lenders and borrowers perform the same function as movements in goods and services and will lead to a more efficient allocation of the world's resources and increase real output. The same applies to capital formation, given the appropriate macro-economic con-

175

ditions. On the other hand, we have argued that capital movements and formation by multinational enterprises are differently generated from those of portfolio investment, and chiefly arise not because the recipient country is short of savings, but of the other ingredients of the package of factor inputs which multinational enterprises provide. To the extent that there are costs to the transmission of productive knowledge, multinational enterprises, by helping to produce domestically goods which would otherwise have to be imported at a higher price, are *ceteris paribus*, increasing allocative efficiency. Whether or not this could be better dealt with by devising alternative methods of compensating the producers of knowledge is another matter (Johnson, 1971). Moreover, to the extent that multinational enterprises help countries to exploit better their full economic potential, they may be fulfilling the principle of comparative advantage. Certainly, too, by their ability to buy inputs more cheaply and their access to wider markets than those available to indigenous firms, they may again make for a better deployment of resources.[19]

The issues become more complicated in other than static competitive conditions and where multinational enterprises are involved. While tariff barriers might induce portfolio capital movements which could either mitigate or worsen the adverse effects of the barriers; the effects are even more uncertain with direct investment, where the tariff might induce the mobility of human capital and productive knowledge as well. On the other hand, where a tariff is imposed to counteract monopoly power or to encourage the more efficient deployment of resources, which in the long run conform to dynamic comparative advantage, then the operations of multinational enterprises (which are essentially concerned with private rather than social ends and cannot be expected to invest in developmental infrastructure) might be to the advantage of host countries. Similarly, differential fiscal penalties or incentives will not only have the usual effects on the flows of capital between independent parties; they will also cause multinational enterprises which engage in intra-company trade, to practise tax deferral or tax avoidance devices, which may or may not improve allocative efficiency, but will certainly have implications for the distribution of income. A fixed exchange rate, like any other price pegging device, will also induce a different type of response from multinational enterprises compared with that of portfolio investors, especially again where substantial intra-group transactions make it possible for firms to shift funds across national boundaries to suit their needs. Finally, the whole gamut of national government controls, except those which are designed to cure market imperfections, will cause a more marked reaction by multinational enterprises and, again, these may not always be in the same direction as in the case of portfolio flows.

19. Assuming they are allowed to exploit these markets.

176

It would be far beyond the reach of this paper to examine all the effects of the capital formation of multinational enterprises. For the remaining space available I propose to concentrate on three areas of interest—(a) national economic management, (b) inflation, and (c) distribution of income.

(a) *National economic management*

Perhaps the most widespread argument used by governments against multinational enterprises or their affiliates is that they make the task of economic management more difficult. The complaints are most vocal from insulated and socialist-type economies or from countries where multinational enterprises have a substantial share of the capital formation in key industries; and they are directed particularly to large multinational enterprises which are interdependent in their operations, and engage in substantial intra-group trading.

The reason for this concern is little different in principle from any other from of open-ness to which an economy might be subject, be it international trade or the integration of financial markets. Open-ness implies interdependence both of economic fortune and disaster. Where an economy can easily and speedily adjust to such open-ness, the costs involved might not be great; but rarely is this the case today, and the costs of interdependence may be substantial.

In discussing the effects of capital movements on national economic management, it is important to distinguish between the cause of these movements, i.e., whether they are endogenous or exogenous, and whether they are in response to movements in interest rates or in expectancy of higher profits (Johnson, 1966). Most of the standard analysis of the effects of capital movements has been to explain these in terms of response to or in anticipation of interest rate changes. Here it is generally accepted that international capital movements weaken domestic monetary policy under fixed exchange rates, although, by the same token, they may help to cure a short-run balance of payments situation. To protect their sovereignty, governments may take various measures ranging from outright prohibition of capital movements (usually exports but sometimes imports), to controlling access by foreign firms to domestic capital markets, or imposing special reserve requirements, to manipulating interest rates to make capital movements less worthwhile.

Many of these problems do not arise with flexible exchange rates, but, even here, capital movements generated by the expectancy of higher profits may reduce the leverage of monetary policy over income and employment, and, in many cases, much depends on expectancies of borrowers and lenders to changes in the interest rate, e.g., whether they expect any change to be permanent or not. On the other hand, a high mobility of portfolio investment, under fixed exchange rates, may increase the effectiveness of fiscal policy, as capital flows tend to eliminate the adverse monetary effects of fiscal policy and to reduce the change in foreign exchange reserves. Under flexible exchange rates, as shown by the experience of Canada in the 50's, (Caves and Reuber, 1971) fiscal policy can be undermined.

Similarly, free capital movements may affect exchange rate policy (Cooper, 1971). In the short run, this is demonstrated primarily by the extent of currency speculation in anticipation of exchange rate changes. In the long run, while exchange risk might inhibit capital flows, Aliber (1970) has shown that in a multiple currency system, this can work to increase the flow of foreign investment, particularly where a higher capitalisation rate is applied to an income earned by a foreign firm than by an indigenous firm. No less important is the effect such flows might have on monetary integration and feasible currency areas. Corden (1971) has suggested that such flows can only help solve the internal and external balance simultaneously in the short run. While monetary integration may end destabilising short-term capital movements, if the exchange rates of the countries within the area, relative to those outside, become more rigid, then destabilising capital movements could increase.

How does the introduction of the multinational enterprise affect these conclusions? Much of what has been said presupposes the existence of an international capital market. Multinational enterprises have most certainly enlarged this market in the last decade or more, particularly the Euro-dollar market, which has helped to finance a good deal of the expansion of such companies in Europe. This, indeed, has been an important source of external funds to multinational enterprises, as well as an outlet for European savings. At the same time, the existence of such a market, coupled with the particular ability and incentive of multinational enterprises speedily to take advantage of it—especially those which engage in international monetary management procedures—has considerably reduced the effectiveness of the monetary policies of individual European countries. This has meant that while, almost certainly, the growth of the international capital market has aided long-run economic development, it may have exacerbated the efforts of national Governments to maintain short-term monetary stability; moreover, because of their easier access to the Euro-dollar market, multinational enterprises—both domestic and foreign-owned—have been given additional competitive edge over national enterprises and this has enabled them further to increase their penetration of the local market.

But the main impact of the multinational enterprise arises from their income-mobility of capital,[20] and from their ability over indigenous firms to engage in internal transactions across national boundaries. Theoretically, the

20. Treating capital, here, in the Fisherian sense, and income the expected stream of benefits to the *investing enterprise*.

effects of income-mobility of capital are rather different from those of inter-est-mobile capital (Johnson, 1966). The former eases national economic management under a fixed exchange rate system, using either monetary or fiscal measures, but reduces the leverage under a floating rate system. More practically, the role of multinational enterprises is shown in a variety of ways. First, because they tend to export more than indigenous firms, fiscal policy is likely to affect their total activities rather less than might otherwise be the case. Second, because the transactions are internal to the company, the possibility of shifting funds from high tax to low tax countries for hedging or speculative purposes are that much greater, through the use of leads and lags. This latter flexibility (which has been demonstrated at various times in recent years) has most certainly led to pressure on weak exchange rates. The fact that this is a perfectly normal and reasonable thing for multinational enterprises (or any enterprise) to do and is a direct reflection of the way in which the international monetary system is organised does nothing to endear them to Governments. For authorities committed to the fixed exchange rates, this can be very disturbing, particularly when one remembers that the liquid assets controlled by multinational enterprises and similar institutions, estimated at the end of 1971 to be $268 billion—well over twice as large as total world reserves ($122 billion) [21] reflects *not* the cash flow which originated from abroad, but the totality of their operations.

Governments can and do respond to the activities of multinational enterprises in the areas just discussed in a number of ways, including the substitution of floating for fixed exchange rates. But, as Maynard (1973) has suggested, multinational enterprises may themselves reduce the effectiveness of such flexibility as their activities may affect the size of the feasible currency area. For this depends on whether or not an economy, by varying its exchange rate, can bring about the necessary changes in relative prices withour employment and output having to suffer; in other words, whether or not real wages (but not money wages) are flexible in a downward direction. It. may be argued that multinational enterprises, prompted, *inter alia*, by the internationalisation of trade unions, are reducing the likelihood of this being achieved by their gradual adoption of harmonised wage settlements. [22] In consequence, any devaluation would encourage unions to press for an increase in money wages, which, if this led, through the wage-transfer mechanism, to an increase in wages throughout the economy, would offset the

21. As observed by the Tariff Commission (*op. cit.* p. 539) 'A movement of a mere 1 per cent. of these assets in response to exchange rate weakness or strength is quite sufficient to produce a first class international financial crisis.'

22. As shown by a resolution passed at a recent conference of the World Automobile Council, the substance of which was that all workers employed by any multinational enterprise should have parity of real wages.

benefits of devaluation and violate the propositions of the feasible currency area. The net result would be a failure to cure unemployment, and an encouragement to countries to consider monetary integration, and so increase the feasible currency area.

(b) *Inflation*

In an essay published in 1968, A. J. Brown argued that the long-term effects of international capital flows on inflation could not be generalised and that everything depended on the amounts of investment in the national and regional economies and on the balance between the amounts of capital formation directed in the world towards increasing capacities to produce goods of flexible and rigid prices respectively. Moreover, at a macro-level, it is possible to argue that multinational enterprises (like other institutions) can only affect the policies pursued by Governments towards inflation but cannot be held responsible for inflation.

Nevertheless, the impact of multinational enterprises on cost-push inflation and the response this generates from trade unions are interesting phenomena. It has sometimes been argued that foreign affiliates contribute to regional inflation by their propensity to pay higher wages to attract labour; it is not difficult to extend to the national level. If this is the case, why is it so? Is it a feature of multinationalism itself or the structure of multinational enterprises? In most cases it is part of both. Multinational enterprises (and their affiliates) tend to be concentrated in capital intensive industries and their productivity is above average. Because of this, they can afford to pay above-average wages, and may be willing to do so to avoid the high cost of industrial unrest or strikes. But this, in itself, will not necessarily lead to higher wages being paid, unless a wage transfer mechanism is operating. This, in turn, will depend, *inter alia*, on the way in which wage agreements are negotiated, e.g., industry-wide agreements are more likely to be related to average profits in an industry etc., while plant bargaining agreements are related more to the ability to pay of the most productive firms. The spread of this type of bargaining technique by United States multinational enterprises has made it more likely that firms competing with their affiliates will ask for the wages paid by them.

More to the point is that the trade unions negotiating with multinational enterprises might themselves try and press for wage parity on an international scale. In these circumstances, and where competition in the goods market is oligopolistic, the goods supplied have a low price-elasticity of demand, the wage transference mechanism may easily cross national boundaries. A low price-elasticity of demand, of course, implies that there is little import competition, or that the prices of imports have also risen. In most industries in which multinational enterprises are operating, there is a substantial trade in goods. But where there are sympathetic movements in wages, both between

180

production units in the same firm across national boundaries, and between firms in the same industry within national boundaries, the consumer is no longer protected and prices will rise.

As yet, little empirical research has been done on the wage transfer mechanism and the rôle played by multinational enterprises in it. But various pieces of evidence are coming to light which tend to support the hypothesis outlined above. Partly this is a structural phenomenon. In the 1960s, for example, wages increased most in advanced industrial countries in those industries in which multinational enterprises are most strongly concentrated. In these same industries, too, United States affiliates pay higher wages than indigenous firms, while between countries, wages tend to be less dispersed than the average. Worker cohesion is strongest and trades unions are the most active where multinational enterprises are concentrated—the motor and chemical industries are cases in point; while, because of the effects on the rest of the enterprise, affiliates can less afford industrial unrest or strikes than indigenous producers. Such facts as these suggest that, in a fully employed economy, capital formation by foreign-owned companies may have more inflationary implications than that of their indigenous competitors; although domestic multinational enterprises may cause similar anxieties. It is one further example of the effects on the open-ness of an economy, where the pressures of costs are internationally transmitted. At the very least, it results in a redistribution of income towards those who work in multinational enterprises away from the rest of the community; at worst, it could result in the twin evils of inflation and unemployment being more difficult to contain. Once again, it has implications for the way in which governments manage the economy for the form and content of national economic planning.

(c) *Distribution of income*

A final, and very brief, comment about the distribution of income arising from the activities of multinational enterprises. Received theory suggests normal capital flows will raise the marginal product of labour in recipient countries and lower it in investing countries. Owners of capital will be affected in the opposite way. This model, however, is hardly appropriate to capital movements generated by multinational enterprises, one of the main results of which is to raise the level of the marginal productivity in host countries, which may benefit *both* labour and capital and, in so far as resources *are* more effectively allocated, raise the level of factor productivity in the investing country.

A more interesting question concerns the distribution of the costs and benefits arising from the operations of multinational enterprises *between* host and investing countries—assuming these can be assessed accurately. In theory, it is possible to draw up a balance sheet of costs and benefits of capital formation by multinational enterprises in a particular country, both to multinational enterprises and to host countries. One could, for example, imagine a cost (dividends remitted royalties and fees, etc.) beyond which host countries would not be prepared to pay for the benefits; this would depend on the alternatives open to them to obtain these benefits. Similarly, one can imagine a price (in the form of foregone profits, etc.) which the investing company is not prepared to pay to the host country, which, again, will depend on the opportunities it foregoes from investing elsewhere. The price finally agreed will depend, *inter alia*, on the bargaining strength of the two parties, and their knowledge of the opportunities open to the other. In practice, costs and benefits are difficult to compute, but recently, research by Vaitsos (1973) has suggested that the benefits to both parties are most substantial than is commonly thought.

Even the above calculation does not get to the root of the sharing problem. An analogy might help here. A multi-regional United Kingdom enterprise might decide to shut down a factory in the North West of England and transfer production to the South East because it is economic so to do. This clearly has certain social consequences; let us assume, however, that this will result in an increase in allocative efficiency and a marked shift in the distribution of income to the South East. Since the United Kingdom Government has a responsibility for the economic welfare of the North West, it is likely to take action to assist the people in that area either to find jobs by moving to the more prosperous South East or encouraging new activity in the North West; if necessary, it can use part of the increased income generated by the company moving to the South East to do this. In other words, the country as whole, out of increased wealth created, may be able to compensate, in part at least, those who have been adversely affected by the (efficient) action of a private company.

There is no device which can compensate for similar type actions of the multinational enterprises. If a United States company closes its Welsh factory to transfer production to the United States, the United Kingdom Government can use the devices of regional policy to help compensate for this. But the contribution of output of the company has been transferred to the United States. A supra-national authority might devise a fiscal system which in some way would compensate for this or at least assist the adjustment to a new pattern of resource allocation. Alternatively, if there were complete mobility of all resources across national boundaries, the readjustment problem would be much easier to deal with.

Again, it may be argued this is no new problem and that free international trade is constantly causing adjustment problems, and that no one suggests that this should result in some distribution of income from nations that gain to those that lose. But here the nature of the problem is different because affiliates of multinational enterprises are much more part of the fabric of the countries in which they operate, and are able to exert more control over decision taking.

VII. *Conclusions*

The impact of multinational enterprises on capital flows differs from that of portfolio investment, due to the fact that the former is primarily a vehicle for moving a package of resources, within the same enterprises, across national boundaries, while the latter is a vehicle for transferring savings between independent lenders and borrowers. This immediately not only affects the determinants of investment of multinational enterprises compared with other firms in the *investing* country, but of the capital formation by affiliates of multinational enterprises compared with indigenous companies in the host countries. A further difference arises from the ability of multinational enterprises to take advantage of differences in input prices and availability and markets throughout the world, and to trade goods and services internally as well as capital. This leads to different types of operations of affiliates of multinational enterprises, which range from truncated production to a commitment covering a wide range of activities on a world scale.

The effects of the capital formation reflect the operations of the affiliates of multinational enterprises and of their group. While portfolio investment is essentially interest (or money capital) mobile, that of the multinational enterprise is essentially income-mobile, income here being the total benefits received on the capital invested by the multinational enterprise *as a whole*. The precise impact will vary according to the type of multinational enterprise and government policies pursued. The general conclusion of the final section in which we briefly examined the impact of multinational enterprises on national economic management, inflation and the distribution of income was that their effects were parallel to those of a free movement in capital and in goods, viz., that domestic management policies became more difficult to achieve the greater the open-ness of the economy. But because multinational enterprises were so much more involved in international transactions than national firms and that a substantial part of these were intra-group; because they were among the world's largest and most powerful financial institutions; and because they operated in a world comprised of sovereign states each with different fiscal, monetary and exchange rate policies designed to meet its own particular objectives, the clash between such firms and national governments was the more dramatically expressed.

None of the alternatives suggested to resolve this dilemma and the balance between equity and efficiency are without cost. Unilateral or multilateral controls over multinational enterprises, the abandonment of national sovereignty to world economic forces, the integration of nations to create an environment offering countervailing power to multinational enterprises but one in which they can operate freely, have all been suggested. But the extent to which any or all of these are possible may depend on how far countries are prepared to abrogate their authority in monetary or fiscal matters and this in the end may be the most crucial question of all.

References·

Arge, R. d' (1969), "Notes on customs unions and foreign direct investment", *Economic Journal*, Vol. 74.

Aharoni, Y. (1971), "The definition of a multinational corporation", *Quarterly Review of Economics and Business*, Autumn.

Aliber, R.Z. (1970), "A theory of direct investment" in C.P. Kindleberger (ed.) *The International Corporation*, M.I.T. Press.

Bandera, V.N. and J.J. White (1968), "US direct investment and domestic markets in Europe", *Economica International*, Vol. 21.

Branson, W.H. and R.D. Hill (1971), *Capital movements in the OECD area*, OECD, Paris.

Brash, D. (1966), *American investment in Australian Industry*, Australian National University Press.

Brown, A.J. (1968), "Capital movements and inflation" in J. Adler (ed.) *Capital movements and economic development*, MacMillan, 1968.

Cairncross, A.K. (1973), *Control over international capital movements*, A. Brookings Staff Paper (forthcoming).

Caves, R. (1971), "International corporations: the industrial economics of foreign investment", *Economica*, Vol. 38.

Caves, R. and G. Reuber (1971), *Capital transfers and economic policy in Canada 1951/62*, Harvard University Press.

Cooper, R.N. (1971), "Towards an international capital market" in C.P. Kindleberger and A. Shonfield, *North American and Western European economic policies*, MacMillan.

Corden, M. (1972), *Monetary integration*, Essays in International Finance No. 93, Princeton University.

Dunning, J.H. (1973(a)), *US industry in Britain: a statistical profile*, an EAG Business Research Study. Financial Times Occasional Paper No. 1.

Dunning, J.H. (1973(b)), "The determinants of international production", *Oxford Economic Papers*, November 1973.

Dunning, J. H. and G. Yannapoulos, "The fiscal factor in the location of affiliates of multinational enterprises" in *Vers une politique fiscale européenne à l'égard des entreprises multinationales*, Centre de Recherches Interdisciplinaires Droit-Economie, Louvain, 1973.

Gray, H. (1972), *Foreign direct investment in Canada*, Government of Canada.

Horst, T. (1972), "The industry composition of US exports and subsidiary sales to the Canadian Market", *American Economic Review*, Vol. 62.

Johnson, H.G. (1966), "International capital movement and economic policy" in T. Bagiotti (ed.) *Essays in honour of Marco Fanno*, Padora.

Johnson, H.G. (1968), *Comparative cost and commercial policy for a developing world economy*, The Wicksell Lectures, 1968.

Johnson, H. (1970), "The efficiency and welfare implications of the international corporation" in C. Kindleberger (ed.), M.I.T. Press, *The International Corporation*, reprinted in J.H. Dunning (ed.) *International Investment*, Penguin Education 1972.

Maynard, G.W. (1974), "The Multinational enterprise and monetary policy" in J.H. Dunning (ed.) *Economic analysis and the multinational enterprise*, Allen and Unwin (forthcoming)

Manser, W. A. P. (1973), *The financial role of multinational enterprises*, International Chamber of Commerce

Mellors, J. (1973), "International tax differentials and the location of overseas direct investment: a pilot study", *University of Reading Research Papers in International Investment and Business*, No. 4.

Polk, J. (1971), *World companies and the new world economy* (unpublished paper prepared for discussion group at Council for Foreign Relations, New York).

Popkin, J. (1965), *Interfirm differences in direct investment behaviour of US Manufacturers*. Unpublished doctoral dissertation. University of Pennsylvania.

Quinn, J.B. (1968), *The role of science and technology in economic development*, UNESCO Paris.

Reddaway, W.B., S.T. Potter and C.T. Taylor (1967 and 1968), *The effects of U.K. direct investment overseas*, Cambridge University Press.

Safarian, A.E. (1966), *Foreign ownership in Canadian industry*, McGraw Hill.

Scaperlanda, A.E. (1967), "The EEC and US foreign investment: some empirical evidence", *Economic Journal*, Vol. 77.

Scaperlanda, A.E. and L.J. Mauer (1969), "The determinants of US direct investment in the EEC", *American Economic Review*, Vol. 59.

Severn, A.J. (1971), "Investment and financial behaviour of American investors in manufacturing Industry" in F. Machlup, L. Tarshis and W. Salant (eds.) *International mobility and the movement of capital*, Universities, N.B.E.R. and Brookings Institution.

Stevens, G.V. (1969), "Fixed investment expenditure of foreign manufacturing affiliates in US firms: theoretical models and empirical evidence", *Yale Economic Essays*, Vol. 9.

Stevens, G.V. (1974), "The multinational enterprise and the determinents of investment" in J.H. Dunning (ed.) *Economic analysis and the multinational enterprise*, Allen and Unwin (forthcoming).

US Tariff Commission (1973), *Implications of multinational firms for world trade and investment and for US trade and investment*. Report for Committee in Finance of US Senate.

Vaitsos, C. (1974), "Inter-country income distribution and trans-national corporations" in J.H. Dunning (ed.) *Economic analysis and the multinational enterprise*, Allen and Unwin (forthcoming).

Vaupel, J. (1971), *Characteristics and motivations of the US corporations which manufacture abroad*, Paper presented to meeting of participatory members of the Atlantic Institute Paris.

Wallis, K.F. (1968), Notes on Scaperlanda's article, *Economic Journal*, Vol 73.

Appendix Summary of shares of plant and equipment spending by United States-owned multinational corporations in gross fixed capital formation in the manufacturing industries of seven key countries, 1966 and 1970

Industry description	Plant and equipment spending by multinational corporations as percent of gross fixed capital formation							Aggregate for all 7 countries		
	United Kingdom	France	W.Germany	Belgium-Luxembourg	Canada	Mexico	Brazil[6]	P&E spending by MNCs (million dollars)	GFCF[1] (million dollars)	P&E as percent of GFCF[7]
1966										
All manufacturing	16.3	4.3	9.2	17.0	42.7	6.7	12.4	3,014	22,407	13
Food	4.6	1.9	1.4	[2]n.a.	22.5	2.7	[2]n.a.	[3]109	[3]2,670	4
Chemicals	15.8	1.9	5.1	23.3	86.6	20.8	16.8	561	4,348	12
Primary and fabricated metals	11.3	1.7	1.8			4.0	[2]n.a.	[4]195	[4]8,579	
Machinery	21.5	15.4	19.4	19.3	64.0	5.3	50.8	748		20
Transportation equipment	47.6	8.8	37.8			3.1	28.2	831		
All other manufacturing	11.6	1.0	1.1	10.6	23.6	.2	6.7	570	6,810	8
1970										
All manufacturing	20.9	5.8	12.3	14.1	32.2	9.3	18.3	4,152	29,739	13
Food	4.4	0.9	2.0	[2]n.a.	23.5	3.1	11.1	[5]163	[5]4,030	4
Chemicals	17.9	2.1	10.4	24.9	68.1	10.7	27.4	691	5,155	13
Primary and fabricated metals	21.1	1.0	8.4			8.3	11.9	457		
Machinery	29.0	23.3	27.8	12.0	57.8	13.9	57.1	1,292	11,482	22
Transportation equipment	45.5	9.8	27.8			17.9	25.6	870		
All other manufacturing	18.2	2.8	2.7	10.8	20.5	13.0	5.9	679	9,072	7

1. "Gross fixed capital formation."
2. Included in "all other industries."
3. Excludes food processing in Belgium-Luxembourg and Brasil. Figures for these countries are included in "all other manufacturing."
4. Excludes primary metals & fabricated metals in Brazil. These figures are included in "all other manufacturing."
5. Excludes food processing in Belgium-Luxembourg, for which the relevant data are included in "all other manufacturing."
6. Figures for 1970 are based on 1969 data for GFCF.
7. Plant and equipment expenditures as percent of gross fixed capital formation.

US Tariff Commission, *Implications of multinational firms for world trade and investment and for US trade and labor*, US Government Printing Office

Chapter XII

MULTINATIONAL FIRMS AND ECONOMIC STABILITY

by *Nils Lundgren*

The objectives of this paper are fairly modest. First, the analysis is of an *a priori* nature with no empirical material to support or test it. Second, we do not work out a complete model suitable for handling the problem, but confine ourselves to analysing some propositions that have been made in public discussion. This approach is, of course, partly explained by the inclinations of the author and the early stage of his own work in the field, but there is also the more general reason that very little generalisation has been done so far on the problem of multinational firms and economic stability. There is thus no body of literature with ready-made models and empirical results to draw upon, though there is a number of studies of more general character.

By multinational firms we shall mean any company having at least one subsidiary or branch in at least one foreign country. This is a less restrictive definition than most. The idea is that all we are interested in are the effects of having companies *which make transactions internal to themselves but external to countries and which make the social and economic conditions and attitudes of one country exert a direct influence on the management of firms in other countries.*

We assume in this paper that the international pattern of production and trade is unaffected by the existence and expansion of multinational firms. This assumption is not founded on the belief that this pattern would have been the same if we had had legislation against direct investment in all countries from the middle of the nineteenth century. It is simply a theoretical device to make it possible to concentrate on the aspects of multinational firms that make them different from other firms. It is common to attribute to multinational firms all sorts of characteristics that they admittedly display but which do not in themselves make firms multinational. Multinational firms are often very big and often use very capital intensive production methods. They are concentrated in industries with rapid technical progress and/or product differentiation. All those characteristics have important consequences for the national economies, but, as those consequences would in principle be there even if all kinds of controlling ownership of equity across national frontiers were to be severed, they will not be dealt with in this paper.

Finally, our discussion is limited to the effects on developed mixed economies. The multinational firms in underdeveloped countries may play a rather different role, because they may dominate whole sectors and create dual economies or even dual societies and because single firms may be very big and powerful in relation to the national governments. Also, monetary mechanisms are rather different due to the lack of developed markets for financial assets in such countries. It should be even more obvious that the discussion could not be valid for those centrally planned economies into which multinational firms are now making inroads.

Economic stability

It is useful for many purposes to divide the targets of public economic policy into three kinds depending on whether the intention is to affect stability, allocation (efficiency) or income distribution (Musgrave 1958). This conference is dedicated to monetary and fiscal policy which, as their names indicate, in principle are instruments that can be used, and are in fact used, to reach targets under all three headings. A progressive income tax, a selective employment tax, and a general value added tax are all fiscal policies presumably intended to realize respectively distribution, allocation and stability targets. Monetary policy may also be given a selective character to favour low interest rates on mortgages to keep down the cost of housing (distribution target) or on agricultural credit to maintain a certain agricultural output (allocation target).

It is clear, however, that in everyday speech the expression monetary and fiscal policy is used in the restricted sense of stabilization policy. By monetary and fiscal policy we normally mean measures by the central bank and the treasury respectively to maintain or restore economic stability, i.e. full employment, a stable price level and equilibrium in the balance of payments. That is also how monetary and fiscal policy has been interpreted for the purpose of this paper. Hence the title multinational firms and economic stability.

The Phillips curve is the locus of feasible combinations of two of the stability targets, namely price level (or wage level) change over time and unemployment. This implies that the economy studied is assumed either to be a closed economy or an economy operated under a regime of flexible exchange rates. Neither assumption seems particulary apt for a study of the mixed economies of today, though the latter might become reasonable in the future if the present trend towards floating exchange rates continues. On the other hand, if we have open economies and fixed exchange rates, price developments in all countries that are small enough to be pricetakers on the international markets would be given from abroad and the trade-off in stabilization policy would be between the current account balance and unemployment.

Now, it is true that all countries have some leeway in the domestic pricing of tradables, because substitution is not perfect between domestic and foreign

188

tradables, particularly not in the short run. Furthermore, some countries do exert an influence on world market prices. Accordingly, the trade off is really a Phillips *surface* in three dimensions: inflation, unemployment and current account balance. But for most countries, and especially in the long run, the main trade off for *national* stabilization policy is between current account balance and unemployment. It is the effects of multinational firms on the possibilities of national governments to cope with shifts in and movements along that "Phillips curve" by means of fiscal and monetary policy that are the main issue here.

This task has not been easy for any country and the basic causes are fairly well known. A country which through inflationary policies or a deterioration of the terms of trade runs into an external deficit, must sooner or later bring about a fall in its domestic price level relative to its trading partners expressed in *their* currencies. Under fixed exchange rates (devaluation ruled out) this must be done through a relative fall in the price level expressed in *domestic* currency which requires a reduction of aggregate demand through fiscal and monetary policy to create overcapacity and unemployment. With good luck, the trick can be done. Demand increases for the country's tradable goods at the expense of trading partners. The current account deficit is eliminated and full employment is restored. The cost of adjustment is temporary unemployment.

This is not a necessary outcome of deflationary economic policies, however. The creation of unused capacity will momentarily reduce the volume of new investment, which in its turn will slow down the rate at which new technology can be introduced into the economy. Productivity will then rise more slowly and unit costs may rise instead of fall in relation to the unit costs of trading partners. The external balance will not improve and may even deteriorate necessitating further deflation in a vicious or semivicious circle.

Countries that are relatively more successful in combining full employment with moderate inflation develop current account surpluses which make for inflationary developments. Under fixed exchange rates they have to export capital to avoid such imported inflation, but that can only be a temporary solution. Eventually, they have to accept a weighted average of the rates of inflation chosen by their trading partners. In addition, the reserve currency country is running a continuous balance of payments deficit creating reserves which boost the world money supply. As there is no pressure built into the system to force the reserve currency country to eliminate its deficit, there is a basic world inflation decided by that country to which the other countries are tied in the long run, while they are busy trying to maintain full employment and external balance.

Such is the picture of economic stability into which we now try to fit the multinational firms.

Direct investment and economic stability

It is common to blame world inflation (to which every country is obliged to conform in the long run under fixed exchange rates) on the direct investments abroad by American companies. The argument then runs as follows. These American firms bring dollars to other countries to buy established firms or to buy and hire productive factors for subsidiaries they establish there themselves. The dollar assets created abroad and held by central banks as reserves increase the money supplies there and cause inflation.

This accusation seems ill-founded. With proper monetary and fiscal policies in the United States the following should happen. American companies decide to invest less at home and more abroad, say in Western Europe. Aggregate demand falls somewhat in the United States and rises in Western Europe. The relative competitiveness of American industry improves and the United States develops a current account surplus, while Western Europe gets a corresponding deficit. This is, of course, the familiar transfer mechanism which raises a host of theoretical and empirical problems that do not concern us here. It is clear that when a flow of direct investment from the United States to Western Europe is initiated or accelerated the effect is to stimulate some extra inflation in the latter area and exert a deflationary pressure in the former. A *steady flow* of direct investment does not have this kind of effect, however, once the relative price levels have been adjusted to that flow. Clearly, the same type of conclusion holds for the balance of payments disturbances in which case the relationships are more obvious. It is easy to see that a stable outflow of direct investment financed by a stable current account surplus is not a stability problem. The general conclusion is that direct investment causes stability problems when it changes in volume under fixed exchange rates.

The relation of American direct investment abroad to world inflation is probably of a more indirect nature. If the United States through expansionary fiscal and monetary policy prevents the fall in aggregate demand that a rise in foreign direct investment tends to create, then there will be a persistent inflationary gap and accumulating dollar holdings in Western Europe, until the price level has risen to a level that establishes the import surplus which eliminates the excess demand. The outcome would be a higher world price level than in the previous case because of the monetary and fiscal policy in the United States.

It seems reasonable to exonerate the American multinational firms of this particular accusation that they contribute to world inflation by investing abroad, as this is only true when they *increase* the flow, no exchange rate adjustments are made, and particular monetary and fiscal policies are applied.

If direct investment was a particularly volatile element of considerable importance to the national economies, it would nevertheless be a stability problem, though not consistently in an inflationary direction. This is hardly the case, however. Changes in the volume of direct foreign investment are usually not of great importance in relation to aggregate demand or even in relation to the foreign payments of a country. In addition, direct investment is often financed locally to a considerable extent which reduces the stability effects of what changes there are in direct investment flows. The fact that so much direct foreign investment is financed locally implies that the capital movement aspect is not of great importance, and it is, of course, the need to effect the real transfer of capital which may create stability problems in connection with direct foreign investment.

Short term capital movements

The existence of multinational firms creates the scope for a much larger volume of short term capital movements. Such movements are to a large extent the results of changes in the structure of leads and lags in current international payments and can be initiated by all economic agents engaging in current international transactions. A company exporting its product to a foreign country may delay payments in the expectation of a devaluation at home or a revaluation of the customer's currency or because interest rates are higher abroad. This can be done either by asking the customers to pay later than usual or by investing the proceeds in the Eurocurrency market. The multinational firms are better placed than national transactors to profit from adjusting their portfolio of short-term assets. First, they can maximize profits for the whole concern when transactions are between affiliates. There are limits to how much and for how long an importer can delay payments to a firm to which it has no ownership relation. An exporter who would like to get his payment earlier than is customary for reasons of exchange rate expectations or interest rate differentials has little possibility to achieve this.

This situation is of growing importance because a rising share of international trade is done between affiliates of the same multinational company. A study has been made comparing the volume of short-term capital movements when all firms trade on an arm's-length basis with the volume obtained when they are members of multinational firms. The difference was very significant, with little variation in the balances of payments in the first case and widely fluctuating payments situations in the second case (Robbins — Stobaugh 1973).

The second reason why multinational firms may make movements of short term capital more sensitive to interest rate differentials and expectations of exchange rate changes is that they bring together information about the situation in international money markets as a by-product of their other activities. Their marginal cost of acquiring such information is therefore lower than for national firms and individuals. A third reason is that multinational firms have the possibility of circumventing exchange regulations against short term movements by means of transfer pricing. Whether this possibility is of significant importance in this context is not known. I have my doubts personally.

What is known, however, is that multinational firms dispose of vast sums of cash and marketable securities, that they account for a large share of world trade, and that they have better facilities and better information than national firms. This does not mean that we are entitled to attribute most of the conspicuous increase in the volume and volatility of short term capital movements in recent years to the expansion of multinational firms. Leads and lags in international payments of national firms and the development of the Eurocurrency markets may still explain most of the change (Hansen 1961, Einzig 1968, Uggla 1970, Grassman 1973). It does follow, however, that short term capital movements are larger and more volatile with multinational firms than they would be without.

We should not jump from this statement to the conclusion that the world economy accordingly is more unstable and more difficult to stabilize for national governments. If we conclude that the international markets for short term securities are dominated by such skilled and well informed speculators as the multinational firms, we should have reason to believe that the speculation is stabilizing, not destabilizing. This does not, of course, seem to be the case. Speculation in those markets has been destabilizing in recent years. The reason for that is that we have fixed exchange rates wich are far from the equilibrium rates and that national governments have too small reserves. Governments cannot make it seem credible that they could hold out at the fixed parity and adjust the domestic price level by fiscal and monetary policy so as to make the equilibrium exchange rate equal to the established fixed parity. Asymmetric expectations develop about the future path of various exchange rate parities and give rise to heavy speculation. Because the reserves of most countries and, in particular, of the countries with overvalued exchange rates, are small in relation to the short term capital movements that can take place, countries are often forced to "validate" the expectations.

The conclusion should accordingly be of the following kind. With multinational firms countries need bigger reserves (and international credit facilities) than they would need in the absence of such firms, if they want to go on with a system of fixed exchange rates where the equilibrium rates are to be allowed to move far away from the parities and remain there for long periods. However, greater exchange rate flexibility and/or larger reserves and automatic international credit facilities could eliminate this difficulty of having multinational firms.

There is another obvious problem connected with a nearly perfect international money market under fixed exchange rates. As has been shown by Mundell and Fleming (Mundell 1962, Fleming 1962) national monetary policy is rendered ineffective under such a system. Any increase in money supply leads to an outflow of short-term capital rather than to a lower rate of interest and higher aggregate demand for goods and services. Under the assumption of perfect international money and capital markets, a country wishing to lower its rate of interest has to increase *world* money supply sufficiently to achieve a global fall in interest rates. This requires international reserves on a scale that no country could hope to have, especially when we take into account the possibilities to sterilize money inflows that countries have.[1] To the extent that the perfection of those markets is due to activities of the multinational firms, the latter can be blamed for the ineffectiveness of monetary policy under fixed exchange rates. There are at least four reasons why the multinational firms may be unfairly debited on this account for the difficulties countries have in maintaining economic stability.

First, and probably most important, the Eurocurrency markets and adjustments in the leads and lags in international payments make capital markets nearly perfect even without multinational firms even though these do add to the perfection. Second, the theory that shows monetary policy to be ineffective under fixed exchange rates and free capital movements also shows fiscal policy to be very effective under the same conditions. There is then no braking influence from the money market and the simple Keynesian model applies. Why should governments insist on using one instrument that has been rendered ineffective instead of using another that has been made more powerful?

Thirdly, if there are reasons to prefer monetary to fiscal policy for the purpose of economic stabilization, which I believe to be true, then we should remember that any country is really free to introduce flexible exchange rates which would reverse the situation and make monetary policy effective in addition to ridding the country of the frustrating problem of external balance and making the determination of the domestic price level a domestic affair.

Fourthly, the "new theory of capital movements" (Grubel 1968, Branson 1970, Leamer and Stern 1970) indicates that the international money and capital markets are not perfectly integrated even when capital movements are completely free. Investors and traders therefore maintain multinational portfolios for purposes of risk diversification. If a country drives down its interest rates, portfolios are adjusted and capital flows out of the country, but the outflow stops when a new stock equilibrium is reached. In principle, therefore, a country *can* establish an interest rate differential against foreign rates.

---

1. The United States may be in a different situation, however, because it is so big in relation to the world economy and because its position as the reserve currency country in principle eliminates the problem of sufficient reserves. In practice, the United States cannot count on other countries accepting unlimited amounts of dollar assets, as we have seen.

In fact there *are* always such differentials. Capital movements arise from *changes* in differentials not from the *existence* of such differentials. Accordingly, changes in money supplies have to be greater to achieve given domestic monetary objectives and international reserves have to be greater when there are multinational firms perfecting the international money and capital markets than when there are not. As there could hardly be any objection to using larger doses in monetary policy[2] and larger international reserves can easily be created if there is the political will to do so, there does not seem to be any reason to worry about the existence of multinational firms on this account.

We thus seem to be able to conclude this section in the following way. With internationally integrated capital markets you need quite large international reserves (including international credit facilities) to be able to maintain fixed exchange rates. Multinational firms raise that level of integration somewhat and so increase the size of the international reserves needed. If there are reasons to stimulate international economic integration, which I think there are, then there is also reason to consider the alternatives of flexible exchange rates and of much larger and automatic international credit facilities rather than looking for ways of interfering with international capital movements initiated by multinational firms.

Monetary distortions

It is often asserted that a contractive monetary policy has biassed effects on the investment activities of different firms. The argument is that subsidiaries of multinational companies and, for that matter, domestic parent companies, have access to financial capital from affiliates abroad so that they can avoid the impact of a credit squeeze. The result is not only that the reduction in the money supply has to go much further to achieve the desired fall in aggregate demand which is an aspect discussed above; it is also asserted that you will then squeeze purely domestic firms, while the multinational firms are little affected, if at all. For every monetary squeeze the latter will then raise their share of the markets and increase their technological lead. The foreign influence in the economy is stepped up, concentration in industry is furthered and smaller firms with a growth potential are killed in their infancy.

There are several objections to this view. One very obvious one is that with the Eurocurrency markets and free capital movements to the country in question, the option to borrow abroad is open to all firms. You do not have to be multinational. However, this objection does not hold, if the country controls capital movements, which is quite common and perhaps rather logical

2. It seems reasonable to assume that the money supply (or changes in it) does not enter the social welfare function.

to do in combination with monetary policy under fixed exchange rates. In that case, multinational firms may have much better facilities to circumvent the controls and finance their investment plans by *direct* capital imports than purely national firms.

But the argument does not stop there. Assume that the central bank contracted the credit supply on the assumption that the control of capital inflow was watertight. If multinational firms can get finance abroad at a lower rate of interest, they will use that facility and the domestic interest rate will not go up as much as expected. Domestic firms will benefit from this indirectly. If the possibilities are unlimited there will be no effect at all of the monetary squeeze. The country then does not control the capital inflow at all. The multinational firms become the institutional channels through which the internal capital market is linked to the world capital market. The result is indeed that they make monetary policy rather ineffective, but *not* that they give rise to discrimination against national firms.

If multinational firms can get only a limited amount of finance from abroad then the monetary policy will be more effective but there is still no discrimination involved. It is only if the monetary policy takes the form of regulations such as that no firm is allowed to borrow from the banks more than a given proportion of their total credit at a given date in the past, that discrimination might follow. Multinational firms could then possibly pass interfirm credits to national firms (they would have an interest as profit maximizers to do that), but the inefficiency of that kind of credit market would put national firms at a disadvantage.

Possibly a very imperfect national credit market could have the same kind of effect as a regulated credit market. It seems natural to put the blame for the *discriminatory* effects on the regulations or the imperfectness, however, and not on the multinational firms as such. But if the government has some good reason to regulate the credit market it is true that it can do so only at the cost of discriminating against national firms when contractive monetary policies are applied.

Multinational firms and wage formation

There is an obvious application of the Stolper-Samuelson (Stolper-Samuelson 1941) theorem on the effects on real wages of the existence of multinational subsidiaries in an economy. Let us assume that such subsidiaries are established not only to increase the parent company's command over the market price of its products, but at least to some extent because it offers a more efficient way to combine resources from various countries in productive activities. In this latter case, the multinational subsidiaries make it possible to increase international specialization in accordance with comparative advantages. The

195

analogy with ordinary international trade is perfect. In that case, we can assume that such subsidiaries hurt the relatively scarce factors of every country and bring gains to the relatively abundant factors. Accordingly, they may reduce real wages in countries where labour is scarce and raise real wages where labour is abundant.

This is a distribution effect which is not our subject here. We bring it up just to define the kind of effects on wage formation that we want to get out of the way. From the point of view of economic stability what matters is whether the existence of multinational firms tends to reduce *nominal* wages so as to exert a contractive effect on some national economies or, whether they on the contrary inflate nominal wages and give rise to accelerated inflation. Both hypotheses are in fact brought forward in political discussions.

The first hypothesis, for obvious reasons often advocated by trade unions, is based on the idea that multinational firms have more bargaining power than national firms in their dealings with trade unions. They can supply customers from their subsidiaries in other countries, if there is a strike in one country. They can move out production if they think that wage claims are excessive and they can rely on the deep pockets of the parent company to cover fixed costs during a long conflict.

The first argument seems reasonable *a priori.* If sales lost through a strike can be replaced by another subsidiary, there is no loss of market share for the concern as a whole. This should be a rather important factor for companies operating in oligopolistic markets, which is what most multinational firms do. The second argument may not always be strong in the short run, as there may be heavy losses if a company tries to sell off specialized equipment. On the other hand, if the product differentiation, that is normally a characteristic of multinational firms, is the result of marketing while the production techniques are of a standard type, it should be quite easy to move production to another country.[3] The third argument finally seems pretty clear. There is, altogether, a case for believing that multinational firms may be more able to resist wage claims than national firms.

It does not necessarily follow that multinational firms for these reasons hold down real wages in the long run. They can probably be assumed to operate in such a way as to get the same return on their marginal investments in all countries. If wage claims in one country are high enough to reduce the marginal return for the multinational companies operating in the country, they will resist those claims to a greater extent. Nominal wages will not rise as much as they would have done in the absence of multinational firms. Now compare the stability effects under the two situations. If the wage claims are

---

3. This reasoning holds for national firms, too, which also have the option of shifting production abroad. However, lacking the experience of multinational firms, national firms probably have higher thresholds for such actions.

compatible with economic stability, this means that the multi-national firms will not experience a fall in their returns on capital and entrepreneurship in the country considered as compared with their returns in other countries. They will then not have any more reason to resist them than national firms.

But if wage claims are in excess of what is compatible with economic stability then we get an interesting difference. If there are multinational firms playing an important role in the economy, then those firms will have the possibilities and reasons mentioned to resist those claims and contribute to wage settlements closer to the ideal ones from the stability point of view. Without the impact of such firms there would be a more difficult problem of stability as the adjustment to the higher wage level is what we have defined as instability. Either an expansionary monetary and fiscal policy is introduced to *validate* the new wage level, which means higher rate of inflation and balance of payments troubles. Or, no monetary expansion is allowed in which case there will be unemployment. This should in the longer run reduce wage drift and make for more moderate wage claims in the next period so that economic balance eventually might be regained. But there will have been unemployment in the meantime and there is a risk of the kind of vicious circle via reduced investment pointed out earlier.

It appears, accordingly, that the kinds of abilities and behaviour on the part of multinational firms that trade unions are worried about, in fact may be a valuable stabilizing factor. This line of reasoning indicates that multinational firms contribute to economic stability. It should be noted, though, that the relation between wages and prices assumed is controversial. We may not be prepared to accept the possibility of cost inflation. Why should trade unions ask for nominal wage increases higher than what they know is possible to squeeze out in real terms? Is it not because they have expectations about further inflation, so that in fact it is the policy of the monetary authorities that is responsible. If this approach is adopted (a "monetarist" approach) then there is no presumption that multinational firms have this stabilizing influence.

The "inflationary" version of wage formation with multinational subsidiaries comes in several forms. One is the exact opposite of the "deflationary" version in that it is based on the idea of such subsidiaries having a *weaker* bargaining position against labour. This is then explained by the fact that the subsidiaries produce components for the international concern which is very vulnerable to interruptions in the deliveries. This is hardly acceptable *a priori*. Any firm, subsidiary or not, that is producing a component of which it is very important for the customer to receive an uninterrupted flow, must be anxious to avoid disturbances. The decisive element here is surely the nature of the international network of production the firm is part of, not the nature of the relationship between firms engaged in that network. One could equally well establish an *a priori* case for why independent suppliers would feel *more*

197

vulnerable than subsidiaries. But the problem is obviously empirical.

Another explanation often brought forth is that multinational firms are so capital intensive or technology intensive that labour costs do not matter much to them. For this reason they give in to excessive wage demands more willingly and stimulate cost inflation (Levinson 1972). This is not because they are multinational, however, and so does not concern us here. But if the argument is that multinational firms give in to excessive wage demands because such firms are necessarily *oligopolistic* this objection does not necessarily hold. An oligopolistic structure requires world production of various goods and commodities to be produced by just a few firms while considerations of transport costs and adaptation to local tastes speak in favour of production taking place in many countries. If it had been impossible (or illegal) to build up multinational firms the structure of many industries might have been considerably more competitive. Whether this would affect wage formation is a question we shall return to below.

A fourth explanation of the presumed wage inflationary bias is that attitudes to wages are formed in the country of origin of the multinational firms where wages are often higher. As the subsidiaries use the technology and production methods of the country of origin they could pay much higher wages and still be profitable. This hypothesis has the testable implication that subsidiaries of firms from high wage countries should be more profitable than the parent companies and/or pay higher wages than the domestic firms of the host country. The evidence is not unambiguous on this point, but may well support the idea.

The problem with all those theories, however, is that they are based on a cost inflation model that is questionable in itself. Again we have to assume that multinational firms are aiming for equalized returns on their marginal investments in various countries. If they are less interested in holding back wage increases in their subsidiaries abroad than national firms in those countries then this should be because those subsidiaries are more profitable than is normal for the industry. This is a reason for investing more in those subsidiaries and hiring more labour. To get that extra labour they may well be prepared to pay more than the normal market wage in the country. This is also what they should do, as this is the way to reallocate labour in a market economy. This behaviour does not increase the rate of inflation.

It is possible, however, that the trade unions do not accept the short term wage differentials that reallocation of labour requires in a market economy, but try to establish the long-run wage equilibrium structure by asking for the same wages for the same jobs here and now. If they do, there will be unemployment in the marginal firms and industries. If the government tries to eliminate that unemployment tendency by expansionary monetary and fiscal policy there will be inflation instead (and balance of payments problems under fixed exchange rates).

198

This is probably a realistic description of the situation in many or most countries. Obviously, there are two things to be said about the role of multinational firms in that drama. Firstly, it is really the existence of companies in general with higher than average profitability and marginal productivity of labour that is the initial factor, not multinational subsidiaries as such. But we should expect a statistical correlation between multinational status and this tendency to set wages higher than the average for the economy. The reason for this is that we live in a period when technical and institutional change is making it more efficient to produce and trade through this institutional instrument that is the multinational firm. And it is characteristic of any period of change that expanding sectors and firms are paying higher wages than contracting ones. This is generally true of all factor rewards outside long-run equilibrium.

Secondly, the inflationary process created by the interplay suggested between multinational subsidiaries (and other growth companies), trade unions and governments cannot easily be blamed on the first set of actors. On the contrary, if we are prepared to accept the principles of the market economy for reallocation of labour to avoid having to *order* employees to go to the growing industries, then the first group is the only one that can be declared *not* guilty on this charge of causing inflation.

There is, finally, an interesting possibility that multinational companies cause the emergence of multinational trade unions. The reason for that can be said to be that multinational companies get a monopsonistic rent on the international labour markets, if trade unions do not organize themselves internationally, too, in order to re-establish the game-theoretical situation that characterizes national labour markets. Now, the experience from the national level is that trade union movements find it difficult to keep their organizations together, if they do not aim for similar or identical wages for the whole area they work in. If that happens at the international level the effects would be tremendous, because that would be tantamount to a move towards basing international trade on absolute rather than comparative advantage.

Regions with lower than average productivity would get unemployment, balance of payments deficts and a dramatic outflow of resources to the areas with higher than average productivity. The experience of *domestic* trade largely based on absolute advantage would repeat itself on the international level. The chances are that multinational trade unions would adopt such "solidaric" wage policies to some extent. In addition to the reason mentioned, trade unions in the richest countries may see such policies as a concealed protection of their own jobs, because it would eliminate the possibility for the less industrialized or just less productive countries to use their *comparative* advantage in industries intensive in semiskilled and unskilled labour. At the same time, *today's* unionized labour in such areas might gain from the higher wages they would get from such an international wage policy while the

199

unemployment that it would create would concern non-unionized labour without influence in the international trade union movement. The heaviest blow would probably fall on *tomorrow's* unskilled labour in those areas, which will then be unemployed.

Again, the conclusion as regards the role of the multinational firms seems to be that those firms are not the *direct* cause of the problem discussed, though they are involved in a very important way. The attempts to maintain economic stability as defined here could be disastrous as there would not be the needed degrees of freedom for that purpose. With factor prices equalized directly by institutional means for regions comprising several countries, which have fixed their exchange rates, or even have a common currency, the stability problem of each country has to be solved by means of regional policy run at the international level. That has proved to be very difficult, to put it mildly.

Conclusions

The general conclusion that seems to emerge from the analysis of multinational firms and economic stability is that not much of the instability experienced in recent years can be blamed on the existence and expansion of such firms. The national economies of today are very open with nearly free trade in goods, services and capital. They are also corporate economies in the sense that big capital intensive oligopolies dominate and make for price rigidity downwards and rapid technical change.

When national economies have those two characteristics of being very open and typically corporate, the adjustment processes have to be very efficient, if stability is to be maintained. But efficient adjustment processes require well functioning markets and suitable international institutions, which we do not have. In fact it seems possible to make the generalization that most of the stability problems discussed above would not exist, if it were not for the presence of various market imperfections. Fixed exchange rates, restrictions on international capital movements, domestic credit market regulations, oligopolistic industry structures and monopoly wages seem to be at the heart of the difficulties. In particular, the institutional arrangements for international payments are not well adapted to the needs of open corporate economies. For such economies could not be expected to maintain economic stability under fixed exchange rates, small reserves and free capital movements. This is the *general* stability problem today.

It is true that multinational firms play an important role in making our national economies both more open and more corporate in the sense used here. At the same time, they can be seen as very efficient institutional instruments for perfecting international markets in inputs and outputs (Baldwin

1970). The problem is accordingly that they improve the international allocation of resources at the same time as they contribute to international instability *given the existing market imperfections and institutional arrangements*. As we are surely interested in further productivity growth, it seems logical to concentrate on reducing market imperfections and developing suitable international institutions for coping with that stability problem rather than to sacrifice real output by trying to prevent the international division of labour done through the international firms.

References

Baldwin, Robert E. (1970), "International Trade in Inputs and Outputs", *American Economic Review, Papers and Proceedings,* vol. LX, No. 2, pp. 435-40.

Branson, William H. (1970), "Monetary Policy and the New View of International Capital Movements", *Brookings Papers on Economic Activity,* 2, 1970.

Einzig, Paul (1968), *Lead and Lags. The Main Cause of Devaluation,* London.

Fleming, J. Marcus (1962), "Domestic Financial Policies under Fixed and under Floating Exchange Rates", *IMF Staff Papers,* vol. 9, No. 3, pp. 369-79.

Grassman, Sven (1973), *Exchange Reserves and the Financial Structure of Foreign Trade: A Study in Commercial Capital Movements,* London.

Grubel, Herbert G. (1968), "Internationally Diversified Portfolios: Welfare Gains and Capital Flows", *American Economic Review,* vol. 58.

Hansen, Bent (1961), *Foreign Trade Credits and Exchange Reserves,* Amsterdam.

Leamer E. and Robert Stern (1970), *Quantitative International Economics,* Boston.

Levinson, Charles (1971), *Capital, Inflation and the Multinationals,* London.

Mundell, Robert A. (1962), "Appropriate Use of Monetary and Fiscal Policy for Internal and External Stability", *IMF Staff Papers,* vol. 9.

Musgrave, Richard (1958), *The Theory of Public Finance.*

Robbins, Sidney and Robert B. Stobaugh (1973), *Money in the Multinational Enterprise: A Study of Financial Policy.*

Stolper, Wolfgang F. and P.A. Samuelson (1941), "Protection and Real Wages", *Review of Economic Studies,* vol. IX, pp. 58-73.

Uggla, Christer (1970), "Commercial Credits and Corporate Covering of Foreign Exchange Positions", *Skandinaviska Banken Quarterly Review,* 1970:3.

Chapter XIII

MULTINATIONAL CORPORATIONS AND NATIONAL MONETARY AND FINANCIAL POLICY

by *Sieghardt Rometsch*

Fitting this paper into the framework of a seminar of this kind poses a twofold problem. First, the "multinational corporation" has become a fashionable topic to wich a large number of distinguished academics, commissions and practitioners have addressed themselves with equal energy and varying success, so that it is difficult to add anything significant. Second, I must attempt in my remarks, without knowing the other papers, to limit my treatment of the subject on which I have been invited to speak—within the extensive range of existing problems—in such a way that overlapping with other papers is kept to a minimum.

Following a definition of multinational corporations, I propose to define their objectives—insofar as these can be generalised at all, and with due regard to the dangers of such generalisations—and then to compare these objectives with those of nationally-oriented monetary and financial policy, again in a general sense and thus with the necessary reservations. This juxtaposition will reveal conflict situations on the one hand, but also mutually strengthening common features on the other. And, finally, a most important matter will be to point out possible ways of resolving the conflicts. Should it be possible only to mitigate the conflicts based on contradictory interests, it will be necessary to weigh them one against the other in a necessarily subjective evaluation to show the implications of a "toleration" of the conflict, which to some extent is unavoidable.

What is, no doubt, the most common definition of the term comes from Jacques G. Maisonrouge, the President of the IBM World Trade Corporation, [1] but this definition is not useful for our purposes because it is ahead of the times and therefore unsuitable for the treatment of current problems. In this paper multinational corporations are to be defined by the criteria which are,

1. A multinational corporation
(*i*) must operate in many countries;
(*ii*) should have foreign subsidiaries carrying out research, development, production, sales and staff functions, etc.;
(*iii*) the subsidiaries should be managed by nationals of the country concerned;
(*iv*) the head office should be multinational;
(*v*) the shares should be dispersed multinationally.

in my view, indispensable and without which, although further qualifications are certainly possible, a corporation does not deserve the label "multinational". Both characteristics lie at the heart—one might say necessarily—of the underlying problems.

First, they must be corporations with "production facilities" in several countries and, second, the worldwide use of the "factors of production"—particularly capital and reserves, know-how and the entrepreneurial concept—must be planned, managed and controlled by a *central* body within the framework of a multinational corporate strategy.

A comparison of the activity of multinational corporations, which is guided by their own best interests, on the one hand, with its influence on the monetary and financial policy of the individual countries, which is guided by national requirements, on the other, must start at the source of possible discrepancies or correspondences, that is to say, with the objectives pursued. In the present context, of course, only that part of the entire range of multinational corporations' objectives is to be singled out that has a direct impact on the monetary and financial policy of separate states.

If it is assumed that the main aim of multinational corporations is the discovery and exploitation of opportunities for division of labour on a worldwide scale, and that the purpose of seizing these opportunities, once identified, must be not only to change existing market positions in one's own favour by means of more-than-proportional growth but also, in the last analysis, to achieve *optimum* profitability (this after all is the natural yardstick for assessing the usefulness of a firm and at the same time the cheapest and in overall terms the most effective investment control), it is necessary to determine those fields of activity of a multinational corporation which have effects that may influence the monetary and financial measures of individual countries. To be concrete, what is meant is a system of rationalised many movements such as is possible, and often already firmly established, within a multinational corporation—a system that guarantees the optimum use of available financial resources while at the same time maintaining friendly and dependable relations with banks.

Specifically, an efficient management of resources contains the following elements:
1. Reduction of the float, not simply within the corporation or between the corporation and its customers but also within the banking system.
2. Minimisation of expenditure on interest
(a) through having a higher level of debt in countries with more advantageous credit terms.
(b) through raising financial credits direct on international money and capital markets.
3. Borrowing, and at the same time structuring the assets, in a way that takes account of expected parity changes.

The system of communicating "money pipes" that is possible within a uniform corporation is attracting, and deserving, particular attention at the moment because the monetarist's theories that were developed and translated into concrete monetary goals in the United States in 1968 and 1969 have in the meantime become major factors in Europe too, and in addition to their general importance for economic policy have assumed a particularly prominent position in the fight against inflation.

Section 4 of the resolution of the EEC Council of Ministers of October 31, 1972, for example, reads as follows:

> "The member countries shall reduce the growth rate of the money supply (the money stock plus quasi-money) in stages until it equals that of the real gross national product plus the normative price increase difined in accordance with the overall economic targets, after taking the structural development of the relationship between money stock and national product into consideration. This target is to be reached not later than the end of 1974. If individual countries are faced with pronounced unemployment, the target might be adjusted accordingly after agreement at community level.
>
> Member countries with full employment must achieve a distinct moderation in the growth of their money supply in 1973, amounting to not less than half of the reduction to be attained by the end of 1974."

Fiscal policy, which plays a dominant role in, for instance, the law on the West German statute book to safeguard stability and growth is conceded little chance of being effective as an instrument of economic and stabilisation policy.

In view of the unfavourable price trend of the goods and services required by the government, a policy of curbing expenditure raises particular problems, so that the temptation to put most emphasis on monetary and credit policy is dangerously strong.

The reason for the use of monetary policy as a means of stabilising prices is primarily that the money stock to a large extent plays an autonomous, i.e., independent, role within the economy, or more precisely aggregate demand, which in relation to the given production potential also determines the level of prices. Even if the direction of this transmission mechanism is still disputed—that is, whether, on the contrary, changes in the money stock simply mirror changes in economic activity—it seems certain that inflationary trends cannot take place without unduly large money creation, regardless of whether the money creation is the cause or only the consequence. It is in the light of this recognition that monetary policy has gained increasing importance as a component of economic policy.

There can therefore be not doubt that a serious conflict potential is inherent in all financial operations of multinational corporations, no matter whether they are internal transactions, exports to other firms, imports from other firms, the management of foreign exchange or the management of financial assets and liabilities; this conflict potential, moreover, increases with the degree of external integration of a country and its restrictive international obligations towards the rest of the world.

I now propose to discuss these problems using as an example the Federal Republic of Germany, which may be taken as representative of comparable problems encountered in the other countries of Europe and, in particular, in the member countries of the European Economic Community.

Since the mid-fifties there has only been one medium-term (4-year) period—that from 1962 to 1965; that is, immediately after the first revaluation of the D-Mark—in which the growth of the money stock in Germany was mainly (70 per cent.) caused by domestic factors and was therefore amenable to control by monetary policy. Prior to this period (from 1954 to 1957) expansion of the money stock was predominantly due to inflows from abroad, and in the ensuing years (from 1968 to mid-1972) it was exclusively due to this influence. In 1970, the money stock would have risen even faster for external reasons had there not been a strong contraction at home on account of the anticyclical reserve.

The dilemma of a national monetary policy that is not sufficiently insulated against external constraints in a country which is closely integrated in the world economy again became manifest in the first two weeks of February 1973 in the case of West Germany. Within 10 days the German money market, which altogether has a money stock of only DM 128 billion, was swamped by dollars equivalent to DM 18 billion. Domestically, these massive inflows of foreign exchange compelled the Bundesbank to take drastic measures to mop up liquidity—the rediscount quotas were reduced to only 60 per cent. of the existing rediscount facility at the central bank—while at the same time the safeguards against external constraints were tightened up:

(a) Purchases of domestic securities by foreigners were prohibited;

(b) Raising credits in excess of DM 50,000.— in foreign countries was made subject to authorisation;

(c) Investments in West Germany by foreigners in excess of DM 500,000.— were made subject to authorisation;

(d) At the same time it was decided to raise the cash deposit ratio from 50 per cent. to a maximum of 100 per cent.

Besides the problems attendant on neutralising such inflows of liquidity from abroad, additional difficulties arise, simply in terms of balances, from the fact that the opening of Germany to such inflows is accompanied by an intensification of the flows of foreign exchange from country to country and therefore entails an increase in other countries' deficits.

The entire problem of the involuntary creation of central bank money in an economy that is "open" in the monetary field affects multinational corporations, which are here in the centre of the storm, only in respect of the finance provided by foreign sources, that is, sources outside the particular host coun-

try. In the balance sheets of multinational corporations they appear, by and large, in three different forms:
(a) as capital stock;
(b) as intra-company loans;
(c) as intra-company trade credits, i.e., as accounts payable.

The finance procured within the country, either through internal cash flow or through domestic borrowing, thus remains unaffected.

In this connection, it is essential to subdivide the cause of this dilemma into two fundamentally different causal areas. The first is a conflict situation which is not based on the existence of multinational firms but must be attributed to the economic interdependence that was made possible, and fostered, by GATT, the EEC Treaty, the world monetary system and the convertibility of the principal currencies of the western world introduced in 1958. This interdependence is inherent in the system and the multinational corporations cannot be made responsible for it.

Second, there are without doubt conflict situations which to a certain extent are potentially present within multinational firms, particularly owing to their manner of operation.

The phenomenon of the Euro-dollar market, which came into being in 1957 and 1958 and today has already become an established part of the European monetary scene, comes into the first category. In the early sixties it had a volume of $1 to 2 billion, but by the end of 1971 it was estimated to total $71 billion and presently as much as $80 billion. In the same period on the Eurobond market, in which only some $100 million was invested in 1963, the volume of issues rose to $4 billion. Medium-term Euro-transactions only got off the ground a few years ago, but already the volume is said to be $10 billion. Thus there has developed in an area free from government intervention and controls a European money and capital market whose financial capacity distinctly exceeds that of any single country in Europe. The problems to which this gives rise are of the following nature:

As America's extra-territorial money market, the Euro-dollar market follows the interest rate structure in the United States in basic tendency. Owing to the unrestricted convertibility of the D-Mark since 1958 and to a well-established foreign exchange market on which exchange risks can be covered for up to a year without great difficulty, the German money and capital market is linked to a source of finance that appreciably enlarges its own intrinsic possibilities. But the crucial factor is that the monetary and financial policy of the United States, no matter whether it is expansionary or restrictive, operating via the transmission belt of the Euro-dollar market, undermines, and often completely frustrates, central bank policies which are guided by domestic economic and monetary requirements. In concrete terms, this means that the interest rate differential between the Eurocurrency market and national money and capital markets results in interest-induced capital movements which on the dependent market—in this case the West German market—tend to even out interest rates. As it was normally possible in past years to borrow on the Euromarket at more favourable rates than in Germany, money and capital imports ensued totalling several billion D-Marks. It was by no means only multinational corporations that took this opportunity of borrowing more cheaply on the Euromarket instead of using the "high interest facilities" supplied by national money and capital markets. On the contrary, both enterprises mainly producing for the domestic market, such as gas and electricity undertakings, breweries or chain stores, and also individuals availed themselves of the advantages accruing from interest rate arbitrage. The *Cash Deposit Act* originally provided for an exempt allowance of DM 2 million, but this amount had to be reduced to DM 500,000 — and finally to as little as DM 50,000 — because individuals continued to borrow on the Euromarket on a large scale. Multinational corporations only did what every sound businessman should do, and did, in his own interest, namely minimise the cost of his business activity—and the measures taken were in no way dependent on the structure of a multinational corporation. Credit brokers and banks provided so-called "offshore financing", without major restrictions regarding the use to which the funds were to be put, as long as the examination of creditworthiness, which was necessary in any case, turned out to their satisfaction. If, therefore, multinational corporations are regarded as one of the indispensable links between the Eurocurrency market and national money markets, this is wrong and the outcome of a basic misunderstanding of the position. Anybody who is reasonably familiar with the activities of the money brokers, mainly in London, but also in Paris and West Germany, knows that they arranged large quantities of direct Eurocurrency credits from London to large and medium-sized enterprises on the Continent. In order to borrow on the Euromarket, one does not need to be a multinational corporation. All that is required is any creditworthy enterprise on the borrowing side and any bank active in the Euromarket on the lending side.

Things are different, however, as soon as domestically-oriented monetary and financial policy is to be safeguarded by restrictive measures or by foreign exchange controls of any kind at all. In such a case, a multinational corporation undoubtedly has means of getting round the measures that are not open to normal enterprises. One may point first in this connection to financial transactions within one corporation. What is meant is not so much straightforward intra-company borrowing, since such borrowing, if it goes across national borders, in most cases is, or can be made, subject to the foreign exchange restrictions in the same way as off-shore bank loans. What is to be brought out here is, rather, those possibilities of exploiting differences in interest rates and expectations of parity changes for which the structure of a multinational corporation is either necessary or particularly advantageous.

However, these opportunities can only be seized—let me repeat it at this

207

juncture—if decisions in the financing field are taken centrally, first from the viewpoint of incurring the lowest interest cost and second with a view to minimising the exchange risk at the same time, so that it is possible to take action, within the framework of a self-consistent strategy, in the superordinate interest of the corporation as a whole.

A matter of central importance in this connection is the wide scope for financing suppliers "invisibly". Within a financially integrated corporation it is an obvious step for subsidiaries to raise loans on the domestic money markets of countries with low rates of interest in order to grant associated companies in countries with high interest rates the longest possible period of credit in connection with intra-corporation deliveries of goods. Conversely, claims arising from deliveries of goods from countries with high interest rates to subsidiaries in low-interest countries are kept low, and where possible even settled by means of advance payments. Calculations made by the German Federal Ministry of Economics in connection with the cash deposit scheme have shown that a delay of 4 weeks in the settlement of liabilities to foreigners arising from merchandise transactions is equivalent to a liquidity creation of DM 10 billion.

A delay of one week in paying for imports and an advance of one week in the settlement of export claims is equal to an increase of DM 6 billion in the money stock. A mobilisation of this potential can have a particularly serious effect in periods of great monetary uncertainty. In West Germany, we have had all too massive experience of this during the ever-more-frequent periods of speculation. I may remind you again of the first 10 days in February 1973. But this wave of speculation again demonstrated—this time with particular clarity—that it is not the multinational corporations that are mainly involved in these upheavals in the monetary sytem. One should, rather, direct one's attention to the balances (running into billions) of foreign banks and other foreign account holders with German credit institutions, since the source of the speculation is to be found there rather than among the multinationals.

Studies suggesting that the resources of multinational corporations that can be mobilised at short notice totalled $258 billion at the end of 1971, and at the same time deriving from this highly questionable sum a responsibility for the monetary crises, should only be given limited attention in this context owing to what seems to me the over-hasty conclusions. On the other hand, it cannot be denied that, at times of particular monetary uncertainty, dividend payments are delayed for months. Liabilities to suppliers in foreign currencies are not settled within the usual periods, but are accumulated on a large scale, D-Mark liabilities of other subsidiaries are settled quickly and D-Mark claims on firms outside the group are generously deferred. Royalties, management fees and other payments are also delayed, thus releasing internal cash flow, which enables internal D-Mark debt to be minimised.

Accurate exchange rate expectations are an essential element in taking

208

advantage of the differences in interest rates on the various money markets, since the raising of a loan does not depend solely on the interest rate differential; exchange rate expectations are of at least equal importance in any money or capital transaction across national borders. The reason for this is that the forward cover transactions, which lead to discounts or premiums, are directly reflected in a reduction or an increase in the interest cost and hence, just like the differences in interest rates, can trigger money and capital movements irrespective of the structure of the enterprise, of whether its commitments are only national or on an international scale.

The factor of overriding importance for the assessment of monetary relationships is the expected course of the overall balance of payments and, within it, particularly of the balance of trade. In addition, the differing rates of inflation and expected changes in political and social fields are taken into consideration before reaching a final decision on the monetary positions to hold. Put concretely, financial managers must find the optimum answer to the following 4 questions:

1. How great is the likelihood of parity changes?
2. How soon is a parity change to be expected?
3. How big will such a change be?
4. How long are the new parities likely to remain unaltered after the change?

Given such a variety of possibilities, the central liquidity management of multinational corporations has undoubtedly become an important element in the present-day financial world. Corporations such as IT&T, Grace & Co., Ford, IBM, General Motors and others each have a senior official whose task it is to keep abreast of developments on the principal money markets of the western world and their currencies and to determine the best possible mix for the investment and raising of funds. The point about this is simply that one does not have to be a multinational corporation to draw the necessary conclusions from monetary expectations, and that in an economy like that of West Germany, where some 19 per cent. of the gross national product is exported and 15 to 17 per cent. imported, it is the recognised task of every enterprise involved in these export and import flows to safeguard itself against the frequently associated exchange risks. It must be conceded, however, that among the totality of conflict situations arising from the freedom of action of large multinational corporations and from their great financial and economic power, international money and capital movements occupy a rather prominent position beside problems such as tax manipulation through internal settlement prices, the export of jobs and capital, technological dependence and the domination of key industries.

This leads us on, finally, to the question of how a country that is firmly integrated in the world economy can plan and implement its monetary and financial policy succesfully as long as the financial managers of a parent company at a head office 5 to 6,000 miles away take decisions that result in

209

changes in payment habits, borrowing or the manner of invoicing, and thus directly influence the course of liquidity policy in the host country. Not infrequently they are able to evade government intervention, so that disruptions of national and international monetary and financial policy of critical proportions may ensue. A discrepancy arises between economic policy and economic reality, a conflict that is rooted somewhere in the increasingly sensitive area between international interdependence in monetary and merchandise matters on the one hand and inadequate international coordination or cooperation in economic and monetary policy matters on the other. The strategic radius of action of multinational corporations, thanks to their international integrative organisation, is thus far in advance of the political structures; it is therefore not congruent with territorially and politically defined units.

The only possible solution to this conflict must be to seek ways of integrating multinational corporations in their political and social environment.

For the contradiction between private motivation and overall objectives in the economic field is as old as the principle of entrepreneurship. Thanks to national regulative policy, aided by an efficient government control of power, it has proved not to be damaging to the general interest, and in a liberal society and economic system it has, in fact, proved extremely fruitful. The high increase rates of output, sales prospects, corporate earnings, income from employment and the social security of the employees are the outcome of the systematic use of knowledge and rules deriving from business administration. Rapid technological evolution and the economic interest of particularly efficient firms in up-to-date products have intensified the trend towards the development of enterprises which, taken as a whole, are no longer a product of a political and social environment formed along uniform lines.

For this reason a movement calling for the abolition of the multinational corporation as a form of organisation and of enterprise must not be allowed to develop. Nobody will be able to deny convincingly that in certain fields, such as the development of modern telecommunications systems, data processing and nuclear energy, systematic long-range research and development, with the associated financial burdens and risks, can only be carried on by enterprises whose turnover and earnings lie above certain minimum levels. Multinational corporations have made a no less important contribution to economic growth and prosperity, to international integration and to the rationalisation of production process. It is, therefore, not the multinational enterprises that have led to the "internationalisation of problems posed by national legal and economic systems", but economic necessity and technological progress. It is they that make international integration and application imperative. For the multinational corporations this means that social integration is essential. The elements of this integration must be, first, that the property of the multinational enterprise is dispersed multinationally, so that the citizens of all the countries concerned can share equally in the growth and in the profits; second, it will be vital to recruit the management of the subsidiaries from nationals of the host country and of other countries, just as the management at the head office should be composed of nationals of numerous countries. This should be accompanied by a far-reaching and indispensable identification of local corporate strategy and its tactical implementation with the interests of the host country. At the same time, however, it should be guaranteed that the overall strategy of the entire group is mapped out in such a way that scope remains for flexible adjustment to other countries' requirements. Laws and regulations, exchange and other controls will only be able to regulate good conduct to a certain extent. In the final analysis, only social integration through the property and the management is able to create a "voluntary" code of good conduct which does not materially differ from that of small and middle-sized local enterprises with the "patriotism" peculiar to them.

This applies without reservations and in identical measure to the conflict situations we have been examining between national monetary and financial policy and the financial management of multinational corporations. Even though the path that has to be taken may be difficult, it still seems more promising to aim at international cooperation not just in economic and monetary policy and in structural and social policy but also in the business policy of major multinational corporations, than for instance to regulate the investment policy of enterprises active throughout the world by controls on foreign investment and government intervention, or even to subject their daily business to dirigistic surveillance.

Part VI

General Report on the Colloquium

Chapter XIV

GENERAL REPORT ON THE COLLOQUIUM

by *Sidney E. Rolfe*

A Colloquium on Financial and Monetary Aspects of Developing Multinational Enterprises was held at the University of Nottingham from April 10 to 13,
1973. The Colloquium was attended by 129 participants from 12 countries.

The Colloquium opened with an address by the Rt. Hon. Lord O'Brien,
Governor of the Bank of England. In his opening remarks, Lord O'Brien
expressed his pleasure at being able to greet SUERF at its first conference to
take place in the United Kingdom. He stated that the Bank has always been in
sympathy with the objectives of SUERF and supported the Association from
the outset. The Governor touched on several key problems relating to multinational corporations which are in need of further and more objective study,
several of which were in fact the subject of Commission deliberations at this
meeting.

His particular interest as a central banker was to know more about the
ability of multinational groups "to shift their liquid assets around in times of
exchange crisis", including the recent dollar crisis of February/March 1973.
He called attention to the study "just published by the United States Tariff
Commission" which put a figure of $268 billion on liquid assets (at the end
of 1971) "of bodies participating in the international money markets, of
which some 70 per cent. were held by United States multinational corporations and banks".

Lord O'Brien cited several recent studies on the subject and, on a more
general level, he mentioned the many benefits which clearly accrue from the
operations of multinational enterprises and suggested that further work remains to be done on "how best . . . to preserve national objectives without
necessarily killing the goose that lays the golden eggs." He predicted that the
enlargement of the European Economic Community will lead, in time, to a
measure of harmonization in these matters in the context of fiscal and monetary policy. In conclusion, he noted that reform of the international monetary system could reduce "the incentive, and the need, for multinational
companies to engage in the operations that have been criticised", allowing
them to concentrate on the business of production and selling and thereby
improving the quality of life of all people.

The Colloquium then turned its attention to five distinct topics for which papers had been provided as follows:

I. General Introduction
    1) "The multinational enterprise" by Edward Thielemans.
    2) "The growth of multinational enterprises—A look into past and future" by G. Y. Bertin.

II. Financial management of multinational corporations
    1) "Financial aspects of a multinational company" by J. Koning.
    2) "Financial management of a multinational enterprise" by A.J.W.S. Leonard and F.H. Brittenden.

III. Multinational corporations and international financial markets.
    1) "The financial role of multinational enterprises" by W.A.P. Manser.
    2) "Multinational companies and international capital markets" by Sylvain Plasschaert.

IV. Financial institutions and the growth of multinational corporations
    1) "Financial institutions and the growth of multinational corporations" by Jack Hendley.
    2) "Financial and monetary aspects of developing multinational enterprises" by Patrice de Vallée.
    3) "Financial institutions and the growth of multinational corporations—An American point of view" by Donald W. Vollmer.

V. Multinational corporations and national monetary and financial policies
    1) "Multinational enterprises and domestic capital formation" by John H. Dunning.
    2) "Multinational firms and economic stability" by Nils Lundgren.
    3) "Multinational corporations and national monetary and financial policy" by Sieghardt Rometsch.

Background

In its terms of reference, the Colloquium was not designed to reach any set of conclusions or anything resembling recommendations. However, a point of view expressed in the discussion was that the financial and monetary problems connected with multinational enterprises are solvable. Each of the Commissions probed the papers before it with a view to discussing the related problems. The results of these discussions are summarized below.

I. *Introduction*

During the introductory plenary session, the question of the relationship of the multinational corporations to the international monetary system was raised. It was noted that the international monetary system is in rapid evolution; the Colloquium therefore was asked to consider the implications for multinational enterprises in a system which may be radically different from Bretton Woods, under which multinational enterprises had expanded enormously. Since the work of reform of the monetary system is by no means complete, it is difficult to envisage the exact form of relationship, a point on which Lord O'Brien had touched. However, the general hypothesis was offered that the export of direct investment capital may to some extent reflect the overvaluation of a currency. Consequently, the relative shift in currency values which has been taking place may well result in changes in the tendency to undertake direct investment, or to a change in the geographic distribution of such direct investment. It may be anticipated that the relative rise in value of the currencies of Europe and Japan may result in enhanced outflows of direct investment capital from those areas to other developed nations or to the developing countries.

II. *Financial management of multinational corporations*

The participants identified three issues for discussion. These were the long-term transfer of capital, short-term capital movements, and the problems of fiscal evasion.

(1) Many participants claimed that the long-term capital requirements of multinational corporations called for relatively little transfer of funds across the exchanges. Most of the funds raised in local markets are through Euro-bonds or in the various domestic or Eurocurrency markets and even more by the plough-back of earnings.

(2) Short-term capital transfers:

(a) It was noted that this is solely the job of the corporate treasurer. The corporation does not distort its production, location or marketing policies in order to profit from expected exchange rate changes or interest rate differentials.

(b) The multinational enterprises, of course, are not the only units in the modern world which engage in short-term capital transfers. Many do. Some participants pointed out that there were two views possible of short-term transfers, whether by multinational corporations or others. They are viewed as "destabilizing" by those who would hold exchange rates fixed, whether those rates are in equilibrium or not. On the other hand, transfers may be viewed as equilibrating forces by those who favour market determination of exchange rates. Consequently, those who tended to favour market equilibration thought capital flows were useful.

(c) Whether switching is protective or speculative is largely a matter of semantics. The result is the same, but it was noted that multinational corporate

217

treasurers who operate in several currencies must switch funds occasionally to avoid losses. Some are more aggressive than others. But many find themselves operating under restrictions which militate against complete freedom to switch, e.g., the United Kingdom parent of a multinational group, which has surplus sterling or big sterling lines of credit, cannot switch into other currencies from those sources, and the same holds true of United States parents of multinational groups under the Office of Foreign Direct Investment regulations.

The exact quantity of such switches is of course unknown. Several studies, some cited by Lord O'Brien for an earlier period, suggest that very little overt speculation had taken place as a result of the operations of multinational corporations during previous crises. The failure of a corporate treasurer to protect himself, however, by switching some balances and by the use of credit lines, sometimes substantial, might make him remiss in the view of top management or shareholders. It was also noted that it is not necessary to indulge in capital transactions, since the objective can be accomplished by means of leads or lags on the trade or dividend account, moving into strong and out of weak currencies. Most of these payments would be made in any event but the timing is changed.

(d) Several times in discussion and in several of the papers, the figure of $268 billion was mentioned. This originally appeared in a study entitled "Implications of Multinational Firms for World Trade and Investment and for United States Trade and Labor", prepared for the Committee on Finance of the United States Senate by the U.S. Tariff Commission.

The allegation that $268 billion is at the disposal of multinational corporations is quite simply a misquote. Appended to this report is the relevant table from that Report and an extract from the summary of its findings. It can be seen that while multinational corporations and banks do control considerable amounts, funds are also available to others, even including the reserves of some unspecified governments.

(3) Controversy also arose over the question of tax policy. Some alleged that by transfer pricing the multinational companies can accumulate profits in low tax countries and thus avoid their fiscal obligations. However, some of those familiar with the operations of multinational corporations minimised the extent to which this abuse is possible. There are very little empirical data on these matters but nevertheless fears that tax avoidance is extensive are often expressed. One participant associated with a Dutch multinational corporation noted that in the case of his company tax havens were rarely used and that their world-wide tax bill is about 48 to 49 per cent. of earnings, approximately the same level as that faced by domestic companies.

The difficulties of switching profits through changes in transfer prices to low tax areas are summarised as follows:

(i) there has to be a high level of inter-company trade which is not true in many industries;

(ii) customs authorities have to be satisfied that dumping was not in progress and also had to be satisfied that tariff revenues were not being evaded;

(iii) tax authorities had to be satisfied that the revenue losses through artificially low profits were not being sustained;

(iv) exchange control authorities had to be satisfied that the export proceeds were not being kept artificially low;

(v) auditors had to be satisfied that reductions in profits were reasonable;

(vi) local management morale in "low profit" companies had to be kept up; and

(vii) some standard of relative company efficiency other than profits had to be found.

Despite these protestations, a number of participants in the Commissions, and in verbal and written comments on the draft report, continued to emphasise the apparent success, particularly of the oil companies, to operate without recorded profits over a period of time.

The residue of comments about multinational corporations centred on the question of tax havens. Many countries, otherwise not tax havens, exempt or rebate withholding taxes on bonds or other obligations held by non-residents. However, tax havens alone permit reduced tax rates on earnings, presumably to induce multinational corporations to establish holding companies there. Many participants pointed out that criticism here should be levelled at the countries which facilitate such arrangements and not at the multinational corporations themselves.

III. *Multinational corporations and international financial markets*

In considering this topic, three main questions were discussed: the terms on which multinational corporations have access to financial markets; the currencies in which multinational corporations borrow; and the international spread of multinational corporation ownership.

(1) As regards the terms on which multinational corporations have access to financial markets, a distinction was drawn between national and international financial markets. In the former, it was not felt that the multinational corporation possessed a comparative advantage over its national counterparts. While the public may regard multinational subsidiaries as desirable investments, host governments frequently impose a queueing system on non-resident foreign-owned subsidiaries seeking local finance—placing the financial needs of indigenous companies before those of foreign-owned subsidiaries. However, government policy of this type is not a significant disadvantage for the foreign

subsidiary since the amount raised by external local finance by such subsidiaries is not great.

As regards access to international capital markets, the main borrowers in these markets are the multinationals. As a consequence, they have an accumulated expertise of international financing and changing financial conditions. While national companies have recently entered the international markets as borrowers, their lack of expertise and credit-rating has placed them at some disadvantage. Thus, multinational corporations do appear to have greater flexibility in meeting their finance requirements, since they can to some extent switch between national and international financial markets. It was noted that lenders in both markets may require a guarantee of loans from the parent company, although parent companies are frequently reluctant to give such guarantees.

(2) The choice of currency in multinational financing was considered from both the borrower's and the lender's point of view. The borrowers are largely United States multinationals, which invariably find dollar financing easy at a time when certain constraints have been placed on borrowings in other currencies. Moreover, insofar as United States multinationals consider the dollar to be weak, dollar borrowings will take on an added attraction.

From the lender's point of view some may feel that the dollar's long term prospects are good. Others would not agree and think that the United States cannot and will not give balance of payments considerations priority over domestic objectives. The United States will go on committing itself in foreign countries, and unless there is a surplus on the current account that would mean a depreciation of the United States dollar in the long run.

Drawing together the views of borrowers and lenders, it was felt that the dollar would continue as the major international transaction currency, notwithstanding interest-rate differentials. Peripherally, it was noted that government oil payments would continue to be denominated in dollars.

(3) It was felt that a greater geographical spread of the ownership of multinational corporations would not ease tensions between these corporations and host countries. The trend towards a divorce of ownership and controls has long been under way and it is the management power of multinationals, not their ownership, which is the source of conflict. Others noted that management is the source of conflict, but it is linked to majority control. In future, some form of worker participation in the decision-making process of multinationals may be equally as relevant for the avoidance of conflicts as a spread of equity ownership, or multinationalisation of management at all levels. Also, in future, new types of relations which do not involve ownership are likely to develop over time, with the Eastern European countries and possibly China, but also with Latin America and other developing areas.

220

IV. *Financial institutions and the growth of multinational corporations*

One form of multinational enterprise is the bank. Three styles of large-scale banking have emerged:

(1) The United States style, characterised by a light network of branches situated in a number of countries. The evolution of the United States style was stimulated by the need to provide banking facilities for the affiliates of United States multinational enterprises.

(2) The European Banks International Corporation (EBIC) style, characterised by an association of several European banks in an especially close relationship which goes much further than the ordinary correspondent bank relationship. This style does not involve an exchange of ownership, but provides the basis for the formation of consortia and joint operations and activities of various kinds, in particular, the ability of a member bank in one country to commit another member bank to make substantial loans locally to a customer of the first bank.

(3) The ORION style, characterised by joint ownership of an international banking group and a three-tier organisational structure analogous to that of the EEC.

Arguments have been put forward in favour of one or other type of structure, but the general consensus was that all three styles had a place in the future development of international financial institutions. Furthermore, some thought that in-house banking, Japanese-style, by multinational enterprises will be part of the future pattern—a phenomenon already starting to emerge. Thus, the multinational enterprise may borrow long and use the funds for short-term money market operations.

It was thought that certain small United States banks did not have a future as international banks, especially local banks with a London branch. However, at least some small United States banks will remain in London to service their customers, lest they lose both the domestic and international business of such clients. Other banks came to London to participate in the Euro-dollar market, especially during the period of United States credit restraint in the late 1960s. These banks are thought likely to disappear from the London scene. As international financial institutions have developed, some tension between them and their multinational clients has been inevitable. In this respect, mention was made of the possible misuse of credit facilities by multinational enterprises, and the alleged inadequacy of services provided by some banks to their clients.

V. *Multinational corporations and national monetary and financial policies*

A number of issues were brought to light in the discussion of this topic, of which the most important were the role of governments in creating market imperfection, and the sensitivity of multinational enterprises to national economic objectives.

A traditional frame of reference in discussing multinational enterprises has been the conflict between the objectives of those enterprises as part of an international economic system, attempting to allocate resources optimally without reference to national borders, and the needs of the nation states. Traditionally, those who place the higher priority on the legitimacy of the objectives of the nation states have seen multinational enterprise as a threat to sovereignty while those who place a higher priority on international economic rationality see the nation state as a residual barrier. One of the papers presented at this meeting, Dr. Nils Lundgren's "Multinational Firms and Economic Stability", and particularly the revision of that paper as presented to his Commission, attempted to bridge this gap. Using recent findings, e.g., with respect to capital market transactions as well as some new theoretical formulations, the burden of the paper, and of its verbal revision, seems to have been that government interventions have proven in many instances to be creators of market imperfections, which very often create more serious problems as secondary consequences. Modern economies may be characterised as "corporate" (i.e., dominated by capital intensive oligopolies) and simultaneously "open" (with nearly free trade in goods, services and capital). Multinational corporations improve the international allocation of resources, while the institutional arrangements under which the modern world exists tend to make them contribute to international instability. The task at hand is to concentrate on developing both national and international policies and institutions to cope with the stability problem rather than sacrifice real growth by interventions to restrict international firms. It was the consensus of the meeting that further work along the lines suggested by the Lundgren paper would focus attention on devices to reduce the conflict between the corporations and the nation states and to maximise simultaneously the benefits from international corporate activity to world economic growth.

(1) Multinational enterprises, national governments and market imperfections: There was some discussion of how and the extent to which national governments should intervene in markets. It was suggested that many features of the markets in which multinational enterprises operated, such as tax differentials, privileged access to finance and the like, were forms of market imperfection arising out of government action. While the existence of such imperfections was generally recognised, there was some disagreement as to how the private benefits multinational enterprises might derive from such imperfections could be eliminated by government intervention. On the one

hand, some held that no great faith should be placed in the operation of market forces as such, and that governments should intervene directly in situations where the private and social costs and benefits of multinational enterprise investment differed. On the other hand, it was noted that direct government interventions, such as those introduced in the United States (e.g., Interest Equalisation Tax and the Office of Foreign Direct Investment measures) had unwittingly encouraged the creation of Euro-dollar markets and stimulated capital flows. It was suggested that government intervention should be directed towards the elimination of market imperfections by working through markets rather than by attempting to replace them with direct controls.

(2) The sensitivity of multinational enterprises to national economic objectives: It was argued that multinational enterprises displayed an insensitivity to national economic objectives and exerted a disruptive influence on national monetary and financial policies. This argument was illustrated by reference to the operation of the Belgian two-tier exchange rate system, and the reaction of multinational enterprises to tax differentials. As regards the two-tier exchange system, it was suggested that, through their ability to purchase foreign exchange in either market, multinational enterprises had contributed to a substantial narrowing of the differential between the rate for each tier, thus undermining the two-tier system.

An opposing point of view was that in the experience of the United Kingdom government, multinational enterprise subsidiaries operating in the United Kingdom had shown a greater sensitivity than United Kingdom companies towards government policies regarding employment, regional planning, and the like. Co-operation between the United Kingdom government and a British multinational enterprise was illustrated by the government/Shell Company agreement on foreign currency holdings by Shell. While it was difficult to generalise, it was held that there seemed to have been no instances of United States multinational enterprises abusing their powers in order that their United Kingdom subsidiaries might thwart United Kingdom government objectives.

(3) As regards the taxation of multinational enterprises, it was argued that
(i) national tax authorities were not incompetent and would intensely scrutinize taxable profits submitted by international enterprise subsidiaries, but that in the absence of co-operation among the different national tax administrations there were limits to their control of the adequacy of the profits submitted by the various subsidiaries;
(ii) while tax systems and rates may well influence the location of new multinational enterprise investment, this could hardly be regarded as an abuse of multinational enterprise power; and
(iii) double taxation may well hit multinational enterprises in a way that their national counterparts do not experience.

223

VI. *Multinationals and flexible exchange rates*

The new element added during the introductory session was the hypothesis that multinational enterprises may now be at a major historic turning point, along with the international monetary system.

American deficits had been associated increasingly with an overvalued dollar. One manifestation of overvaluation was the extent of direct investment from the United States. Now greater flexibility of exchange rates should restore a payments equilibrium; this would reduce the level, but not eliminate, United States direct investments. At the same time, the United States capital controls are to be eliminated by 1974.

The Colloquium was therefore asked to look ahead, if the hypotheses above are correct, to assess:
(a) the future growth of United States-based multinational corporations;
(b) the impact on Europe, and upon European- and Japanese-based multinational corporate expansion; and
(c) the impact on the Eurocurrency and Eurobond markets.

In reply (to a and b), the Colloquium seems to have rejected the idea of a slower growth for multinational corporations. The balance of opinion indicated continued belief that multinational corporations would grow at about the same rate as in the past, nearly 10 per cent. per year. But some distinctions were made with respect to future patterns by many participants. There would be some levelling off of United States multinational growth and increased growth from European (notably German) and Japanese firms; and aggregate growth would take place even with a strong reduction in outflows from the United States.

Some participants noted that tariff barriers are evidences of non-free trade and still provide a defensive motive for direct investment. If trade barriers are in future reduced, so may be this motive. But if American protectionism increases, so will direct investment in the United States.
(d) With respect to financial markets, the response was:

1) General agreement that a turning-point could result in considerable shrinkage of the dollar-denominated Euro-dollar and Eurobond markets.

2) Several factors operate to ensure that these markets will not disappear completely:
(i) Bank secrecy laws in certain European centres.
(ii) As regards Euromoney markets, the American Regulation Q; reserve requirements for deposits; lack of interest payments for short-term deposits; a different "tax morality"; and the time factor;
(iii) As regards Eurobonds, Securities Exchange Commission requirements; withholding tax considerations; and underwriters' preferences; and
(iv) There may be some substitution effects: loans to the Less Developed Countries, Eastern Europe, and for new services from Euromoney sources, and for an Atlantic capital market, along lines suggested by Professor Plasschaert.

Appendix

EXTRACT FROM SUMMARY OF FINDINGS OF: *"Implications of multinational firms for world trade and investment and for United States trade and labor"*

(Prepared for the Committee on Finance of the United States Senate by the United States Tariff Commission)

The international money markets have many participants. It is beyond dispute that the persons and institutions operating in these markets have the resources with which to generate international monetary crises of the sort that have plagued the major central banks in recent years. As a group, private institutions on the international financial scene controlled some $268 billion in short-term liquid assets at the end of 1971—and the lion's share of these assets was under the control of multinational firms and banks headquartered in the United States. This $268 billion, all managed by private persons and traded in private markets virtually uncontrolled by official institutions anywhere, was more than twice the total of all international reserves held by all central banks and international monetary institutions in the world at the same date. These are the reserves with which central banks fight to defend their exchange rates. The resources of the private sector outclass them.

Because $268 billion is such an immense number, it is clear that only a small fraction of the assets which it measures needs to move in order for a genuine crisis to develop. The international money market, possessing such a *masse de manœuvre* as well as an efficiency and flexibility unknown in the past (even the recent past), can focus with telling effect on a crisis-prone situation—some weak currency which repels funds and some strong one which attracts them.

Because such a small proportion of the resources of the multinational corporations is needed to produce monetary explosions, it appears appropriate to conclude that destructive, predatory motivations do not characterize the sophisticated international financial activities of most multinational corporations, even though much of the funds which flow internationally during the crisis doubtlessly is of multinational corporation origin. Rather, the important role of the multinational corporations has been to provide the primary creative force in the development of the international money market, a market which is now fully institutionalized as a reality of international financial life. This is the sense in which the multinational corporations indeed have altered the conditions around which the policies of governments are framed.

Table T: *Estimated short-term asset and liability positions of principal institutions in International Money Markets, 1969-1971*
(Billion of U.S. dollars)

Holder of assets or liabilities	Denominated in dollars		Denominated in foreign currencies		Total	
	Assets	Liabilities	Assets	Liabilities	Assets	Liabilities
United States banks:[1]						
1969	8.9	28.1	0.5	0.2	9.4	28.3
1970	10.1	21.8	0.6	0.2	10.7	22.0
1971	12.1	15.8	0.9	0.2	13.0	16.0
United States nonbanks:						
1969	3.5	1.7	0.7	0.4	4.2	2.1
1970	3.6	2.2	0.6	0.5	4.2	2.7
1971	4.7	2.2	0.5	0.4	5.2	2.6
Foreign banks:[2]						
1969	64.9[3]	52.3[3]	10.7[3]	10.6[3]	75.6[3]	63.0[3]
1970	43.0	31.7	5.8	5.8	48.8	37.5
1971	44.3	38.3	8.4	8.2	52.7	46.5
Foreign governments, central banks, and international organizations:[4]						
1969	4.9	NA	0.4	NA	5.3	NA
1970	10.0	NA	2.8	NA	12.8	NA
1971	10.7	NA	8.0	NA	18.7	NA
Foreign nonbanks:[5]						
1969	7.3	6.2	NA	NA	7.3	6.2
1970	7.6	9.4	NA	NA	7.6	9.4
1971	6.8	11.4	NA	NA	6.8	11.4
Foreign affiliates of United States nonbanks:[6]						
1969	NA	NA	NA	NA	59.9	34.9
1970	NA	NA	NA	NA	80.6	46.9
1971	NA	NA	NA	NA	110.0	63.0
Foreign branches of United States banks:[8]						
1969	[7]	[7]	[7]	[7]	[7]	[7]
1970	34.6	36.1	12.7	11.3	47.3	47.4
1971	40.2	42.1	21.2	19.4	61.4	61.5
Totals:						
1969	89.5	88.3	12.3	11.2	161.7	134.5
1970	108.9	101.2	22.5	17.8	212.0	165.9
1971	118.8	109.8	39.0	28.2	267.8	201.0

1. Data are total foreign short-term assets and liabilities of United States banks as reported in United States sources, *less* claims on and liabilities to official monetary institutions.

2. Basically, these data are those reported to the BIS by banks in eight European countries (Belgium-Luxembourg, France, Germany, Italy, Netherlands, Sweden, Switzerland, and the United Kingdom), plus Canada and Japan. Figures from United States sources relating to foreign branches of United States banks have been subtracted from these figures and are shown separately in the table for 1970 and 1971. Also the eight European countries' asset and liabilities vis-à-vis the United States (denominated in dollars) were removed from the totals, and data from United States sources on *total* dollar claims and liabilities against foreigners were added.

3. Includes foreign branches of United States banks.

4. Data cover (1) identified official holdings of Euro-dollars, (2) unidentified holdings of Eurocurrencies plus residual sources of reserves—both as estimated by the IMF—plus (3) claims on United States banks of nonmonetary official institutions such as the IBRD and IADB. "NA" = not available.

5. Available data cover United States., and foreign banks' claims on and liabilities to all foreign members, including foreign branches/affiliates of United States nonbanks. To insure elimination of double-counting, since positions of the United States-affiliated firms are shown separately, the available data have been reduced by 50 per cent.—i.e. it is assumed that half of the assets and liabilities reported by United States and foreign banks against foreign nonbanks actually are liabilities and assets, respectively, of foreign affiliates of United States nonbanks.

6. Data are estimated current assets and liabilities of non-financial affiliates of United States firms.

7. Included under "foreign banks".

8. Figures are from United States sources citing *total* assets and liabilities of branches. Therefore, some long-term items are included.

Sources: *Federal Reserve Bulletin*, Sept. 1972; *U.S. Treasury Bulletin*, Sept. 1972; Bank for International Settlements, *Annual Report*, 1971 and 1972; International Monetary Fund, *Annual Report*, 1972; United States Commerce Department, Office of Foreign Direct Investment, *Foreign Affiliate Financial Survey*, July 1971 and *Foreign Direct Investment Program, Selected Statistics*, July 1971; and data furnished by United States Department of Commerce, Bureau of Economic Analysis, Foreign Investment Division.

Appendix

MULTINATIONAL CORPORATIONS AND CAPITAL MARKET INTEGRATION

by *John Mellors* [*]

At the fourth colloquium of the Société Universitaire Européenne de Recherches Financières (SUERF) a number of the papers and discussions concerned the link between multinational corporations and the evolution of integrated capital markets.[1] This paper draws on the SUERF proceedings in an attempt to answer three questions. First, what direct rôle have multinational corporations played in fostering the integration of national capital markets? Second, to what extent have multinational corporations contributed indirectly to such capital market integration by fostering the growth of financial intermediaries with links across national boundaries? Finally, what problems does such integration pose for national governments? Before turning to these questions it must be stressed that while the author has benefited greatly from the papers and discussions of the SUERF colloquium, there is no attempt here to summarise these proceedings.

The direct rôle of multinationals

The ability of multinational corporations to narrow cost differentials between different national capital markets depends upon two factors, the volume of funds raised by multinational corporations relative to the total volume of funds traded in all capital markets, and the relative abilities of all market participants to switch the location of their activities. Since we have no quantitative information as regards either factor, we can provide no more than a qualitative assessment of the rôle of multinational corporations in integrating national capital markets. We consider the direct contribution of multinational corporations to this process of integration in two stages. First, we examine the integration of national capital markets that arises as a consequence of the multinational corporations financing activities in these national markets. Sec-

[*] Reprinted from *The Bankers' Magazine*, June 1973.

1. Fourth SUERF Colloquium on "Financial and Monetary Aspects of Developing Multinational Enterprises", held at Nottingham University, 10th–13th April, 1973.

ond, we assess the rôle of multinational corporations in the international capital markets for Eurocurrencies and Eurobonds.

As regards national markets for the issue of new equity capital, no discernable international integration has taken place to date. Some multinational corporations contribute to the development of *national* equity markets by the issue of minority shares in their subsidiaries. Since the affiliates of multinational corporations may be dominant companies in certain less-developed host countries, issues by such affiliates assist in the actual creation of national primary and secondary markets.

Equity capital

The cost of equity capital is peculiar to a particular company—far more so than the cost of loan finance—and depends on the expectations of potential shareholders regarding future earnings. Thus primary (new issue) markets for equity capital can only be integrated in the sense that a given company can obtain the same proceeds from a simultaneous share issue in two or more national markets. In fact, it is relatively rare for companies to make simultaneous issues in different regional markets within one country. To our knowledge, no companies have contemplated such simultaneous issues across national boundaries.

The fragmentation of national capital markets for equity issues is attributable to two factors external to the multinational corporations: the restrictions common to most capital markets on foreign outflows of funds and the structural weaknesses of many national equity markets. Within Western Europe, only the United Kingdom can be said to possess a well-developed capital market for new equity issues. As the Segré Report[2] noted, elsewhere in Europe the long-term capital for companies is provided mainly through the media of banks and other lending institutions rather than through primary equity markets. Thus a sizable issue of equity shares in these countries would currently cause large price fluctuations in the secondary markets for equities.

While no integration of equity markets has yet taken place, the multinational corporations have created pressures for such integration in one way. In terms of both numbers and size, multinational corporations owned by United States shareholders dominate the ranks of multinational corporations. Given the fears of "Economic imperialism" that such multinational corporations provoke, their growth stimulates demands for the internationalisation of shareholdings in multinational corporations. Whether or not such a diffusion of shareholdings would diminish conflicts between multinational corporations

2. EEC Commission, *The Development of a European Capital Market*, (The Segré Report), EEC, 1966.

and nation states is debatable. However, given that pressures for such diffusion exist, the integration of primary equity markets may be brought closer as a result of the internationalisation of shareholdings.

National loan capital markets

Turning to the integration of national markets for loan capital, we can make a more positive assessment. The first point to be noted is that multinational corporations face distinct problems in raising loan capital, due to what Manser[3] has termed their "extra-territorial posture". Funds raised in the country of the parent company become capital exports when used to finance overseas affiliates and, as such, are frequently subject to government measures designed to restrict capital outflows. From the point of view of multinational corporation development, the most notable restrictions on capital outflows in the last decade have been those imposed by the United States government. As members of large multinational corporation groups, foreign-owned subsidiaries may possess certain advantages over their host-country competitors in approaching the capital markets of their host-countries for loan finance.
Again, however, restrictions on the foreign subsidiary's access to such markets, imposed by host-country governments, may make access to these markets difficult.

Notwithstanding these problems, multinational corporations do raise substantial amounts of loan capital in national markets—particularly in the form of short-term bank credit extended to multinational corporation affiliates. Thus Brooke and Remmers[4], in a study of 115 foreign subsidiaries operating in the United Kingdom, found that bank credit as a percentage of their investment in net assets amounted to 12.7 per cent. over the period 1959—67, compared to a figure of 7.5 per cent. for a comparable group of British quoted companies (p. 189). As regards the possible narrowing of inter-nation interest differentials, the significance of loan capital raised in the national markets depends on the ability and willingness of multinational corporations to shift these funds from one subsidiary to another. In the absence of restrictions on its funds flows, the multinational corporation can transfer funds raised by subsidiaries faced with low-cost capital markets to subsidiaries faced with high borrowing costs in a straightforward fashion, making due allowance for any forward exchange cover required. Of course, things are rarely this simple, and the existence of restrictions on funds flows may en-

An asterisk (*) denotes a paper presented at the fourth SUERF Colloquium.
   *3. Manser, W.A.P., Extract from *The Financial Role of Multinational Enterprises* (Chapter 7).
   4. Brooke, M.Z., and Remmers, H.L., *The Strategy of Multinational Enterprise*, London, 1970.

courage the use of more indirect transfer mechanisms. Thus the transferor may decrease prices charged on inter-group sales to the transferee or speed up payment for goods purchased from the transferee on inter-group credit. Koning[5] has outlined a number of such indirect transfer methods.

In passing, we are doubtful of the extent to which transfer prices may be manipulated—either to faciliate funds transfers or for tax purposes—although generalisations are dangerous. There is a fair body of evidence from both businessmen and independent researchers to the effect that transfer prices are either arm's length prices or differ from arm's length prices under the scrutiny of (or direction of) tax and customs authorities. As Shulman[6] points out, the manipulation of transfer prices involves a potentially serious loss of usable control information, unless accounts are consistently prepared on both a "rigged" and "unrigged" transfer price basis.

Transferring funds

To the extent that multinational corporations do transfer funds from one subsidiary to another (by either direct or indirect means) with a view to benefiting from capital market imperfections, they promote a reduction in these imperfections. Given two countries with "cheap" and "dear" capital market rates respectively, the cost of funds to borrowers in the country where the "cheap" finance has been raised by a multinational corporation is higher than it would have been in the absence of this borrowing. Similarly, the cost of funds to borrowers in the country where the raising of "dear" finance has been avoided by the multinational corporation is lower than would otherwise have been the case. Insofar as the suppliers of loan capital to multinational corporations can also choose which market they will enter, the integration of the two markets is obviously enhanced. Note that while the above discussion has been framed in terms of the external financing of multinational corporations the same processes will promote narrower cost differentials if the internal financing of multinational corporations is planned on a global scale. For example such narrowing arises if a subsidiary that faces a "dear" capital market is supplied by transfers of internal finance from other subsidiaries-funds that could otherwise be lent in "cheap" capital markets, or remitted to the multinational corporation parent company for dividend distribution to shareholders.

*5. Koning, J., "Financial Aspects of a Multinational Company".
6. Shulman, J.S., "When the Price is Wrong—By Design", *Columbia Journal of World Business*, May/June, 1967, pp. 69–76.

The difficulties noted above that face multinational corporations in raising loan capital in national markets have been a significant factor in stimulating the demands made by multinational corporations in the emerging Euro-currency and Eurobond markets. Borrowings in these markets are particularly attractive to multinational corporations in that they are free from exchange control restrictions, may be arranged quickly, and the interest payments may be made free of withholding taxes (subject to the suitable location of the multinational corporation's finance subsidiary). The rapid growth of the Euromarkets is a well documented phenomenon. Plasschaert[7] puts the current total size of the Eurocurrency pool at around $85 billion and records (Table II) a growth in the new issues of Eurobonds made by private companies from some $0.7 billion in 1965 to $3.7 billion in 1972. This latter figure represents some 59 per cent. of the total Eurobond issues of that year. Manser, (p. 152), calculates that over the period 1964—68, around 30 per - cent. of all capital remitted by multinational corporation parent companies to their overseas subsidiaries was drawn from the Euromarkets. Thus multinational corporations have represented a major stimulus to the demand side of these markets. Naturally, insofar as a multinational corporation possesses a sizeable liquid balance of funds, it is free to enter the Eurocurrency market on the supply side also.

Given the existence of the Euromarkets and their freedom from restrictions on funds flows, switches of funds between these Euromarkets and national capital markets in response to covered interest rate differentials have the effect of reducing the magnitude of such differentials. However, two reservations should be borne in mind. Firstly, the extent to which multinational corporations themselves promote capital market integration through switching between national and Euromarkets is open to debate. Notwithstanding their advantages, the Euromarkets do not offer a complete alternative to national capital markets as a source of external finance for multinational corporations. As regards their contribution to the total financing of multinational corporations, both internal and external, net borrowings in the Euromarkets have perhaps amounted to around 10 per cent. of the total funds employed by multinational corporations (Manser p. 152). Secondly, we cannot be sure of the extent to which funds used to purchase multinational corporation Euro-issues are made up of funds switched out of national capital markets or represent net additions to the total volume of savings.

Cooper[8] has demonstrated the tendency of differentials between national

*7. Plasschaert, S., "Multinational Companies and International Capital Markets."
8. Cooper, R.N., "Towards an International Capital Market?" in Kindleberger and

capital markets to narrow over time, both as regards short-term money market rates and as regards interest rates on long-term government bonds. There is no doubt that multinational corporations have played a significant direct rôle in the narrowing of interest rate differentials between national capital markets.

Multinationals and institutional development

We now turn to the more indirect pressure that multinational corporations have exerted in encouraging the development of integrated capital markets. The integration of any market depends upon the development of institutional channels whereby buyers and sellers of commodities may be brought together. In the case of capital markets, multinational corporations have played a significant part in encouraging the development of the institutions required for the integration of national short- and medium-term capital markets; namely, the development of multinational banks and banks with extensive international links. While many other factors (such as United States banking regulations limiting the extent of branch networks within the United States) have also played a part, we discern two significant links between the development of international banking and the growth of multinational corporations from the papers of Hendley,[9] de Vallée,[10] and Vollmer.[11]

Firstly, there is the natural tendency for banks to follow their multinational corporation clients as these clients develop globally—a tendency encouraged by the possible loss of a multinational corporation's domestic business if its expanding overseas needs are not also catered for. Why have multinational corporations not turned to local banks overseas for the short-term financing and other facilities required by their affiliates? In many cases, of course, the overseas affiliates of multinational corporations do employ the services of local banks. However, from the point of view of a local bank, the newly-established affiliate of a multinational corporation represents more of an unknown quantity than does a newly-established domestic firm. The local bank may be only casually acquainted with the activities and financial standing of the multinational corporation group as a whole and may experience difficulties in improving its information on the group. Reservations on the part of local banks may be increased by the reluctance of the parent company of a multi-

Shonfield, (eds). *North American and Western European Economic Policies,* Macmillan, 1971.

*9. Hendley, J., "Financial Institutions and the Growth of Multinational Corporations."

*10. de Vallée, P., "Les Institutions Financières et le Développement des Entreprises Multinationales."

*11. Vollmer, D.W., "Financial Institutions and the Growth of Multinational Corporations: An American Point of View."

national corporation to guarantee the debts of its overseas subsidiaries and, as de Vallée suggests, the fact that newly-formed overseas affiliates are typically thinly capitalised and may expect losses during the first years of operation. From the point of view of multinational corporations, banking with the foreign branches of its domestic bank (or overseas banks related to it) may be more convenient in terms of both the efficiency of general services provided and the existence of credit facilities negotiated between the parent companies of the multinational corporation and its domestic bank.

International branch and consortium banking

Another major factor behind the growth of international branch and consortium banking has been the emergence of the Eurocurrency and Eurobond markets—the growth of these markets in turn having been stimulated on the demand side by the borrowing of multinational corporations. The magnitude of individual issues made in the Eurobond market by multinational corporations has required the services of banking consortia comprising both commercial and investment banks of different nationalities in sponsoring such issues. In view of United States intentions of reducing the United States balance of payments deficit and to re-open New York as an international banking centre, the extent of future growth in the Euromarkets is not easily predictable. However, it seems probable that several of the international banking consortia formed in response to past growth in the Euromarkets will continue to provide international banking services for the clients of the member banks.

In response to these and other factors, the last decade saw a rapid expansion of international branch banking and the development of international banking links beyond the traditional correspondent relationships. Thus in 1960, eight United States banks had 131 overseas branches whereas by mid-1972, 106 United States banks had 558 foreign branches. United States banks have also taken an active part in the formation of international banking consortia such as the Orion Group. Not all the recent developments have increased the dependence of multinational corporations on international banking services. The application of sophisticated techniques of cash management may reduce the total cash float required by the multinational corporation group as a whole. Central clearing systems for inter-group payments, the establishment of finance subsidiaries and the like often reduce the multinational corporations' need for external banking services.

Insofar as the internationalisation of banking institutions has contributed to the efficient workings of the Euromarkets, the development of international banking has already promoted closer integration of national short- and medium-term capital markets in the manner noted earlier. Moreover some banks have unwittingly contributed to the narrowing of money market diffe-

237

rentials through the short-term credit facilities extended to multinational corporations, with some multinational corporations drawing on these facilities and relending the funds when interest rate differentials have made such arbitraging profitable (Hendley). The existing links between the banks of different countries and the growth of international branch banking provide the institutional base on which further integration of short- and medium-term capital markets will be founded, if and when restrictions on capital flows are relaxed.

Money market integration

The existence of well-developed institutional links is crucial to the provision of timely and accurate information on exchange risks and the capital market conditions in different countries if interest rate differentials between these markets are to be narrowed by arbitraging activities. The development of information flows between and within international banks is of service to individuals in the same way that information flows within the multinational corporation group assist the multinational corporation in borrowing funds cheaply and lending surplus cash at the best rates. Finally, the creation of international banking links assists money market integration by encouraging national commercial banks to develop their thinking in global terms. Previously, the organisation of such banks has been geared primarily to the needs of domestic customers.

In view of the fact that capital market integration to date has been confined to increased links between national markets for loan finance, it is not surprising that multinational corporations have had virtually no impact on institutional developments outside of the commercial and investment banking spheres. Links between the institutions of national equity markets have certainly not strengthened in response to any internationalisation of shareholdings in multinational corporations to date. While there has been some growth of national mutual funds that hold portfolios of both domestic and overseas shares, the activities of multinational corporations have played no part in stimulating the growth of such funds. Some international links between national stock exchange dealers have been formed, particularly as regards the United Kingdom and United States equity markets, but such links have not developed as a response to any obvious stimulus provided by the operations of multinational corporations. Institutional developments promoting the integration of national equity markets will continue to be inhibited by the structural weaknesses of certain of the markets involved and by continuing restrictions on the purchase of foreign share issues by individuals.

238

We have seen that multinational corporations play a substantial part, both directly and indirectly, in fostering the integration of national capital markets for loan finance. In view of the fact that both multinational corporations and purely national firms stand to gain from capital market integration, why may such integration be impeded by national governments? The answer is not hard to find. The operations of multinational corporations contribute to a number of the difficulties that governments encounter in formulating macroeconomic stabilisation policies. These problems were discussed at the SUERF colloquium by Dunning,[12] Lundgren[13] and Rometsch,[14] and have been considered elsewhere by Cooper and Maynard[15] among others. Since the extent to which capital market integration is feasible depends primarily upon the freedom with which capital may flow across national boundaries, we concentrate upon the implications of such capital flows for the attainment of internal and external economic balance.

One can readily construct plausible models to indicate the kind of difficulties that may arise for a national government from such flows.

Suppose that a country wishes to maintain unrestricted capital flows and a fixed exchange rate, and that a "temporary" deficit develops on this country's balance of trade. The government seeks to correct this temporary imbalance by restraining domestic economic activity and it attempts to achieve this by curtailing government expenditure. For simplicity assume that interest rates are initially equal in all national capital markets and that no new capital is being demanded. As domestic activity declines in response to reduced government expenditure, a decline in the transactions demand for money, coupled with the reduced demands for capital from the government will tend to lower interest rates. Now, a once-and-for-all adjustment to security portfolios takes place as a consequence of lower interest rates (relative to rates overseas). These portfolio adjustments involve a capital outflow for the country until such time as portfolios have adjusted to the new pattern of interest rates. Eventually, the government will have created a situation in which (i) domestic output and employment have fallen, (ii) the deficit on the balance of trade has been reduced or eliminated, and (iii) the country's interest rates are lower than those prevailing in other countries.

---

*12. Dunning, J.H., "Multinational Enterprises and International Capital Formation."

*13. Lundgren, N., "Multinational Firms and Economic Stability."

*14. Rometsch, S., "Multinational Corporations and National Monetary and Financial Policy."

15. Maynard, G.W., "Monetary Policy and the Multinational Enterprise," *University of Reading Discussion Papers in International Investment and Business Studies No. 3* (1973).

Suppose now that a demand for new capital arises. Given fixed exchange rates, borrowers of new capital have little or no incentive to diversify their borrowings. They will all be attracted to the primary capital market in the country seeking to cure the deficit on its balance of trade. Thus a demand for new capital will develop in this country that gives rise to new capital outflows. These capital outflows will continue until such time as interest rates have been bid up to those prevailing in other countries, aggravating the balance of payments adjustment problem of the country experiencing the outflow. The adjusting country must attempt a delicate balancing of fiscal and monetary policy in an effort to remedy the balance of trade deficit while preventing the emergence of cost differentials in different primary capital markets. In fact, in order to counteract the consequences of allowing foreigners access to its primary capital markets, the adjusting country must attempt to eliminate the cost advantage to overseas borrowers that accrues from such access.

Exchange rate problems

The above example is highly simplified but it illustrates the difficulty of achieving internal and external balance under a system of unrestricted capital flows and fixed exchange rates. This difficulty is substantially increased when we allow for the fact that capital flows depend on exchange rate expectations in addition to interest differentials. Above, we assumed that the country's trade deficit was only "temporary"–implying no fundamental difference between an equilibrium exchange rate and the rate actually fixed. In practice, some governments develop an affection for given rates that other people regard as indefensible. When market participants hold "one-way" expectations regarding the future of a given fixed rate, free capital movements, internal balance and the maintenance of that rate become irreconcilable. In this context, the ability of multinational corporations to switch a large float of liquid assets between different currencies may considerably increase the pressures on parities that are already suspect for more fundamental reasons.

Up to this point we have assumed that governments seek to maintain fixed exchange rates over long periods of time. Given the difficulties of reconciling internal and external balance, free capital movements and fixed exchange rates, most governments have sought to restrict capital flows in some manner or another. It may well be argued that since the integration of national capital markets would benefit both multinational corporations and national firms, governments should adopt flexible exchange rate systems rather than place restrictions on international capital flows. In fact, the choice between restrictions and flexible exchange rates is not this simple. One of the problems involved may be appreciated from the analysis of "feasible currency areas". A full discussion of feasible currency areas is beyond the scope of this article, but we summarise the problem briefly. Given an initial deficit on a country's balance of payments, a devaluation can only restore equilibrium at full output and employment levels if real wages in the deficit country are reduced as a consequence of the devaluation. The extent to which real wages in the deficit country are reduced depends upon the degree to which money wages in the deficit country are related to the money wage levels of other countries. If a devaluation was followed by pressures that restored money wages in the deficit country to their former level (in foreign currency terms), the devaluation would not succeed in restoring balance of payments equilibrium at full output and employment levels. Maynard discusses the problem in detail and suggests that multinational corporations may reduce the effectiveness of devaluations as a method of eliminating external deficits while preserving full output and employment levels. For example, the stimulus that multinational corporations provide to multinational trade union activity makes it more difficult for the real wage levels of different countries to be varied independently of each other by means of exchange rate changes. Thus while a government possesses some measure of choice between restricting capital flows and introducing a flexible exchange rate system, its latitude in this matter depends, among other things, upon the extent to which real wages in the country concerned can be varied independently of real wage levels in other countries.

Conclusion

We have indicated that multinational corporations stimulate, both directly and indirectly, the integration of national capital markets, but that the unrestricted capital flows implied by complete integration could create serious problems for national governments as regards their macroeconomic stabilisation policies. We have not discussed many less important but nonetheless significant obstacles inhibiting the full integration of national capital markets. As a consequence of these problems, such integration is not a real possibility in the foreseeable future.